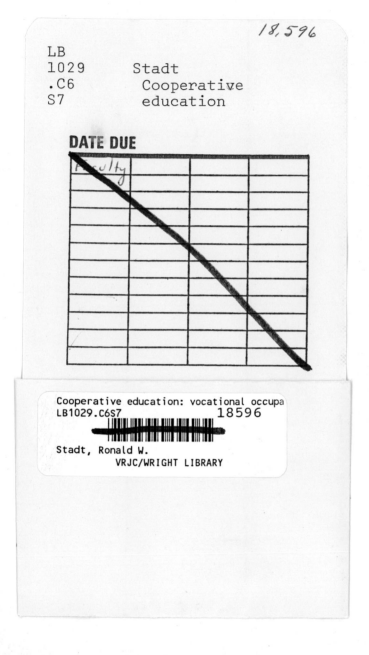

# COOPERATIVE EDUCATION:

## VOCATIONAL

## OCCUPATIONAL

## CAREER

# COOPERATIVE EDUCATION:

## VOCATIONAL

## OCCUPATIONAL

## CAREER

Ronald W. Stadt

and

Bill G. Gooch

Department of Occupational Education
Southern Illinois University, Carbondale

A Howard W. Sams Book

PUBLISHED BY THE BOBBS-MERRILL COMPANY, INC.
INDIANAPOLIS

To

Lorraine

and

Lou

FIRST EDITION

FIRST PRINTING—1977

A Howard W. Sams Book

International Standard Book Number: 0-672-97110-0
Library of Congress Catalog Card Number: 75-36917

# Contents

Types of Publics and How to Reach Them
Vehicles for Public Relations
Techniques for Using Public Relations Vehicles
Calendar of Public Relations
A Public Relations Plan

Planning an Evaluation System
Student Followup Survey
Employer Followup Survey
Team Reviews
Checklists

Planning and Implementing Change
Utilizing Results of Followup Surveys
Adjusting Occupational Emphases

# Foreword

Criticisms of Educational programs for youth and adults continue to mandate flexibility, increased options, and interfaces between theory and occupational experiences. Currently, there is a need to reassess education at all levels. Most of the ills of public education are known to us, e.g., dropout rates, reading levels, achievement scores, lack of "best educational fit," and other criticisms in lay literature and professional research. Rather than continuing diagnoses of the same ills, there is need for educational leadership which can provide new prescriptions for treatment of chronic ills. The authors of this book have helped leaders focus on cooperative education which unifies learning in a community setting.

The focus on cooperative education emphasizes the individual's career aspirations and integrates classroom and field experiences in a clear and comprehensive manner. These efforts are especially appropriate at a time when the national focus is on vocational or occupational education, career education, and career development. This book is an ambitious but successful treatment of the needs of individuals, the community, program implementation, and evaluation.

Many of the chapters are useful entities and have application in a variety of educational settings. Together they display a special interrelatedness. The authors have shown clearly symbiotic relationships which should exist among the various components of cooperative education.

James D. McComas
  Dean, College of Education
  University of Tennessee

# Preface

Unavoidably, this book assumes that readers will attach rather common meanings to the numerous terms that are used. This assumption is necessary and quite dangerous. Definitions are given as the terms are introduced, which alleviates many difficulties. Career education is seldom used, since (a) it connotes career-related learning experiences from preschool through adulthood and (b) a type of delivery system primarily for the preparation levels of career education is dealt with. Consistent use of four acronyms avoids many nomenclature problems. (1) Cooperative vocational/occupational education (CVOE) is used throughout, because the words "vocational" and "occupational" are in common and overlapping usage. (2) Federal education agencies are sometimes referred to as FEA's. (3) The term *state education agency* (SEA) is used occasionally. (4) Local education agency (LEA) is used often to connote school, college, institute, or any other agency at the student services, professional forefront. Hopefully, this usage will be pleasing to post-secondary educators who dislike generic use of the term *school*.

By design, this is a book with scope and focus. Every possible attempt has been made to assure applicablity to cooperative programs, regardless of occupational specialties, characteristics of clientele, or sponsoring agency. It is intended to be as applicable to public or private post-secondary programs and to alternative programs, such as Comprehensive Employment and Training Act programs, as to high school programs.

The book focuses on lesser than baccalaurate, career-oriented programs. Little is said regarding baccalaurate or graduate programs; but, much of the detail of chapters which deal with program conduct is applicable to programs at any level, so long as work experience is related to classroom and laboratory experience and to student career goals. Whereas much of the book might serve to improve higher education work experience programs not directly related to career goals, such programs are not its focus.

The book has five sections which parallel the problem definition, planning, implementation, conduct, and evaluation sequence.

Section One, Foundations of Cooperative Education, establishes basic understanding and many definitions. Chapter 1, "Role Segmentation vs Community," builds a rationale for cooperative education in four new ways. Chapter 2, "Types of CVOE Programs," defines programs by learner motivation, occupations, clientele characteristics, and educational levels.

Section Two, Planning and Initiating Cooperative Vocational/ Occupational Education (CVOE) Programs, deals with three determinations which must be made prior to what too many take to be first steps. Chapter 3, "Determining Program Constraints," treats institutional, state and federal agency, community, legal, and financial limitations. Chapter 4, "Determining Needs for CVOE," deals with major ways for assessing student needs and aspirations and with primary and secondary sources of area manpower information. Chapter 5, "Determining Cooperative Program Types," describes methods for deciding upon total and individual program features in keeping with constraints and needs.

Section Three, Development and Implementation of Cooperative Education, explains details of five processes which must be begun long before students come to class and journey to training stations. Chapter 6, "Working With a Steering Committee," describes a sequence of tasks which should be accomplished together with a committee broadly representative of the community. Chapter 7, "Providing Internal Resources," describes essential staff, facilities, equipment, and operating budget provisions, which LEA's must allocate for CVOE. Chapter 8, "Utilizing External Resources," contains a lengthy treatment of working with advisory committees and describes ways to maximize use of community facilities, free and inexpensive materials and resource persons, and field trips. Chapter 9, "Student Ingression and Orientation," describes a sequence of tasks for matching student profiles and program purposes and for orienting students to program components. Chapter 10, "Establishing Training Stations," defines characteristics of desirable employers and training stations, procedures for initiating partnerships, and procedures for developing training agreements and training plans.

Section Four, Conduct and Operation of Cooperative Vocational/ Occupational Education (CVOE) Programs, details processes for effecting learning in classrooms and at training stations and for assuring functioning student organizations and public relation efforts. Chapter 11 "Planning Instruction," provides strategies for selecting and organizing learning units and for correlating classroom and on-the-job experiences. Chapter 12, "Executing Instruction,' provides strategies for accomplishing desired classroom learnings. Chapter 13,"The Training Station," details procedures for tasks such as assisting training sponsors and assessing student progress at training stations. Chapter 14, "Program Management," provides methods for controlling program elements which are not treated elsewhere in the book. Chapter 15, "Vocational/Occupational Student Organizations," describes efforts of such groups and the teacher-coordinator-advisor's responsibilities. Chapter 16, "Public Relations," defines methods for providing information to various publics and for scheduling public relations items.

Section Five, Evaluation and Program Change, deals at length with evaluation activities which have special relevance to cooperative education and with a system for regularizing products of evaluation into plans for implementing change. Chapter 17, "Evaluation," describes procedures for planning an evaluation system, conducting followup studies, managing team reviews, and using checklists for eleven areas of concern. Chapter 18, "Program Change," details steps in planning changes, based on inputs from various evaluation activities, and provides special hints for benefiting from results of followup surveys and from various studies of student interest and aspirations and of labor market demands.

We acknowledge the support of our families for the usual sacrifices. We are grateful to students who pretested the several chapters, to Dorothy Thompson and Debbie Tedford who managed our calendars and were very helpful to our other pursuits, to Billy J. Taylor who prepared the bibliography, and to Wayne A. Morella who prepared the illustrations.

# Sample Forms and Illustrations

# Foundations of Cooperative Education

# Chapter 1

# Role Segmentation vs Community: Rationale for Program

The theme of this chapter is that Cooperative Vocational/Occupational Education (CVOE) is uniquely suited to the task of developing the community by linking major societal components. The first section deals with building wholesome, meaningful, and productive relationships between young and old, employer and employee, and education and work.[1] The second section describes cooperative education as a viable pattern—as demonstrated later in Chapter 2, it is really a number of patterns with similarities—of community education. The third section describes cooperative education as a major, acceptable response to contemporary criticism of schools and colleges. The fourth section submits that cooperative education improves vocational/occupational education.

Some of the outcomes of reading this chapter are:

1. Understanding of linkages of student, school, community, and world of work.
2. Understanding cooperative education and community education, as contrasted to self-centered and cloistered education.
3. Understanding several major criticisms of education and how cooperative education turns criticism from negative to positive.
4. Facility for explaining the benefits of cooperative education to several kinds of people.

## IMPROVES RELATIONSHIPS AMONG GROUPS

Several segments of society cry out for improved relationships among various groups. Perhaps foremost among these are opponents of age grouping. Community planners and other practicing behavioral scien-

---

[1]The intent is not to argue that society must return to some previous condition which entailed community. As students, colleagues, and educational practitioners have submitted during discussions of various of the ideas presented here, the concern is to project ways to solve problems of the present and near future with means readily at hand and proven in situations limited only in scale. This is not to say that much or all of what is proposed has not been demonstrated in decades long past.

tists have realized values of mixed age groupings largely by observing negative features of retirement villages and convalescent homes, which restrict contact between young and old. Arguments for ungraded elementary schooling typically submit that increased age span enhances development of intellect and aspects of personality such as poise and responsibility. Arguments for educational parks, for selective secondary school student participation in community college programs, and for the "mainstreaming" of people who have interrupted schooling for various reasons and are older by more than several years than their student peers contain similar and other claims. Alleged benefits of nonschool-based youth groups include various learnings from older people. Retirees who prefer to continue working make similar claims, emphasizing understandings which can be developed only over several decades and which need to be shared with younger workers who are assuming leadership positions in private and public sectors. Increasingly, criticism of schooling and imposed adolescence evidences concern about narrow age grouping and the near isolation of teenagers, as in *Youth: Transition to Adulthood* (65,78).

Concern about relationships between employers and employees is equally widespread and often voiced with caution lest the ire of organized pressure groups be raised. Academics and political figures underscore the evils of the wage-price spiral and the significance of productivity levels during economic stress, recommending greater understanding of commonalities of purpose and benefit between employer and worker groups. Concern about bargaining and work-stoppage rights of public employees of various kinds and professionals in both public and private sectors appears to be very high. Government and foundation-sponsored analyses of worker alienation deal pointedly with the need to apprise young and old of such matters as the history and principles of unionism, economics of free and public enterprises, and patterns of participatory management which appear to benefit all parties. Management and labor groups foster various in-school and out-of-school educational programs. But, these are nearly all fostered by one or the other and tend to emphasize differences rather than emphasize means to common ends.

Little need be added to commentary regarding the dearth of meaningful relationships between schooling and work. Popular books and magazines deal profusely with the oversupply of credentials and lack of match between specialties studied in schools, colleges, and universities and the employment market. Leaders in career and vocational/occupational education submit that programs must facilitate ease of movement into and within a rapidly changing labor market. Analyses of actual experiences of graduates find many programs wanting and some programs very successful in this regard.

As will be seen in subsequent chapters, well-conducted CVOE programs have essential and interrelated components which make for improved relationships across the above gateways to adulthood, which too often are barriers to full citizenship—the young/old, employer/employee, and education/work thresholds. The major of these essential features are:

1. Programs with breadth across occupations and depth along the responsibility ladder in keeping with student and community needs,
2. Continuous input to program design and conduct, from various segments of the community,
3. Functioning advisory committee(s),
4. High-quality student services, including testing, selection, orientation, career guidance, personal counseling, and placement,
5. High-quality classroom learning experiences and high-quality learning experiences at appropriate training stations, according to carefully designed, individual plans,
6. Pay and credit for students,
7. Multifaceted public relations programs, and
8. Multifaceted evaluation systems, including followup of both students and employers.

For the moment, the fact that CVOE bridges gaps between major groups is best demonstrated by lists of benefits to students, community, employer/employee individuals and groups, and educational enterprises. The following are inclusive of the kinds of statements found in state education agency manuals, texts, and journal articles on cooperative education. They are not the result of carefully conducted research and evaluation.[2] In part, they represent the teacher-coordinator experiences of one of the authors and the on-site evaluation experiences of the other. They are cautiously drawn and represent the viewpoint of people who have been privileged to relate closely in various capacities to successful programs. Obviously, items within and among the four lists are not mutually exclusive. They are nearly exhaustive. Obviously, these benefits support viewpoints offered in the remainder of the chapter.

### Benefits to Students

Students work in real situations which are in keeping with interests and abilities. *Contact with several levels of management and employee representatives* and other community leaders via work site, club, and social functions has many positive, salutary effects.

---

[2] There have been few cost/benefit or cost/effectiveness analyses of vocational and occupational education programs and even fewer of cooperative education per se. See Hennessy (21) for recommendations regarding such studies.

*Career Decisionmaking* is made more judicious, accurate, and flexible by cooperative education. Students refine knowledge which is useful to later decisions regarding such matters as type of employer, place of employment, and opportunity for and requirements of advancement.

*Good work habits* are among the most significant benefits. Transition to and from work and/or other educational experiences is eased by skilled guidance of a teacher-coordinator. Cooperative education students live the concept that life consists of various balances of education and work and develop a sense of agency regarding the selection of both training and employment opportunities.

*Placement, advancement, and rewards and benefits* are maximized if no other reason than that cooperative education students "get the jump" on others, especially at understanding the synergistic effects of sound preparation for learning and earning.

*Responsibility and other leadership characteristics* are extended by cooperative education experiences. Students learn the importance of such traits as dependability and initiative in themselves and their superiors. Motivation for knowledge acquisition is improved by use. Cognitive development and values for subjects such as science, mathematics, and communications are enhanced by contact with the world of application and reality. Education and career development are understood in relation.

*Problem-solving skills* are greatly improved over what is achieved in programs which are limited to local education agency (LEA) experiences.

*Articulation of vocational and occupational programs with the world of work* is greatly improved by communications which are shared by students, teacher-coordinators, job supervisors, and advisors. Learnings are more relevant to individual students.

*Attitude development* is improved in scope, depth, and accuracy. Employability improves development of self-concept, especially attitudes regarding one's self-worth, earning power and financial independence, and wholesome contribution to the common welfare. Sense of community and cultural belongings are enhanced.

*Interpersonal relations at work* are improved. The social psychology of work is much better learned via combinations of coordinated work and formal educational experiences than by one or the other—or by both, separated in time.

*Home, school or college, and employer are coordinated* in the interest of students. These linkages resemble associations which were common when very few of the young were unemployed and which affect very few of the young today.

*Financial* benefits are obvious. *Economic education* benefits are less so. As wage earners, students learn much about microeconomics and are motivated to learn macroeconomics, i.e., they gain insight into financial relationships of employers, individuals, and governments.

*Personal characteristics* basic to employment are valued in new ways, e.g., punctuality, appearance, attendance, realiability.

### Benefits to Community

A *pool of skilled and experienced manpower* is developed. Furthermore, cooperative education incorporates features which work to balance manpower supply and demand.

*Citizenship and responsibility* and what Law (36), p.36, calls *civic competence* are more evident in communities with cooperative education programs. Students, employers and their associations, workers and their associations, and schoolmen are more aware and appreciative of community.

*Retention of young* (and older) *people* in the community is increased because people become aware of opportunities for meaningful and progressive careers in the immediate area.

Educational institutions are encouraged in new ways to satisfy *training and social needs of the community*.

*The number of people who take* more *from a community* than they contribute to financial, social, recreational, etc., aspects of life *is reduced* by widely participatory CVOE programs. Communities become much more attractive to private and public sector employers who have opportunities to locate new or expand existing enterprises.

### Benefits to Employers and Employees (individual and group, private and public)

Supervisors learn *job analysis and educational principles and practices* which are essential to on-the-job training of all workers. Supervisors are released from elementary tasks, which can be done by student-learners.

*Training occurs at low cost to employer and employee groups.* Both benefit from guidance functions such as *testing and placement services*. People are moved to *permanent employment, economic participation, and union membership* with better knowledge and attitudes.

*Introduction of minority employees* in a wider range of establishments and occupations is eased by cooperative education.

*Employee turnover is reduced* because of better matching of individuals to jobs and flexibility of employees who have both in-school and on-the-job experiences.

*Opportunity for influencing vocational and occupational programs* is provided by cooperative education.

Cooperative education *provides a pool of temporary and seasonal employees*.

Cooperative education *contributes to "good will,"* i.e., both management and labor benefit from recognition and clear demonstration of belonging in the community.

Employers and labor *develop understanding of educational problems,* which is useful at election time and in general and specialized advisory roles.

Employers and employees *work together in programs which benefit* the larger community and foster communication and understanding of other matters.

### Benefits to Local Education Agencies (LEA's)

*Broader programs satisfy more student needs*. Cooperative education is especially well-equipped to accommodate new and emerging occupations, exceptional students, and occupations which require broad competencies and/or expensive facilities which cannot be provided by LEA's.

*Retention and attendance* are improved.

*Student/faculty relations* are improved.

*Faculty updating* occurs on regular bases by observation and the work of coordinating.

*Facilities* otherwise not available to learners and on scales unattainable by other educational models *are used*.

*Programs are affected by knowledge* of outstanding people in the productive community. Curriculum revision is more rapid and reflective of occupational requirements. In-school experiences are more sensitive to the need for balance along dimensions of the world of work.

*Counseling is improved* by knowledge of changing employment conditions.

The *placement function* operates on more continuous bases.

*Feedback re program success and failures* is more continuous and current re practice in business, industry, commerce, and government. Students make almost immediate evaluations of in-school learnings and are themselves involved in adjusting in-school and out-of-school learnings one to the other and according to competency requirements.

## CVOE IS COMMUNITY EDUCATION

Far too few leaders in state and local education agencies have realized that CVOE is a viable pattern of community education. Purposes and principles of community and cooperative education have great similarity.

### Community Education Essentials

A short-form definition of community education is: improvement of the individual, i.e., development of skills and knowledge for a better livelihood, and community improvement via social action [Minzey and le Tarte (46), p.7]. Community education agencies serve people of wide age ranges and with various motivations. Their motivations can be categorized as: to acquire basic and/or liberal education, to participate in recreation activities, or to develop along career patterns. Their participation ranges a great deal in terms of time and in terms of balance of learner and presenter responsibilites. Community education is conducted in a large variety of facilities under the auspices of a large variety of public and private agencies—all orchestrated by one agency, which is responsible for total programming. Community education is process-oriented, i.e., is not only the sum of several programs. It entails (1) the process of fitting experiences to motivations, time constraints, and other variables in the interest of individuals, community, and social action and (2) the process of involving all components of the community in the delivery of services.

Kerensky and Melby (32) idealized community education as consisting of twelve components.[3]

1. Maximized Use of Existing Human and Physical Resources
2. Establishment of Cooperative Procedures with Government Service Agencies
3. Establishment of Cooperative Procedures with Volunteer and Civic Service Organizations
4. The Development of Cooperative Procedures with Business and Industry
5. The Establishment of Cooperative Procedures with Other Educational Institutions
6. The Establishment of Procedures for Self-Generating Activities
7. The Initiation and Coordination of Special Community Events
8. The Establishment of Problem Solving Procedures through the Creation of a Citizen's Advisory Council
9. The Employment of a Community School Director or Coordinator Who Serves to Tie All of the Above Together and Serves in the Capacity of an Ombudsman for His Entire Community

---

[3]Serious students and/or practitioners of community education should read this and other works of Melby to note that community education, cooperative education, and aleviation of educational criticism "go together".

10. The Establishment of a Climate for Innovation and Change
11. Provisions for Heuristics
12. Provisions for Serendipity

Obviously, CVOE entails all, with the exception of component nine, to some degree. Many of Kerensky and Melby's (32) definitions of these components are well-satisfied by cooperative education. The full list of components, including the more subtle heuristics and serendipity, are evidenced where cooperative education is successful. Futhermore, where cooperative education flourishes without other aspects of community education, effective teacher-coordinators serve many of the functions of community education directors,i.e., component nine.

A newer list of community education components facilitates closer comparisons. Minzey (45) lists the following components of community education.

1. An Educational Program for School Age Children
2. Use of Community Facilities
3. Additional Programs for School Age Children and Youth
4. Programs for Adults
5. Delivery and Coordination of Community Services
6. Community Involvement

It is essential to note that the first four components are programs and the last two are processes.

### Comparison of CVOE and Community Education

Thoroughgoing and successful cooperative education programs include each of the six components of community education to at least minimal degree. As the lists of essentials and benefits presented earlier in this chapter and as even cursory examinations of best-quality, ongoing programs indicate, cooperative education is illustrative of community education. Each of the components of community education is easily matched with elements of cooperative education:

1. *An Educational Program for School Age Children.* In typical LEA's, cooperative education is much more than a program. It is usually a system of programs across occupational areas or clusters and across ability and interest categories. Furthermore, a typical community has cooperative education at two or more levels on the educational ladder.
2. *Use of Community Facilities.* Cooperative education uses a great variety of community facilities in both public and private sectors. Advanced programs utilize nearly all available types of wholesome employment establishments, including private homes and selected

work stations in LEA's themselves. Furthermore, related experiences are not restricted to classroom experiences but typically involve visits to financial institutions, private and public job placement agencies, and health service agencies, as well as special presentations in employer facilities, e.g., demonstration of expensive or large machines.

3. *Additional Programs for School Age Children and Youth.* Student personnel services which are essential to cooperative education are best provided in community education settings. Both community and cooperative education depend upon inventories (and use) of social service agencies, free and inexpensive equipment, material and supplies, resource persons, etc. Reward and recognition programs serve students and contributors alike.

4. *Programs for Adults.* In addition to participation as advisors, in-school presentors, contributors of free materials, etc., those adults who are supervisors of student-learners receive instruction re supervision and training and perhaps some updating re their specialties. This instruction ranges from informal presentations during teacher-coordinator visits to job sites to formal classes in LEA's outside working hours. Students are the vehicle for some updating of both supervisors and teacher-coordinators. Teacher-coordinators also learn from supervisors and others at work sites. Furthermore, there is a trend toward cooperative adult education programs sponsored by industry or business and education. See for example the publications by Ohio State University (51,52, 53, and 54).

5. *Delivery and Coordination of Community Services.* Placement services are the best example of CVOE's contribution to this component of community education. It is not unusual to find that an LEA which has prime responsibility for community education has used placement services for cooperative and other vocational or occupational education graduates as a base for developing job placement services for all residents—and in far fewer instances for ex-residents. Cooperative education students clubs often have community service projects. These fit nicely into community education services. Some of them have the further advantage of relating directly to occupational preparation, e.g., child care students offer free babysitting for single parents, building trades students construct park and playgrond equipment prior to more ambitious projects in their regular sequence of learnings.

6. *Community Involvement.* As Chapter 8, Utilizing External Resources, illustrates, cooperative education functions best when program phases from intial survey and design to evaluation and graduation involve community members. Where cooperative education works best, it is not an LEA's program; it is the community's program and everyone

speaks of it that way, of *our* program. Authorities concerning the introducton of cooperative or community education programs advocate very similar sequences of events, including community surveys, steering committees, and advisory committees.

In addition to community projects undertaken by student clubs, cooperative education has impact upon community problems, e.g., alienation of youth, delinquency, school leaving, poverty, unemployment. Granted, the approach to these and other social, economic, and political matters is not direct. But, like some other aspects of full-blown community education programs, cooperative education makes differences in a community. These differences are in aspects of life which are little altered by LEA's which define roles and functions quite apart from their publics, e.g., to transmit culture or organized knowledge. After all, cooperative education shares the concerns of community education to develop people who are fully and freely engaged in wholesome work, recreation, and learning for citizenship and self-betterment.

Perhaps more than any other pattern of community education, cooperative education contributes immensely to the breaking down of traditional, segment organizational patterns of LEA's. Sans community education, LEA's may be oriented to (1) the content of instruction, (2) and/or to the clientele served, and/or (3) to the employers of graduates. Very few LEA's are oriented to more than one or two of the three. With community education, LEA's are oriented to all three. Community education greatly reduces role segmentation and leads inevitably to cooperative linkages between individuals and groups.

## ALLAYS EDUCATIONAL CRITICISM

It is not the present concern to detail various major criticisms of education. This is a vast literature, which is from time-to-time analyzed according to major categories of complaint.[4] The intent here is to illustrate briefly in only four ways that CVOE is a major and appropriate response to educational criticism.

### Cooperative Education and Disadvantaged and Target Groups

One contemporary complaint re LEA's is that they fail to serve certain groups. It is widely maintained that cooperative education is a viable delivery mode for various groups, e.g., socioeconomic disadvantaged, educationally disadvantaged, handicapped, minorities, women. Weisman (82), Kerensky and Melby (32), *Youth: Transition to Adulthood* (65 and

---

[4]See for example: McNally and Passow, (38) Purpel and Belanger (63), and Bailey and Stadt (4), especially Chapters 1 and 2.

78), Bailey and Stadt (4), and Silberman (69) make this point in different ways and with varying degrees of caution. State manuals on cooperative education, texts, and journal articles on cooperative education make the point more directly and forcefully. This is in no small part because federal legislation and state plans for vocational-technical education have provided for special programming for specified kinds of people. With far from sound empirical evidence, but based upon the principle that methodologies which work with special needs clientele tend to work with all others, the authors submit that cooperative education has a long history of and a bright future for launching individuals of any description on wholesome careers which involve various balances of educational preparation, work experience, and advancement. Because it links LEA's, employer and employee groups, community agencies, and individuals aspiring to brighter futures, cooperative education is especially well suited to emerging peoples.

### Cooperative Education and Accountabilty

Much of contemporary criticism asks that education be accountable to its various publics. Bailey and Stadt (4) deal at some length with this matter, concluding that career education, better than less well-organized components of LEA's, has great potential for responding to accountability demands.

One of the controversies in the literature of accountability concerns the appropriateness of cost/benefit analyses. It is now widely held that such analyses are unmanageable. Yet, it would seem that cooperative education would fare very well under economic scrutiny insofar as students and most graduates earn wages and insofar as community resources of various kinds accrue benefits at minimal additional costs. More manageable *cost/ effectiveness* analyses compare dollar inputs with social and psychological outcomes which are the responsibility for the community, LEA's, and educational professionals. Employability, earning power, and other benefits of cooperative education are certain to be of increasing concern to mature critics of education. Again, because of its work-a-day linkages, CVOE fares well under such analyses. Each of several parties works to assure the success and effectiveness of other parties. An open and circular system is almost certain to have greater effect on human variables than can a closed and linear system such as content-centered, college preparatory instruction. (See also Financial Constraints in Chapter 3.)

### Cooperative Education and Advocacy

A less widely publicized complaint about LEA's is that as their size increases, say beyond 500, students and staff become less well acquainted and tend to become alienated. Everyone knows only the few whom he contacts regularly and no one feels part of the whole. Study commissions stress this phenomenon. One response to alienation within LEA's is "child advocacy." This has been the theme of conventions and a growing literature. In sum, child advocacy says that all LEA personnel must foster and support the best interests—however varied—of individual students. This is not a new idea. But, especially in large population centers, it is a welcome, professional response to the idea of child advocacy in cooperative education.

There is no better model of student advocacy than cooperative vocational/occupational education. The teacher-coordinator enlists a wide array of resources in the interest of individual students and manages a checks and balances system, which assures economic, social, psychological, and educational benefits. Each cooperative student does indeed have a chief advocate. Furthermore, because there is a career plan and a more immediate training plan, other teachers, counselors, job supervisors, and other student contact personnel, in LEA's and at work, bolster the interest of individual students or advocacy function in cooperative education.

### Cooperative Education and Transition to Adulthood

It is not surprising to experienced vocational/occupational educators that serious examinations of transition from childhood and schooling to adulthood and economic responsibility recommend cooperative education as an alternative for many people. Even though they are largely done by other than vocational/occupational educators, large-scale studies are increasingly appreciative of the benefits of cooperative education, apprenticeship, and other work-experience programs. Yet, it is sad to note that the full breadth and depth of cooperative education have not been compared with the sweeping recommendations of large-scale studies. Such comparison cannot be undertaken here. Suffice it to say that cooperative education has a long history of success and is clearly worthy of great expansion to assure smooth transition to responsible adulthood. This is obvious to a great many LEA's at university, college, and secondary school levels, which are expanding cooperative education many fold. The point of the argument here is that cooperative education—really career education with cooperative work experiences at various levels, beginning at least as early as age fourteen for some—is a way to avoid "throwing the baby out with the wash." That is, career education and especially the capstone experience, i.e., CVOE, is the great hope for LEA's.

## IMPROVES VOCATIONAL/OCCUPATIONAL EDUCATION

It is fair to ask: Does cooperative education make a difference over vocational/occupational education done in classrooms and laboratories without live experiences in the world of work? Needless to say, some things are best learned within "ivied halls." Such things as nomenclature of any occupational area, electronic fundamentals, and a new computer programming language are best learned thoroughly and with minimum interruption in cloistered situations. But, especially for the young, who have not learned productive, economic responsibility gradually—as is possible for some who are reared in or on small enterprises such as family shops and farms—cooperative education is a viable method for assuring that the junction of schooling and working is a "merge" as contrasted to a "yield" or a "stop" intersection.

### Summary

A rationale for CVOE is easily built in many ways. Anyone who has attended a student/employer awards and recognition banquet could strengthen the above arguments: (1) That there are a great many positive linkages between and among students, employer/employee individuals and groups, community agencies, and LEA's which participate in cooperative education programs. (2) That cooperative education is a form of and often the stepping stone to full-blown community education. (3) That cooperative education—as part of career education—is at once a response to concern for the special learning and employability-related needs of target groups, to accountability demands, to insistence upon student advocacy, and to national commitment to smooth transition to adulthood via early and growing involvement in economic, social, and political affairs. (4) That cooperative education improves vocational/occupational education. Cooperative education sounds ambitious; it must be; it is an essential institution in America. Subsequent sections of this book deal with matters which maximize its success/failure ratio.

### Activities

1. Interview a teacher-coordinator, a school or college counselor, and an educational administor, asking each to enumerate the benefits of CVOE to students and the LEA. Plan questions beforehand.
2. Interview a chamber of commerce and a labor union official, asking each to enumerate advantages and disadvantages of CVOE to management, labor, and students.
3. Consult an expert on community education to discover whether he/she has recognized the similarities of community and CVOE.

4. Identify two newspaper or journal articles which criticize education. Draft a response to the criticism, indicating how CVOE might strengthen positive criticism and challenge negative criticism.
5. Interview a director of vocational/occupational education in an LEA, asking whether or not CVOE improves vocational/occupational education and in what ways and under what conditions.
6. Write a critique of this chapter, emphasizing what research is necessary to substantiate or refute the claim that CVOE is an essential American institution.

# Chapter 2

# Types of CVOE Programs

Cooperative Vocational/Occupational Education (CVOE) cannot be described satisfactorily along any one dimension. Several variables must be managed simultaneously for full understanding. This chapter begins with several definitions from State Education Agency (SEA) manuals. Major sections describe types of programs along the following dimensions.

Learner Motivations

Occupational Areas or Clusters

Special Student Groups

Levels on the Educational Ladder

These dimensions are not and cannot be mutually exclusive. There is much overlap between categories on one dimension and on another.

Some of the outcomes of reading this chapter are *understanding:*

1. Standard definitions of cooperative vocational/occupational education (CVOE).
2. Similarities and dissimilarities of types of programs by learner motivations, occupational areas, special student groups, and levels on the educational ladder.

## CVOE DEFINED

It is essential to differentiate cooperative vocational/occupational education (CVOE) from other work experience programs. This section begins this task. The Tennessee handbook (73), p. 4, contains a good working definition of cooperative education.

A program of vocational education for persons who, through a cooperative arrangement between the school and employers, receive instruction by alternation of study in school with a job in any occupational field, but these two experiences must be planned and supervised by the school and employers so that each contributes to the student's education and to his employability. Work periods and school attendance may be on alternate half-days, full days, weeks, or other periods of time in fulfilling the cooperative work-study program.

The type of cooperative education adopted by a school should be determined by the occupational needs of its students and the occupational opportunities within the community. Specialized or occupational area type vocational cooperative education programs should be instituted wherever feasible, especially where a school has a multiplicity of vocational cooperative education programs.

The Minnesota handbook (44), p. 9, for cooperative vocational education defines cooperative vocational education with emphasis upon requirements of the Vocational Education Amendments of 1968.

1. Cooperative education is an arrangement for bringing relevancy to formal instruction through alternating employment in the community with classroom instruction. The term encompasses plans employing a wide variety of practices, policies, and procedures.

2. The legal definition of cooperative vocational education contains the minimal requirements for reimbursement for this type of education which equals or exceeds the Federal requirements.

3. The legal definition contains three criteria for cooperative vocational education: (1) students must receive instruction, including required academic courses and related vocational instruction by alternation of study in school with a job in any occupational field, (2) these two experiences must be planned and supervised by the school and employers so that each contributes to the student's education and to his employability, and (3) work periods and school attendance may be on alternate half-days, full days, weeks, or other periods of time.

4. Cooperative vocational education may be funded under two parts of the Amendments of 1968: Part B—State Vocational Education Programs, and Part G—Cooperative Vocational Education Programs. The purpose of Part G is to aid the states in expanding cooperative vocational education to include students in areas with high rates of school dropouts and youth unemployment.

5. Since there are alternative objectives for local cooperative vocational education, some of which may conflict in program operation, choices should be made during the planning stage.

6. In selecting program objectives, local planners should be fully aware of the vocational attitudes of prospective students and the range of student attitudes toward school.

7. Vocational planners are strongly encouraged to heed the needs of special groups of students such as those with academic, cultural, and other handicaps.

The Vermont (79) and other state manuals contain comparisons of cooperative education and work-study (Table 2-1), as provided for by the VEA (1968).

The Illinois guide (28), p. 1, provides definitions which contrast cooperative vocational education, and cooperative work training and work-study.

Cooperative Vocational Education (CVE) is an instructional plan which combines learning experiences gained through regularly scheduled supervised employment in the community and vocationally oriented in-school instruction. The employing community serves as a laboratory where students have an opportunity to apply the principles and practices they have learned in school in the changing world of work. Cooperative occupational education is a general term used to describe various types of cooperative plan programs specifically designed to prepare youth for occupations in proportion to the distribution of employment and career opportunities.

Cooperative Work Training (CWT) is a program designed to provide students with maturing experiences through employment that will help them become productive, responsible individuals. The part-time work need not be related to the occupational goals of the students. This type of program is termed Cooperative Work Training or CWT. This program is designed specifically to serve disadvantaged youth and adults who are dropouts and who need the social, emotional, maturation and career exploration essential for success. All elements of the cooperative plan are present in the operatior. of the program; only the level of employment is lower than in cooperative vocational education.

Work-study is a program designed to provide financial assistance, through part-time employment, to students who have been accepted for full-time enrollment in vocational training. The part-time employment, in a nonprofit institution, is based on the financial need of the student and is not necessarily related to his career objective. This type of program is done by special contract with the Division of Vocational and Technical Education.

Cooperative vocational/occupational education is to be distinguished from two other forms of work experience education. One of these is called *extended laboratory*, especially by health occupations educators. These experiences occur by plan in accord with in-school learnings. But, they are short term and unpaid. In essence, they make use of equipment and/or clients or customers which are not available in the LEA. For example, an auto mechanics class might rotate in pairs through several days of experiences re wheel balancing and front-end alignment. A dental hygiene class might work in pairs with elementary teachers on oral hygiene instruction.

The other work experience program which is not cooperative education is internship. Mason and Haines (41), p. 17, lists eight characteristics of internships.

1. Is used in professional or sub-professional curricula at collegiate levels (in two-year or four-year institutions).
2. Is undertaken typically as a culminating experience prior to the student's graduation, but after preliminary classroom work.
3. Occurs in an actual professional job situation where the intern experiences the requirements of employment.
4. Was conceived as a way primarily of enabling the student to apply the

## Table 2-1. Comparative Analysis of Cooperative Education Programs and Work-Study Programs Vocational Education Amendments of 1968

| Part B State Vocational Education Programs | Part G Cooperative Vocational Education Programs | Part H Work-Study Programs for Vocational Education Students |
|---|---|---|
| 1. Money appropriated under Part B and allotted to the states may be expended for cooperative education programs | 1. Money appropriated under Part G and allotted to the States shall be expended for developing new programs of cooperative education | 1. Money appropriated under Part H and allotted to the States shall be expended for work-study programs |
| 2. Purpose<br>* To provide on-the-job work experience related to the student's course of study and chosen occupation | 2. Purpose<br>* To provide on-the-job work experience related to the student's course of study and chosen occupation | 2. Purpose<br>* To provide financial assistance to students who are in need of earnings from employment to commence or continue their vocational education program |
| 3. Students Served<br>* Individuals who desire and need such education and training in all communities of the State | 3. Students Served<br>* Individuals who desire and need such education and training in all communities of the State<br>* Priority is given to areas of high rates of school dropouts and youth unemployment | 3. Students Served<br>* Economically disadvantaged full-time vocational education students |
| 4. Uses of Funds<br>* Program operation and ancillary services | 4. Uses of Funds<br>* Programs operation and ancillary services<br>* Reimbursement of added training cost to employers, when necessary<br>* Payment for certain services or unusual costs to students while in cooperative training | 4. Uses of Funds<br>* Compensation of students employed<br>* Development and administration of program |
| 5. Federal Portion of Support<br>* Based upon Statewide matching (50/50) for all basic grant vocational education programs. Application of State criteria for allocation of funds determines level of assistance. | 5. Federal Portion of Support<br>* All or part (100%) | 5. Federal Portion of Support<br>* 80% |

## Part B
### State Vocational Education Programs

6. Instruction
* In-school vocational instruction related to occupational field and training job

7. Work Periods
* Alternate half days, full days, weeks, or other periods of time. (Number of hours of work generally equal the number of hours spent in school)

8. Wage Payments
* Regular wages established for the occupational field
* Usually at least minimum wage or student-learner rate established by Department of Labor
* Wages paid by employer

9. Age Limitations
* Minimum age 14 as per Child Labor Laws

10. Eligible Employers
* Public or private

11. Administration
* Administered by the State or local educational agencies under supervision of the State Board for Vocational Education in accordance with State Plan provisions

## Part G
### Cooperative Vocational Education Programs

6. Instruction
* In-school vocational instruction related to occupational field and training job

7. Work Periods
* Alternate half days, full days, weeks, or other periods of time. (Number of hours of work need not equal the number of hours spent in school)

8. Wage Payments
* Regular wages established for the occupational field
* Usually at least minimum wage or student-learner rate established by Department of Labor
* Wages paid by employer

9. Age Limitations
* Minimum wage 14 as per Child Labor Laws

10. Eligible Employers
* Public or private

11. Administration
* Administered by the State or local educational agencies under supervision of the State Board for Vocational Education in accordance with State Plan provisions

## Part H
### Work-Study Programs for Vocational Education Students

6. Instruction
* In-school vocational instruction not necessarily related to the job

7. Work Periods
* Maximum of 15 hours per week while attending school

8. Wage Payments
* $45 per month, $350 per academic year or in certain cases $60 per month, $500 per academic year
* Public funds are used for compensation

9. Age Limitations
* 15 through 20 years of age

10. Eligible Employers
* Limited to public, non-profit employers

11. Administration
* Administered by the State or local educational agencies under supervision of the State Board for Vocational Education in accordance with State Plan provisions

concepts and skills he has learned in the college classroom rather than a way of learning new skills and knowledges.

5. Is usually a full-time, resident experience and typically at least three months in length in order to provide a complete experience.
6. Places the intern usually in a firm or agency that is selected by the college for its progressive method of operation.
7. Has the student supervised at his internship agency by a professional person who has been selected for his ability in his profession and for his competence as a trainer.
8. Pays the intern a salary because he is productive person; but his pay is usually at a reduced rate because he is a trainee and not all of his time is fully productive.

Internships are used in graduate and baccalaureate programs in professional and paraprofessional fields, including engineering, education, and public administration. Community college and technical institute programs for health and public service occupations make good use of the internship plan. When done well, it has nearly all the benefits and advantages of cooperative education. The major contrast from cooperative education is that internships are done *after* theory and other in-school experiences, whereas cooperative education incorporates elements of both.

The "Report of a National Conference on Cooperative Education" (64), p. 13, provides a succinct definition of cooperative education.

Cooperative vocational education is an interdependent combination of vocational instruction and employment related to that instruction.

Cooperative vocational education is an instructional plan which combines learning experiences gained through regularly scheduled employment in the community and vocationally oriented in-school instruction.

Cooperative vocational education is a purposeful blending of vocational instruction and employment which meet job preparatory objectives.

Cooperative vocational education is, therefore, a school initiated and school-supervised program which involves persons enrolled in or brought back into the formal school setting. School, for our purposes, means any level of education, including community colleges and technical institutes.

## CVOE AND LEARNER MOTIVATIONS

One way to describe types of cooperative education is to define learner goals or motivations for cooperative work experiences. As the previous section indicated, CVOE and work study are quite different in this regard. This section illustrates the fact that within career and vocational/ occupational education there are a range of learner motivations for cooperative work experience. This range parallels the educational ladder—for most people.

### Career Exploration

"Exploratory work experience education is primarily a career guidance program." [Kimbrel and Vineyard (33), p. 1]. Such programs involve short-term nonpaid experiences which contribute to decisions toward or away from occupations. [Mason and Haines (41), p. 81.] Observation and supervised participation provide information necessary to free and intelligent choices. These experiences are credit bearing, usually as units in courses at the 8-10 grade levels.

### Occupational Orientation

Some preparatory level programs are preceded by occupational orientation—or begin with occupational orientation—which shows "what can be done." People who have made career and/or occupational choices are placed in unpaid or paid positions for several days or weeks or a summer term to learn from practitioners and via "hands on." Best quality programs entail scheduled samplings of assignments and tasks. These provide information regarding individual interests, strengths, weaknesses, and aptitudes, which are helpful to educational programming and later placements in cooperative and permanent work situations.

### Vocational/Occupational Preparation via Cooperative Experiences

This is the overriding concern of this book.

### General Work Experience Education

This is not a form of vocational/occupational cooperative education and is not the concern of this book. Very few secondary schools, a small percentage of colleges, and a very rapidly increasing number of four-year colleges and universities afford students opportunities to earn credit via work experience which may or may not by related to career pattern development. These experiences add many dimensions to otherwise limited social-psychological and economic development and are worthy of claims laid by proponents of work experience. But, they are the concern of vocational and occupational education only insofar as they require clarification, i.e., contrast to programs wherein work, schooling, and training plans coincide, and insofar as they might confuse employers and affect the provision of training stations for students whose motives are more direct.

**Remediation**

Lest the parallel of orientation, exploration, and preparation with the educational ladder be overemphasized, it is well to appreciate that cooperative education has utility in remedial programs for out-of-school youth and unemployed or underemployed adults or adults returning to the work force as it does for secondary and post-secondary programs for people of typical ages. All too few students in the various public and private programs which serve such clientele are provided live experiences which aid and assure career decisions and refine entry level knowledges and skills. Remedial, upgrading, and returning students deserve the benefits of cooperative education as well as do "main line" students.

## OCCUPATIONAL AREAS OR CLUSTERS

The major way to describe types of cooperative programs is according to occupational areas or clusters or as is very often the case, according to "service areas" which stemmed from vocational education legislation prior to 1968. Whereas these areas persist as identifiable programs with cooperative experiences near the ends of programs, it should be noted that some states have structured vocational and occupational education in new ways. For example, since 1969 the Illinois State Plan for Vocational and Technical Education has specified the following occupational areas:

1. Applied Biological and Agriculture
2. Business, Marketing, and Management
3. Health
4. Industrial Oriented
5. Personal and Public Service.

Obviously, these categories (1) extend agriculture education as the following section describes, (2) accommodate other than traditional office and distributive occupations, e.g., middle management and computer programming programs in community colleges, (3) emphasize health occupations as contrasted to their earlier inclusion in trades and industry, when only practical nursing was reimbursable, (4) use a more manageable term than trade and industrial (to which some had added technical to the chagrin of people in other areas which also include technician-level occupations), and (5) emphasizes the major growth areas of public service and personal service—again moving some occupations, such as cosmetology, from industrial to a more unified category.

The following sections appear because (1) programs exist in these areas in many states, (2) identifiable programs with these labels persist (and rightfully so) even in states, such as Illinois, which have changed the next-higher level of categories of occupational areas, and (3) these terms are used by professional associations, teacher educators, and publishers. It is important to note that the nomenclature or alphabet soup of cooperative education varies greatly from state to state. The following headings are followed by one or more acronyms, which are spelled out in the respective descriptions.

### Agricultural and Agribusiness (AO, ABO, ARO)

Three categories of agricultural and related occupations are appropriate for cooperative education.

1. Animal and plant, food and fiber, production entails a number of occupations. Especially, as farm and ranch operations increase in size and diversity, the number of specialties which make for appropriate work stations and opportunity for placing students with varying interests and abilities increases. It is important to note that garden and decorative seed and plant production, e.g., sod farm, nursery, seed house, greenhouse, and pet and pleasure animal breeding and training are part of Agriculture Occupations (AO).
2. Agribusiness Occupations (ABO) require agricultural competencies, but are situated along the route of material coming to or leaving production facilities. Some categories of these occupations are grain storage and transportation; animal health, feed, seed, and chemical supply and application; livestock and ag products brokerage; and ornamental horticulture.
3. Ag-Related Occupations (ARO) may also be classified in other areas such as distributive education or trades and industry. They require some of the knowledges which agricultural and agribusiness occupations require but major competencies are in other areas. Some of these are on-farm and agribusiness office workers, engine mechanics, salespersons in florist shops, and food processors. Classroom and on-job experiences for ag-related students will often be individualized.

Some SEA's and LEA's use terms such as natural resources, and environmental to depict a wider range of occupations than did the older connotations of agriculture and agribusiness. How occupations are grouped should depend upon local matters such as labor market characteristics and the diversity of occupations represented in preparatory programs. Many occupations are not obviously within one or another area or cluster—no matter what the categorical system.

Secondary school agricultural programs which involve cooperative experiences can serve students who are concerned to enter the above mentioned occupations. This is also the case for post-secondary programs. Some occupations are typically the concern of post-secondary LEA's and rarely of secondary schools. Most of these, such as turf management or agricultural mechanics include management and/or technician-level competencies, which require more in-school specialization than can be afforded by most high schools.

### Distributive and Marketing (DE)

Distributive occupations differ from industrial and office occupations. Distributive Education (DE) is concerned with the movement of goods and services from production to consumption, i.e., with marketing, transportation, advertising, financing, wholesaling, displaying, retailing, and the like. These occupations occur in all manner of retail stores, markets and dealerships, eating and drinking establishments, amusement centers, supply houses, wholesale establishments, banks and other financial institutions, rooming establishments, travel agencies, etc. Some jobs in distribution are buyer, sales clerk, store clerk, order clerk, inventory clerk, display designer, manager, sales supervisor, supervisor, cashier, and route clerk. As is the case in agriculture, distributive education in post-secondary LEA's includes preparation for some occupations which require greater supervisory, managerial, and financial responsibility and/or technical knowledge, e.g., business administration, public administration, midmanagement, and supermarket management.

### Health (HOE)

Health Occupations Education (HOE) programs in secondary and post-secondary programs prepare people for cooperative experiences in hospitals, clinics, convalescent homes, and related establishments, such as medical laboratories. The Illinois manual (29) for health occupations programs lists the following occupations as appropriate to secondary school programs.

Dental Aide
Dental Laboratory Aide
Geriatric Aide
Home Health Aide
Hospital Admissions Clerk
Hospital Housekeeping Aide
Hospital Central Service Aide
Hospital Food Services
Hospital Laundry Aide

Inhalation Therapy Aide
Medical Laboratory Aide
Medical Office Aide
Medical Records Clerk
Mental Health Aide
Nurse Aide, Orderly or Attendant
Occupational Therapy Aide
Operating Room Aide
Physical Therapy Aide
Psychiatric Aide, Orderly or Attendant
Public Health Aide, including Environment Control Aide
Recreational Therapy Aide
Small Animal or Large Animal Veterinary Aide (when no Agricultural
    Cooperative Program is included in the curriculum)
Ward Clerk
X-ray Aide (minimum age 18 years)

As do many students in other areas, such as agriculture and distributive education, many secondary school health occupations students plan to and are well-equipped to pursue post-secondary programs. A great many of these programs have cooperative and other forms of work experience. Some post-secondary programs which are suited to cooperative experiences are medical laboratory, dental laboratory, social welfare assistant, inhalation therapist, and child care. Many post-secondary health occupations programs are controlled in no small part by state licensing agencies and accrediting bodies. Many programs entail learning experiences with minimum responsibility at work sites, followed by rotating internships, usually unpaid. Many of these programs would be improved by cooperative education, i.e., by coordinated, in-school and paid training station experiences. There are more than a few indicators of trends in this direction.

**Home Economics (HERO)**

Since 1963, some home economics educators have been concerned to adapt experiences so that students move to gainful employment. Home Economics Related Occupations (HERO) are gainful or wage-earning education and function in much the same manner as other secondary school cooperative programs. But, typically, the in-school curriculum is designed for homemaking and family living and some students are enrolled in cooperative and related classes in the senior year. Some of the occupations they pursue are child care or nursery aide, institutional housekeeper, visiting homemaker, food service, clothing maintenance, and needle trades.

In better- and best-quality programs, job competency requirements and the processes of cooperative education, functioning via student and advisor groups, serve to modify substantive courses so that employability is a primary rather than a secondary objective. Not enough home economics departments have foreseen conflicts between homemaking and gainful programs. Some have the resources to do both just as some secondary school or community college business or industrial departments do vocational and practical or hobby programs quite apart from one another.

### Industrial (ICE)

Industrial Cooperative Education (ICE) occupations range from semi-skilled to technical. The older designation trade and industrial is no longer used in some states. One way to categorize industrial occupations is (1) in plant, (2) on-site, and (3) service, i.e., as (a) manufacturing, (b) construction, and (c) maintenance and repair. Another common category is transportation. Some are apprenticeable occupations (in some areas of the country) and some LEA's arrange for advanced placement in apprenticeship programs. Most industrial occupations entail opportunities for advancement.

Some occupations appropriate to secondary school preparation are automotive body, automotive mechanic, draftsman, appliance repair, motor repair, electrician, meat cutting, building trades (or a single building trade) radio and television servicing, sign painting, welding, machine operator, and upholstering. Some occupations appropriate to post-secondary preparation are automotive technician, diesel mechanic, engineering draftsman, air conditioning and refrigeration mechanic, civil engineering assistant, concrete construction, automotive service manager, supervision, electronics technician, mechanical engineering technician, welding, numerical control, quality control, and aviation electronics.

### Office (OO, COE)

Office Occupations (OO) or Cooperative Office Education (COE) programs place students in almost all manner of private and public agencies. Almost the full ranges of size and function of enterprises have appropriate entry positions. Student-learners acquire office skills in preparatory courses such as typing, shorthand, bookkeeping, and data processing. Cooperative experiences are usually scheduled for grade twelve or the second year of post-secondary programs. Some programs involve cooperative experiences for two years. Nearly all programs entail a one-period related class, typically called office practice. In some large schools, cooperative experiences are separate for stenographic and clerical-bookkeeping students [Mason and Haines (41), p. 113] in Office Occupations (OO).

In most secondary situations, office occupations programs prepare high-quality students for highly skilled positions. There are a number of programs in large cities for students who might otherwise leave school because of academic problems. These programs are not called "OO" and usually move people to employment in clerical jobs. Most begin with cooperative experience in grade ten and continue until the student leaves school.

Many advanced office and clerical programs at the post-secondary level involve cooperative experiences. Some of these are court recorder, executive secretary, legal secretary, medical secretary, and accounting.

### Service (SOC)

Service Occupations Cooperative (SOC) education is an emerging area, primarily in post-secondary LEA's. Some specialty areas are (1) entertainment: theatrical staging, dance, broadcasting, film production, (2) recreation and hospitality: supervision, resort and club management, (3) public services: corrections, early childhood education, fire prevention and control, law enforcement, social services, (4) personal services: cosmetology, mortuary science, private security, building and grounds custodian, legal assistant. All these involve cooperative experience for Service Occupations Cooperative (SOC) education students.

### Diversified (DO)

Diversified Occupations (DO) programs are nearly always conducted by teacher-coordinators with industrial education backgrounds. One difference between these programs and industrial cooperative programs is the breadth of occupations. In diversified occupations programs, students are typically found in manufacturing, health, automotive retailing, off-farm agriculture, and food service occupations. DO programs are also contrasted from ICE programs in that seniors (or juniors, in some instances) in high school are enrolled in coop and a related class and have not had a sequence of orientation and preparatory-level courses. ICE students nearly always take a sequence of industrial courses prior to the cooperative experience. In large secondary schools, diversified occupations programs wane as occupational areas, such as health, develop more specialized cooperative programs.

**Interrelated (IRCE)**

Interrelated cooperative education (IRCE) programs were initiated in a great many schools in response to emphasis placed upon cooperative education in the 1960's. By definition, interrelated programs purport to serve all manner of occupations and all manner of students (excepting special education), regardless of whether they have had a sequence of occupational courses. Comparable terms are "Diversified Vocational" and "Cooperative Occupational Education" [Smith (70), p. 26]. Usually, students work in the afternoon and have one related class and two or three other classes in the morning. Interrelated cooperative education functions well in small schools. One or two teachers manage the cooperative education component and the several other vocational teachers are spared trips to training stations. Often in small communities there are not enough training stations or enough students to warrant separate cooperative programs in several occupational areas.

The term *interrelated* refers to two formats, both of which concern more than one broad area of occupations. In the most diversified format, one teacher-coordinator serves the full spectrum. In "sectional cooperative programs," teacher-coordinators specialize [Cook (12), p. 27]. The most common sectional program is business occupations. Retail, marketing, and office occupations students attend the same related class and are coordinated by one teacher.

As subsequent chapters indicate, there are many ways to schedule teachers so that teams of professionals serve students in concert. Small schools can use a great many staffing and transportation modes to increase employability.

The interrelated plan also functions well as an introductory phase, leading to specialized programs. Many schools and some colleges have developed cooperative education programs by beginning with one teacher coordinator and developing one or more programs in such areas as business, industrial, and agriculture, after community and student response merits—say two or three years. Often, the first teacher-coordinator serves as in-service educator to orient other personnel to teacher-coordinator tasks.

**CVOE Differentiated From Other JOB-ORIENTED Curricular Components**

It is essential to differentiate some of the above from other than job-oriented curricular components. Some of these differentiations are:

1. Agricultural from agriculture for general education and personal use, e.g., gardening and pet care.
2. Distributive and office programs from business courses for general

education and personal use, e.g., consumer education, personal typing, college note taking.

3. Health occupations education from health education.
4. Home economics gainful from homemaking.
5. Industrial-oriented from industrial arts courses for general education and personal use.
6. Community college university parallel courses taken primarily by transfer students, e.g., accounting for future CPA's or chemistry for prenursing students.

Types of cooperative education by occupational areas are certain to grow. Especially, as LEA's align programs with job markets, clusters such as public services are sure to yield new programs with rather common terminology, nationally. This is as it should be and is in no way threatening to existing programs which make the best of the processes of cooperative education—which working together, ensure employability of program product.

## SPECIAL STUDENT GROUPS

Another way to describe types of cooperative education is to identify special groups which might be served. The Illinois guide (28), p. 3, lists some of these: (1) rural youth preparing for nonfarm agricultural related occupations, (2) inner-city youth with home backgrounds and ethnic factors which inhibit education and employment, (3) the physically handicapped, (4) slow learners and mentally retarded, (5) emotionally disturbed youth and adults, (6) juvenile delinquents, (7) college dropouts, (8) college-oriented, and (9) academically or otherwise gifted or talented students.

Whereas it is well to consider groups such as these when assessing needs, designing programs, and recruiting enrollees, it is well to provide for as many as possible via heterogeneous groupings. That is, "mainstreaming" is recommended wherever possible. Nevertheless, cooperative education is a very workable solution to the vocational/ occupational education needs of some special populations.

### Special Students

The most obvious of these are classified as special education students. Many of the physically handicapped and mentally handicapped who cannot function effectively in regular vocational programs can be served in special programs. Special schools or programs for blind and partially sighted, for deaf or hard of hearing, and for amputees and people with motor handicaps can and should use cooperative education. This requires only a few special elements such as greater care in establishing work stations, transportation, and relationships with various public and philanthropic agencies which provide financial support and services for the handicapped. The success of these and other special education schools and programs are best assured by professional teams which include special education teachers, vocational/occupational education teachers, and rehabilitation counselors.

Programs for the mentally handicapped often entail cooperative education. The typical instance is a group of educable mentally handicapped (EMH) youngsters who (1) work for periods ranging from six months to several years in janitorial or food service work in school or an in-school sheltered workshop (which typically has a catchy name) and then (2) work at training stations in the community as dishwashers, busboys, housekeeping assistants, stockroom assistants, etc., for a period of several months to a year before they assume full-time work. All of the elements of cooperative education, including pay and training plans, are evident in such programs; and it is not unusual to find that some of the other vocational programs in the same institution are variously unsuccessful, primarily because they do not entail cooperative experiences—and thus lose contact with the labor market. Put another way, EMH cooperative education often shows what can be done.

Programs for the emotionally disturbed are not nearly so numerous as are special programs for retarded. Emotionally disturbed are often served in sheltered workshops and cooperative programs together with retarded. In many instances, success in meaningful, paid work, however menial, is the turning point toward recovery and normal responsibilities for learning and earning.

Another special group is not a special education classification. Many alienated, delinquent, potential delinquent, and probable early leavers, some of whom are educationally (and often socioeconomically) disadvantaged can be served by cooperative education. In the typical situation, high-risk students are placed in a school within the school. This might entail a special counselor, specially oriented teachers for the required academic courses, and several kinds of vocational teachers and teacher-coordinators. In one extremely successful small city program, such students are graduated from three special programs. One is very much like distributive education and includes experience in school stores, followed by cooperative experiences in the community, usually in lower-level jobs than mainstream DE students. Another involves a related class and a progression of experiences in a school-owned service station. Many of the students in this program are tempted to assume full-time work elsewhere before graduation. Some are well prepared to be owner-managers. A third program has features of a sheltered workshop and of diversified occupations. It operates behind a storefront and involves making and selling decorative items, such as plaques, repairing small appliances and lawnmowers, contracting to decorate dance halls, making party favors, etc. Most students in these programs are no longer alienated from authority and use primary abilities in relation to their work and in the conduct of their personal, social, and financial affairs well before graduation. Some "mainstream" before graduation and some matriculate to post-secondary occupational programs.

A special cooperative education program for 14- and 15-year olds is called *Work Experience and Career Exploration Program* (WECEP). It serves "students who develop a feeling of frustration or failure in academic achievements and wait for their sixteenth birthday to quit school" [WECEP Guide (31), p. 2 ]. Inception of WECEP required that the Employment Standards Division of the United States Department of Labor waive the age restriction for experimental programs. The waiver stipulated ages 14 and 15 and up to 8 hours of work a week and up to 4 hours a day when school is in session, any portion of which may be during school hours. The related class involves major units of study such as understanding self, how to get a job, and career fields. Students work in a great variety of establishments, for the most part at jobs which require little skill training.

A number of states provided special CVOE experiences for early school leavers. In Illinois, programs for people who have left secondary schools, have employment problems, and want to upgrade themselves are served by emerging community college programs. High schools refer potential students to college counselors and teacher-coordinators. Students may concentrate on vocational skills development and work experience. But, they are encouraged to complete high school graduation requirements via G.E.D. classes and/or self-study.

## Prison Inmates

The incarcerated are served by two forms of cooperative education. In some instances, work in prison industries or other jobs such as maintenance and food service is related to study and the individuals progress according to plan. In the main, work and study in penal institutions are unrelated and thus not labeled cooperative education. Some work-release programs are more nearly like cooperative education. Often, prisoners who are released for full-day work are placed in jobs which relate to vocational or occupational programs completed prior to transfer to a work-release center. Typically, group sessions with counselors are akin to related classes. These sessions deal with social psychology of work, managing financial affairs, etc., much after the fashion of WECEP, inter-related, and DO-related classes.

One of the most rapidly growing segments of secondary school and community college vocational/occupational education is programs in cor-rectional institutions. With qualifications, of course, it seems apparent that cooperative education will parallel these developments because of inherent benefits.

## LEVELS ON THE EDUCATIONAL LADDER

Cooperative education is a viable method from secondary school—for people as young as 14—to post-graduate study. Because the focus of this book is upon secondary and post-secondary vocational/occupational edu-cation below the baccalaureate level only brief descriptions of bac-calaureate and graduate programs are given below. More thorough treat-ments of collegiate programs are given by Knowles (34) and Barbeau (5).

### Community and Junior College Programs

By far, most community and junior college cooperative programs are occupational programs. The diversity of these programs was described in the earlier section on occupational areas and clusters. According to Knowles (34), p. 39, programs occur in approximate order of frequency in business and office, engineering, industrial, agricultural, health, social services, and public services. Knowles emphasizes the need for growth in the latter categories. Other chapters of this book apply as well to commun-ity and junior college occupational programs as to secondary school programs.

### Baccalaureate Programs

Two plans predominate in baccalaureate programs. The four-year plan is the more common and serves liberal arts majors, primarily. Depending upon academic calendars, i.e., whether an institution is on the quarter, semester, or other schedule, and upon proximity to jobs, colleges schedule work periods for one or more terms. Most entail the equivalent of one year of work. Several summers of work is the most common plan. The other baccalaureate plan is the five-year plan. The five-year plan is the older of the two plans. It was begun in engineering occupations and has incorporated a variety of schedules. Often, students are paired, i.e., one works and one studies. [Knowles (34), p. 33.] This has many practical advantages. Many universities have industrial vocational teacher education programs with options very much like five-year plans which are used in occupations they will later teach. Perhaps, some day, all teacher education majors will have extensive, paid cooperative experiences in schools.

There are other plans in baccalaureate institutions. For example, many institutions schedule a short work period in the senior year. Plans vary in many ways, e.g., whether work is required or optional, whether a teacher visits the work site or not, whether work is related to career plans and study or not, the schedule and duration of work, and program goals.

It is interesting to note that a few baccalaureate and very few graduate cooperative programs are sponsored by single corporations, single industries, groups of corporations, and (rarely) agencies of government. Again, the serious student of baccalaureate and other cooperative education should see Knowles (34), pp. 79-88. The best-known industry-sponsored five-year program is General Motors Institute at Flint, Michigan. Knowles and the GMI college bulletin make fascinating reading for professional educators who are especially concerned with accountability on the employability criterion.

### Graduate Programs

Knowles (34),p. 70, reports a study which discovered fourteen graduate programs with cooperative education components. Graduate cooperative education has most of the same benefits and constraints as do programs at other levels. By one way of thinking, it has an additional advantage. Insofar as advanced study brings a professional, a scientist, or an artist to the forefront of knowledge and/or technique and insofar as the leading edge of a field is done for pay in other than academic enterprises, e.g., corporations, think tanks, government agencies, churches, cooperative education is an appropriate capstone experience for those who will be highly creative in pursuits which are essential to various fields of human progress.

### Summary

Cooperative education is at once easy and difficult to define. It can readily be defined as a planned program which is student and process-oriented, rather than institution or teacher- and content-oriented. It can easily be compared to other work experience education such as work study, extended laboratory, and internship. It is difficult to understand various types of cooperative education programs. Nuances are subtle indeed. To categorize ongoing programs, it is best to consider learner motivations, occupational areas or clusters, special student groups, and levels on the educational ladder simultaneously. Thus, for example, one can understand that WECEP is a program for alienated youth, involves a large variety of unskilled occupations, serves only 14- and 15-year-old potential dropouts, and occurs in senior high schools. Or, one can understand that DE is a program for rather highly motivated students, some of whom are college or university-bound, involves distribution and marketing occupations, and entails cooperative experience at the end of high school or college programs.

### Activities

1. Secure two LEA plans for vocational/occupational education. List and define the types of cooperative described by each LEA. Visit the LEA's to determine whether your definitions are accurate and whether the plans are being pursued. Obtain lists of occupations and sponsoring firms for each ongoing program.
2. Secure a state manual(s) for cooperative education. List and define the types of cooperative education and requirements and funding levels for each.
3. Visit a cooperative education program and interview three or more students to determine (a) career aspirations before and after cooperative experiences, (b) student assessment of the "match" of in-school and out-of-school experiences, and (c) benefits and values which students attribute to cooperative education. Compare these with the lists of benefits in Chapter 1.
4. Visit a school, college, or technical institute without cooperative education. Secure program and course descriptions and definitions of employment projections for graduates. Write a fifteen hundred word proposal re how cooperative education might be structured for the institution.
5. Visit the personnel director of a major employer in your community. Determine past, present, and projected involvement with cooperative education. Discover if programs in several LEA's are adequate, overlapping, etc. Visit several work stations and students if possible. Discover students' opinions re benefits, limitations, career patterns, etc.
6. Visit a chamber of commerce office or a management association and interview the director to determine past, present, and future involvement in different types of cooperative programs. Discover what the chamber does re planning, conduct, public relations, awards, evaluation of cooperative education.
7. Visit a union office and interview an officer or a business agent to discover the same kinds of things as Activity 5 discovers from management.

Section **Two**

# *Planning and Initiating Cooperative Vocational/Occupational Education (CVOE) Programs*

# Chapter 3

# Determining Program Constraints

Highly successful cooperative vocational/occupational education (CVOE) programs do not materialize through mysterious or spontaneous processes. They are planned, developed, and implemented by individuals who are cognizant of prevailing needs, values, constraints, potentials, pitfalls, opportunities, and limitations. Because cooperative education operates in an arena influenced by many countervailing forces and sub-populations, planning is an essential ingredient of the program development process.

Most vocational education practitioners start the planning process by surveying manpower needs of the community and career aspirations of students. Determining manpower demands and student aspirations are very important to the program planning process. However, planners should consider several factors prior to the adoption of a planning strategy. The Project Aristotle Task Group on the Systems Approach to Education and Training (1967) referred to these factors as "real world, limiting conditions which must be satisfied by any acceptable system designed to attain education objectives." These constraints are normal environmental forces which affect applications of all types of planning models.

Planners must understand various aspects of the environment in which planning takes place. Each environment entails constraints which impinge upon planning. Failure to consider real world, limiting factors during development processes can lead to inefficiency, failure, and frustration in the program.

This chapter examines some constraints which should be considered before establishing CVOE programs. Consideration is given to institutional constraints, community constraints, and legal constraints.

Some of the outcomes of reading this chapter are:

1. Awareness of the several publics which relate to CVOE programs.
2. Understanding how various constraints and requirements may be alleviated and/or satisfied.

## LOCAL EDUCATIONAL AGENCY (LEA) CONSTRAINTS

The theoretical base of the local educational agency (LEA) plays an important part in determining commitment to, and consequently, success of, the cooperative plan of education. Attitudes, feelings, and beliefs of people associated with the LEA produce a psychological climate which has important ramifications for program implementation processes. The term *institutional philosophy,* though widely used, is very misleading. Program planners should appreciate that LEA's are made up of various publics and that publics frequently operate from diverse psychological and philosophical bases.

Implementation of successful CVOE programs depends upon support of students, teachers, counselors, administrators, and other personnel. It may be unreasonable to assume that all personnel will be actively supportive of cooperative vocational education. However, program planners should take steps to alleviate active opposition to cooperative education and to enlist support from as many colleagues as possible. CVOE assumes (1) that properly structured and supervised work experiences are as valuable as classroom experiences to the educational development of individuals, and (2) that the cooperative plan makes demands on the institution which education programs limited to in-house experiences do not make.

### Administrative Concern

All levels of administration should be committed to cooperative education. Decisions and actions re such matters as facilities, staffing, scheduling, budgeting, and programs are affected by the philosophy of administrators and governing board members. In addition to awarding regular credit for experiential learning, institutional leaders will have to sanction major deviations from normal scheduling patterns. Most states specify courses which students must complete to be graduated from high school or from certain post-secondary programs. Because the cooperative education plan requires that students be away from the LEA on half-day or whole-day bases, required courses have to be scheduled during periods when cooperative students are in attendance.

The cooperative plan also introduces elements of the open campus concept. This is not a matter of concern to most post-secondary institutions. However, many secondary schools have to revise institutional policy to accommodate student arrivals and departures at times throughout the day. Because many cooperative students provide their own transportation to training stations in the community, automobile usage policies may also have to be revised in some LEA's.

**Faculty Concerns**

Many of the negative concerns of instructional staff regarding CVOE center on the issue of educational respectability. The idea of community involvement in the process of education is looked upon with skepticism by many of the faculty members who have not had work experience outside of education. Human deprivation occurs at all levels of human existence. Individuals who have not had to function beyond the walls of an educational institution are culturally deprived.

Therefore, people who are responsible for initiating cooperative vocational education programs must be cautious, thorough, and tactful with colleagues. The concept of equating work with learning (though not at all new) is not as acceptable to some members of educational communities as it is to others. Some educators abhor the concept and, alas, some are unchangeable. Thus, novice program developers can unwittingly precipitate active opposition of some faculty members and jeopardize approvals and/or program success.

It is important to know the types of concerns which faculty members have relative to cooperative education. Educational respectability is a legitimate and often-voiced concern. It is easily satisfied by explanations and illustrations of the demand of CVOE upon students. Other concerns may be more pragmatic, but are just as important to successful initiation of CVOE programs. Some questions often raised by faculty are:

1. What affect will implementation of a cooperative vocational education program have upon enrollment in my program?
2. Will I have anything to say about the educational credibility of the CVOE program?
3. Is the CVOE program going to be primarily for those who can't succeed in the "regular" program?

Such questions can be answered to the satisfaction of most parties before they are elevated to serious proportions. (See Chapter 16, Public Relations, which deals with internal and external information programs.)

What has been said relative to concerns of instructional staff is even more applicable to the concerns of counselors. One could plan, develop, and implement an excellent CVOE program, and find it wanting of students and failing if counselors are not convinced of its values and working in its behalf.

**Economic Concerns**

One of the most popular patterns of comtemporary CVOE at the secondary educational level is the half-day pattern. Students spend a part of the school day in regular classes, and part of the day at training stations. Such programs usually enroll 30-45 students, and are coordinated by one teacher-coordinator. The teacher-coordinator usually teaches two related classes and coordinates everything from student selection to followup on program completers.

Economy-conscious educators often question this pattern, pointing out that a full-time faculty member serves only 30-45 students, whereas "regular staff members" are assigned five "regular" classes of 20 to 30 students. At first blush, this pattern of CVOE seems to some to be extremely uneconomical. However, what may seem to be economically unsound is cost-saving for at least three reasons.

First, teacher-coordinators of CVOE programs operating on the half-day pattern are responsible for 30-45 students for three, four, and even five periods of the school day. The cooperative student spends one hour per day in a related class and three to five hours per day on the job. Thus, a teacher-coordinator's load is comparable to loads of "regular" faculty members. Furthermore, some positive economic benefits accrue to the institution because 30-45 students are away for one-half of the school day, e.g., space requirements are reduced and teaching loads of other faculty members are reduced. Second, such programs benefit from facilities, equipment, and supplies used at training stations without incurring additional expense. Furthermore, such programs result in student wages and, in most instances, improved earnings of employing enterprises, which improve community economics, including tax bases for public LEA's.

## STATE AND FEDERAL EDUCATION AGENCY CONSTRAINTS

The ultimate authority for public education rests in state governments. Local governing boards function according to rules, regulations, codes, plans, and guidelines which are generated by state education agencies (SEA's). Vocational education was the first curriculum area to experience major federal directives. Since the Smith-Hughes Act of 1917, states have been required to prepare plans for expenditure of federal funds allocated for vocational education. State plans for vocational education are the legal bases for eligibility for federal funds. In effect, state plans are contracts with the federal government. They provide a degree of accountability. That is, they ensure that federal monies are expended for purposes delineated in various legislative enactments.

State vocational education agencies provide valuable assistance for planning and conducting vocational programs at the local level. Consultative services, financial assistance, and curriculum materials are only some of the many services which most SEA's provide LEA's.

State plans establish (1) certification requirements for personnel who administer, supervise, and conduct vocational/occupational programs, (2) program planning, approval, implementation, and evaluation procedures, and (3) various procedures relative to the conduct of reimbursable vocational/occupational programs.

Whether an SEA is a barrier or a gateway to program success is, in the main, dependent upon an LEA's understanding of the role and function of the SEA. If an SEA is perceived to be a positive resource and if an LEA maintains close liaison with the SEA during initiation stages, CVOE programs can be very effective.

The following statements from the Illinois State Plan for Vocational and Technical Education (1976) are typical of guidelines established by SEA's. (These guidelines relate to the development of several types of CVOE programs under provisions of Part G of the Vocational Educational Amendments of 1968. (See Table 2-1.)

*Cooperative Vocational Education Programs*

In addition to the provisions in 1.0 and 2.0 of this part of the State Plan, the following special provisions apply to cooperative vocational education programs supported with Federal funds under Part G of the Act.

*Procedures for Approval of Cooperative Vocational Education Programs*

The Division of Vocational and Technical Education will accept from local educational agencies applications for approval of cooperative vocational education programs. Funds under Part G may also be used for ancillary services and activities which are necessary to assure quality in such programs as the Director deems appropriate.

*Submittal of Applications*

Application for a special cooperative vocational education program is made by the local educational agency submitting a properly executed application to the Division of Vocational and Technical Education. The application shall include information of the nature, duration, purpose, and plan of the project; value to vocational education, staff qualifications, financial arrangements, and participation of public and private employers; and any other data which will substantiate the proposal.

*Review of Applications*

State staff will review all applications. Priorities will be accorded applications submitted by local educational agencies serving areas having concentrations of youth unemployment and school dropouts. Other evaluative criteria include the potential impact on needs of disadvantaged students, impact on reducing youth employment, promotion of cooperation between public education and public and private employers, relevance to annual and long-range plans, staff, facilities, reasonable cost, and expected outcomes.

*Action on Applications*

The State Director shall approve, disapprove, or defer action on the application. The applicant shall be notified in writing of the disposition of the application.

*Requirements of Cooperative Vocational Education Programs Purpose*

The program will meet the definition of a cooperative vocational educational program in Regulation 102.3(g) and will be administered by the local educational agency with the participation of public or private employers providing on-the-job training opportunities that may not otherwise be available to persons who can benefit from such a program.

*On-The-Job Training Standards*

The cooperative vocational program shall provide on-the-job training that: (1) is related to existing career opportunities with potential for promotion and advancement, (2) does not displace other workers who perform such work, (3) employs student learners in conformity with Federal, State, and local laws and regulations and in a manner not resulting in exploitation of the student-learner for private gain, and (4) is conducted in accordance with written training agreements between local educational agencies and employers, of which copies shall be submitted to the State for filing with the local application. (See DVTE Bulletin No. 34, "Articulated Guide for Cooperative Occupational Education.")

*Identification of Jobs*

Cooperative vocational education programs will be approved only if it is determined, on the basis of information in local applications, that neccessary procedures have been established for cooperation with employment agencies in identifying suitable jobs for persons who enroll in cooperative vocational educational programs.

*Additional Costs to Employers*

Approval of cooperative vocational programs under this section of the Act, using Part G funds, requires local educational agencies to assure the following:

(a) The payment of added employer costs will be made only when it is apparent that without such reimbursement employers will not be able to provide quality on-the-job training.

(b) Such added employers' costs will include only that part of the compensation to students which represents the difference between the compensation to be paid and the fair dollar value of services rendered by the student, as determined by negotiations between local educational agencies and the employers.

(c) Such added employers' costs will not include the cost of construction of facilities, purchases of equipment, and other capital costs which would inure to the benefit of the employers.

(d) Such added employers' costs as set forth in training agreements between local educational agencies and employers shall indicate the cost factors applied, the amount of funds to be paid, and the duration of reimbursement.

*Cost to Students*

The State Board shall insure that any unusual costs incurred by students enrolled in an approved vocational cooperative education program shall be reimbursed either to the student, or directly to the vender, for goods or services rendered. Nonpersonal items purchased for use in this program become the property of the local educational agency. Payments will be made only for those costs which

(a) are not usually required of persons engaged in the field of employ- ment for which cooperative vocational education is being provided, such as special tools, equipment and clothing, transportation, safety, and other protective devices;

(b) do not have the effect of underwriting personal obligations and expenses which students in similar circumstances are reasonably expected to assume.

*Participation of Students in Nonprofit Private Schools*

The State Board shall, to the extent consistent with the number of students enrolled in private nonprofit schools in the geographic area served by a project or program, provide vocational education services which will meet the needs of such students. These services may be provided through such arrangements as dual enrollment, educational radio and television, mobile or portable equipment, and may include professional and subprofes- sional services.

Plans will be developed in consultation with representatives of the non- public schools involved and shall include the number of students who are expected to participate in each program and shall further define the extent and manner of their expected participation.

Public school personnel may be made available on other than public school premises only to the extent necessary to provide vocational educa- tion services required by the students for whose needs such services were designed and only when such services are not normally provided at the private school.

The local educational agency providing such programs shall maintain administrative control and direction over such programs and each applica- tion shall so provide.

Federal funds shall not be used to pay for the salaries of teachers or other employees of private schools, except for services performed outside their regular hours of duty and then shall be under public supervision and control, nor shall these services include the use of equipment, other than mobile or portable, on private school facilities.

Provisions shall be made to insure that classes enrolling students from both private and public schools be formulated so as to avoid forming classes that are separated by school enrollment or religious affiliation.

*Noncommingling of Funds*

State and local accounting procedures shall guarantee that Federal funds made available under Part G of the Act will not be commingled with State or local funds but will be separately identified as expenditures of Federal funds.

*Evaluation and Follow-up Procedure*

Each cooperative program identified under this section of the Act shall provide adequate staff to assure continuous supervision and evaluation of on-the job training programs. Each local educational agency will keep a record of all visitations made during the year to the training station and shall make them readily available to the Division of Vocational and Technical Education. As part of the agreement by the State, each agency will conduct a follow-up study of students as set forth in the agreement. The teacher-coordinator along with vocational guidance personnel will be responsible for conducting these follow-up studies.

*Ancillary Services and Activities*

Appropriate State staff in the Special Programs Unit shall assist in the administration, supervision, and evaluation of cooperative vocational education programs, professional development activities for teacher-coordinators, development of curriculum and instructional materials, research, and special demonstration and experimental programs. The Professional and Curriculum Development Unit and the Research and Development Unit shall coordinate those activities which are unique to the responsibilities of each unit.

Obviously, State and Federal education agencies influence the development of vocational programs in many ways. Federal influence concerning the initiation of CVOE programs upon SEA's is very direct insofar as State plans are responsive to Federal guidelines.

Opportunity and danger are juxtaposed in the real-world, i.e., in the constraints discussed above. Such is the nature of professional pursuits. By becoming aware of prevailing needs, values, potentials, pitfalls, opportunities, and limitations CVOE program planners can substantially reduce the chance of failure.

## COMMUNITY CONSTRAINTS

The cooperative method of helping individuals develop salable skills relies heavily upon human and physical resources of the local community. Therefore, consideration must be given to such things as prevailing and projected unemployment and employment patterns, diversity of job opportunities, geographic relationship of campus and community, and prevailing values and mores.

The employment milieu has serious implications for CVOE program planning. For example, some labor groups may be strongly opposed to the cooperative plan of vocational/occupational education, especially during times of severe economic depression. Even during expansionary times, improperly informed workers can easily come to view proposed CVOE programs as threats to their economic well-being.

· CVOE programs are limited by the range of available job opportunities in a community. (Graduates are usually more mobile than in times past.) Planners must ask: "Are there adequate numbers and types of occupations available to warrant consideration of a cooperative program?" This question must be answered affirmatively before funds are expended for planning, developing, and implementing CVOE programs. Some LEA's may choose to develop vocational/technical programs to meet needs of graduates who travel great distances from the community for initial employment experiences. However, because the laboratories of CVOE programs are work stations in the community, such programs are fully dependent upon local labor markets.

The geographic relationship of attendance centers to the community is a primary consideration. CVOE students must travel to jobs and coordinators must visit training stations. In most situations, distance is not prohibitive. However, in sparsely populated regions, it can be a significant deterrent to program success. Scheduling and provisions for transportation must be dealt with in various ways. For example, students might attend classes for two or three days and be bused to an industrial park or shopping center on the other two or three days. Schedules and transportation should depend upon characteristics and needs of CVOE programs and occupations and upon characteristics of clientele, e.g., family income and willingness to provide transportation to distant jobs.

## LEGAL LIMITATIONS

Conformance of CVOE programs to Federal, State, and local laws and regulations must be assured. Various laws regulate and control employment of minors. The issue of legal responsibility for CVOE students at work sites can be a major barrier to cooperative education. It is important to understand both legal responsibilities and professional responsibilities. LEA's should define responsibility as something to be shared with participating employers. It is easy to say that employers are responsible for people they hire and that LEA's need not be concerned. But, it is difficult to defend this position because schools are responsible for students in attendance. Because CVOE programs are bona fide school programs, LEA's do not relinquish responsibility by using laboratories in the world of work. Cooperating employers are responsibile for complying with labor laws which relate to employment of minors and LEA's are responsible for educational matters. To explain responsibilities, alleviate fears, and illustrate proper practices, teacher-coordinators must know all laws which pertain to youth employment. They must share this knowledge fully with employers involved in CVOE programs.

Labor laws are obviously restrictive. But, they were developed for the protection and benefit of workers, especially young workers. When CVOE employers unknowingly violate the law, the LEA has a responsibility to inform them and offer solutions. Needless to say, employers who willfully and wantonly violate child labor provisions should not be utilized.

The Minnesota handbook for cooperative education (44), p.75, lists six concerns regarding labor-law compliance.

1.  Students enrolled in cooperative vocational education and receiving on-the-job training are subject to the provisions of all local, State, and Federal labor laws, unless exempt by special application and approval.
2.  The coordinator is expected to know the regulations which apply to the students, the occupations and the participating training stations.
3.  The principal kinds of regulations pertain to: (1) age restrictions, (2) minimum wages and overtime pay, (3) hours of work, (4) hazardous occupations, (5) insurance, and (6) minimum wage exemptions for student-learners.
4.  The coordinator does not enforce the laws; however, he informs the employers of provisions which apply to students and avoids placing students in training stations which do not comply with the laws.
5.  Failure to comply with labor laws is damaging to the image of the program and, in instances where students' health or safety are impaired, make the coordinator vulnerable to criticism, or even legal action.
6.  Information on labor laws should be obtained from the regional office of the Wage and Hours and Public Contracts Division of the United States Department of Labor, and from the appropriate State Department of Labor.

Nearly every state has developed laws, regulations, and guidelines relative to the employment of minors. When there is a variance between the provisions of federal and state laws, the law establishing the most restrictive conditions prevails.

### Age Limitations

Most states require minors who are less than 18 years old to obtain a work permit or age certificate. Certificates may usually be obtained from local school authorities.

The best initial source of information concerning legal requirements for wages, hours, and working conditions for minors in a variety of occupations is usually the area employment office. This agency not only provides information re labor laws, but can also provide assistance to vocational testing, counseling, and placement functions.

The United States Department of Labor publication, *Child-Labor Provisions of the Fair Labor Standards Act (1969)*, contains most necessary information relative to employment of minors (1969).

Generally, the minimum employment age for other than hazardous occupations is 16. Individuals must be at least 18 years old before they can work in an occupation which has been declared hazardous by the Secretary of Labor.

The Fair Labor Standards Act contains the following provisions relative to employment of 14- and 15-year-old minors.

Employment of 14- and 15-year-old minors is limited to certain occupations under conditions which do not interfere with their schooling, health, or well-being.

(a) 14- and 15-year-old minors may not be employed:
   (1) DURING SCHOOL HOURS, except as provided in paragraph (b).
   (2) BEFORE 7 A.M. or AFTER 7 P.M., except 9 P.M. from June 1 through Labor Day (time depends on local standards).
   (3) MORE THAN 3 HOURS A DAY — on school days.
   (4) MORE THAN 18 HOURS A WEEK — in school weeks.
   (5) MORE THAN 18 HOURS A DAY — on nonschool days.
   (6) MORE THAN 40 HOURS A WEEK — in nonschool weeks.

(b) In the case of enrollees in work training programs conducted under Part B of Title I of the Economic Opportunity Act of 1964, there is an exception to the requirement of paragraph (a) (1) of this section if the employer has on file with his records kept pursuant to Part 516 of this title an unrevoked written statement of the Administrator of the Bureau of Work Programs or his representative setting out the periods which the minor will work and certifying that his employment confined to such periods will not interfere with his health and well-being, countersigned by the principal of the school which the minor is attending with his certificate that such employment will not interfere with the minor's schooling.

**PERMITTED OCCUPATIONS FOR 14- and 15-YEAR-OLD MINORS IN RETAIL, FOOD SERVICE, AND GASOLINE SERVICE ESTABLISHMENTS**

(a) 14- and 15-year-old minors may be employed in —
   (1) OFFICE and CLERICAL WORK (including operation of office machines).
   (2) CASHIERING, SELLING, MODELING, ART WORK, WORK IN ADVERTISING DEPARTMENTS, WINDOW TRIMMING and COMPARATIVE SHOPPING.
   (3) PRICE MARKING and TAGGING by hand or by machine, ASSEMBLING ORDERS, PACKING and SHELVING.
   (4) BAGGING and CARRYING OUT CUSTOMER'S ORDERS.
   (5) ERRAND and DELIVERY WORK by foot, bicycle, and public transportation.
   (6) CLEAN UP WORK, including the use of vacuum cleaners and floor waxers, and MAINTENANCE OF GROUNDS, but not including

the use of power-driven mowers or cutters.

(7) KITCHEN WORK and other work involved in preparing and serving food and beverages, including the operation of machines and devices used in the performance of such work, such as, but not limited to, dishwashers, toasters, dumbwaiters, popcorn poppers, milk shake blenders, and coffee grinders.

(8) WORK IN CONNECTION WITH CARS AND TRUCKS if confined to the following:

Dispensing gasoline and oil.

Courtesy service.

Car cleaning, washing and polishing.

Other occupations permitted by this section.

BUT NOT INCLUDING WORK:

Involving the use of pits, racks or lifting apparatus or involving the inflation of any tire mounted on a rim equipped with a removable retaining ring.

(9) CLEANING VEGETABLES and FRUITS, and WRAPPING, SEALING, LABELING, WEIGHING, PRICING and STOCKING GOODS when performed in areas physically separate from areas where meat is prepared for sale and outside freezers or meat coolers.

In Any Other Place of Employment 14- and 15-Year-Old Minors May Be Employed In—any occupation except the excluded occupations listed below:

(b) 14- and 15-Year-Old Minors May Not Be Employed in—

(1) Any MANUFACTURING occupation.

(2) Any MINING occupation.

(3) PROCESSING occupations (except in a retail, food service, or gasoline service establishment in those specific occupations expressly permitted there in accordance with the foregoing list).

(4) Occupations requiring the performance of any duties IN WORK-ROOMS OR WORKPLACES WHERE GOODS ARE MANUFACTURED, MINED, OR OTHERWISE PROCESSED (except to the extent expressly permitted in retail, food service, or gasoline service establishments in accordance with the foregoing list).

(5) PUBLIC MESSENGER SERVICE.

(6) OPERATION OR TENDING of HOISTING APPARATUS or of ANY POWER-DRIVEN MACHINERY (other than office machines and machines in retail, food service, and gasoline service establishments which are specified in the foregoing list as machines which such minors may operate in such establishments).

(7) ANY OCCUPATIONS FOUND AND DECLARED TO BE HAZARDOUS.

(8) OCCUPATIONS IN CONNECTION WITH:

(a) TRANSPORTATION of persons or property by rail, highway, air, on water, pipeline or other means.

(b) WAREHOUSING and STORAGE

(c) COMMUNICATIONS and PUBLIC UTILITIES

(d) CONSTRUCTION (including repair)
Except Office or Sales Work in connection with these Occupations (not performed on transportation media or at the actual construction site).

(9) ANY OF THE FOLLOWING OCCUPATIONS IN A RETAIL, FOOD SERVICE, OR GASOLINE SERVICE ESTABLISHMENT:

(a) WORK performed IN or ABOUT BOILER or ENGINE ROOMS.

(b) WORK in connection with MAINTENANCE or REPAIR OF THE ESTABLISHMENT, MACHINES or EQUIPMENT.

(c) OUTSIDE WINDOW WASHING that involves working from window sills, and all work requiring the use of LADDERS, SCAFFOLDS, or their substitutes.

(d) COOKING (except at soda fountains, lunch counters, snack bars, or cafeteria serving counters) and BAKING.

(e) Occupations which involve OPERATING, SETTING UP, ADJUSTING, CLEANING, OILING, or REPAIRING power-driven FOOD SLICERS and GRINDERS, FOOD CHOPPERS and CUTTERS, and BAKERY-TYPE MIXERS.

(f) Work in FREEZERS and MEAT COOLERS and all work in PREPARATION OF MEATS for sale (except wrapping, sealing, labeling, weighing, pricing and stocking when performed in other areas).

(g) LOADING and UNLOADING GOODS to and from trucks, railroad cars or conveyors.

(h) All occupations in WAREHOUSES except office and clerical work.

These provisions prevent conduct of CVOE programs for youth under 16. However, a large number of CVOE programs have been developed specifically to serve the occupational/education needs of students 14 and 15 years old. These programs are conducted by special agreement between SEA's and the Department of Labor. (See description of WECEP in Chapter 2.)

**Wage Limitations**

The various state and federal wage and hour laws are applicable to the employment of CVOE students. These laws establish prevailing minimum wage rates. Whenever there is not congruence between federal and state stipulations, the higher rate must be paid. Some examples of enterprises covered by the Federal Wage and Hour law are:

1. Any retail or service enterprise having an annual gross sales of $250,000.00.

OMB Appi ival No. 44-R0308

U.S. DEPARTMENT OF LABOR
Employment Standards Administration

| OFFICIAL USE ONLY |
|---|
| A. Control number_____ |
| B. Effective date_____ |
| C. Expiration date_____ |
| D. Reviewing official _____ |

## APPLICATION FOR AUTHORIZATION TO EMPLOY A STUDENT-LEARNER AT SUBMINIMUM WAGES

The school official's certification in Item 27 of the application provides temporary authority to employ the named student-learner under the terms proposed in the application which are in accordance with section 3(c) of the Student-Learner Regulations (29 CFR 520). The authority begins on the date the application is forwarded to the Regional Office of the Employment Standards Administration. At the end of 30 days, this authority is extended to become the approved certificate unless the Administrator or his authorized representative denies the application, issues a certificate with modified terms and conditions, or expressly extends the period of review. Note that the certificate is valid for no more than 1 school year and does not extend beyond the date of graduation.

**READ CAREFULLY THE INSTRUCTIONS FOR COMPLETING THIS FORM. PRINT OR TYPE ALL ANSWERS.**

| | |
|---|---|
| 1. NAME AND ADDRESS, INCLUDING ZIP CODE, OF ESTABLISH-MENT MAKING APPLICATION: | 3A. NAME AND ADDRESS OF STUDENT-LEARNER:<br><br><br><br>B: DATE OF BIRTH:<br>(Month, day, year) |
| 2. TYPE OF BUSINESS AND PRODUCTS MANUFACTURED, SOLD, OR SERVICES RENDERED: | 4. NAME AND ADDRESS, INCLUDING ZIP CODE, OF SCHOOL IN WHICH STUDENT-LEARNER IS ENROLLED: |
| 5. PROPOSED BEGINNING DATE OF EMPLOYMENT (Month, day, year) | 17. TITLE OF STUDENT-LEARNER OCCUPATION: |
| 6. PROPOSED ENDING DATE OF EMPLOYMENT (Month, day, year) | 18. NUMBER OF EMPLOYEES IN THIS ESTABLISHMENT |
| 7. PROPOSED GRADUATION DATE (Month, day, year) | 19. NUMBER OF EXPERIENCED EMPLOYEES IN STUDENT-LEARNER'S OCCUPATION |
| 8. NUMBER OF WEEKS IN SCHOOL YEAR | 20. MINIMUM HOURLY WAGE RATE OF EXPERIENCED WORKERS IN ITEM 19 |
| 9. TOTAL HOURS OF SCHOOL INSTRUCTION PER WEEK | 21. SUBMINIMUM WAGE(S) TO BE PAID STUDENT-LEARNER (if a progressive wage schedule is proposed, enter each rate and specify the period during which it will be paid): |
| 10. NUMBER OF SCHOOL HOURS DIRECTLY RELATED TO EMPLOYMENT TRAINING | |
| 11. HOW IS EMPLOYMENT TRAINING SCHEDULED (Weekly, alternate weeks, etc.)? | |
| 12. NUMBER OF WEEKS OF EMPLOYMENT TRAINING AT SUBMINIMUM WAGES | |
| 13. NUMBER OF HOURS OF EMPLOYMENT TRAINING A WEEK | |
| 14. ARE FEDERAL VOCATIONAL EDUCATION FUNDS BEING USED FOR THIS PROGRAM? | 22. IS AN AGE OR EMPLOYMENT CERTIFICATE ON FILE IN THIS ESTABLISHMENT FOR THIS STUDENT-LEARNER? (If not, see instructions). |
| 15. WAS THIS PROGRAM AUTHORIZED BY THE STATE BOARD OF VOCATIONAL EDUCATION? | |
| 16. IF THE ANSWER TO ITEM 15 IS "NO", GIVE THE NAME OF THE RECOGNIZED EDUCATIONAL BODY WHICH APPROVED THIS PROGRAM: | 23. IS IT ANTICIPATED THAT THE STUDENT-LEARNER WILL BE EMPLOYED IN THE PERFORMANCE OF A GOVERNMENT CONTRACT SUBJECT TO THE WALSH-HEALEY PUBLIC CONTRACTS ACT OR THE SERVICE CONTRACT ACT? |

**ATTACH SEPARATE PAGES IF NECESSARY**

Form WH-205
Rev. June 1973

**Fig. 3-1. U.S. Department of Labor application for a certificate to employ a student-learner.**

2. Banks.
3. Insurance companies and agencies.
4. Construction.
5. Laundry and dry cleaning establishments.
6. Hospitals, schools, and nursing homes.

Some examples of exempt enterprises are:

1. Retail enterprises with less than $250,000.00/annum sales.
2. State, county, and city government offices. (See section 3D of Fair Labor Standards Act.)
3. Certain farm workers.

Employment associated with CVOE programs should, as nearly as possible, entail working conditions identical to those of other beginning workers. Nevertheless, there are circumstances under which employers are hardpressed to provide both the training emphasis demanded by CVOE and the minimum wage. Thus the USDL recognizes students enrolled in "bona fide" CVOE programs as student-learners and permits employers to apply for approval to pay not less than 75 percent of the statutory minimum wage. (See Fig. 3-1.)

Most employers pay CVOE students the minimum wage or more and do not find it necessary to apply for the special student-learner minimum wage rate. Applications are *not* approved if:

1. The occupation does not require a sufficient degree of skill to necessitate a substantial learning period.
2. Another worker is displaced.
3. Wage rates or working standards of experienced workers would be depressed.
4. The occupational needs of the community or industry do not warrant the training of students at less than the statutory minimum.
5. There are serious outstanding violations of the Fair Labor Standards Act.
6. The number of students at certificate rates is more than a small proportion of the establishment's working force.

Employers who apply for approval of student-learner subminimum wage rates should observe the following:

1. The hourly wage rate paid a student-learner must be at least 75 percent of the applicable statutory minimum wage under the Fair Labor Standards Act.
2. Application must be filed at least 30 days in advance of the time a student is to begin employment.

3. Students under 16 years of age are not eligible to receive student-learner certificates and student-learners under 18 years of age cannot receive certificates to work in hazardous occupations, excepting for exemptions explained in the hazardous occupations section of the Fair Labor Standards Act.

4. Permission to employ student-learners at subminimum rates is usually not granted during the summer months. In exceptional cases, such employment may be authorized, if it is an integral part of the vocational training program. Requests for summer vacation employment must be accompanied by a statement explaining the extraordinary circumstances justifying such employment and the number of hours per week for which special minimum wages are requested. The certificate will spell out such conditions.

5. A student-learner may not work or attend school over 40 hours per week unless justified by extraordinary circumstances. These must be explained at the time of application.

6. Even if the student-learner is not in school, he can only work 8 hours per day and 40 hours per week, at subminimum wages.

7. Student-learners cannot be employed during any week at a special wage rate for hours in addition to 40 hours of school and on-the job training.

Because some enterprises which may provide training stations are not within the jurisdiction of state or federal wage laws, LEA's should be very careful to ensure that CVOE programs do not become sources of inexpensive manpower for mercenary employers. Carefully developed training plans and supervision at work sites are the major means to assuring fair standards and that the training stations do not become merely sources of inexpensive manpower.

### Hazardous Occupations

Occupations are classified as hazardous endeavors after thorough investigation by the United States Department of Labor, Bureau of Labor Standards. The Secretary of Labor issues what is referred to as a hazardous occupations order. Presently, 17 hazardous occupations orders are in effect. That is, 17 occupations have been declared to be particularly dangerous for minors between 16 and 18 years of age. Those occupations are:

1. Occupations in or about plants or establishments manufacturing or storing explosives or articles containing explosive components.

2. Occupations of motor-vehicle driver and outside helper.

3. Coal-mine occupations.
4. Logging occupations and occupations in the operation of any saw-mill, lathe mill, shingle mill, or cooperage-stock mill.
5. Occupations involved in the operation of power-driven woodworking machines.
6. Occupations involving exposure to radioactive substances and to ionizing radiations.
7. Occupations involved in the operation of elevators and other power-driven hoisting apparatus.
8. Occupations involved in the operation of power-driven metal hoisting apparatus.
9. Occupations in connection with mining, other than coal.
10. Occupations involving slaughtering, meat-packing, or processing or rendering.
11. Occupations involved in the operation of certain power-driven bakery machines.
12. Occupations involved in the operation of certain power-driven paper-products machines.
13. Occupations involved in the manufacture of brick, tile, and kindred products.
14. Occupations involved in the operation of circular saws, band saws, and guillotine shears.
15. Occupations involved in wrecking, demolition, and shipbreaking operations.
16. Occupations involved in roofing operations.
17. Occupations involved in excavation operations.

**Child Labor Provisions of the Fair Labor Standards Act.**

The United States Department of Labor, WHPC Publication 1258, January, 1969, pp. 5-30 for complete text of the 17 hazardous occupations orders.

Hazardous occupations orders numbers 5, 8, 10, 12, 14, 16, and 17 contain exemptions for student-learners employed under the following conditions:

1. The student-learner is enrolled in a course of study and training in a CVOE program under a recognized State or local authority or in a course of study in a substantially similar program conducted by a private school; and
2. Such student-learner is employed under a written agreement which provides:
   a. That the work of the student-learner in the occupations declared particularly hazardous shall be incidental to his training;
   b. That work shall be intermittent and for short periods of time, and

    under the direct and close supervision of a qualified and experienced person;

  c. That safety instructions shall be given by the school and correlated by the employer with on-the job training; and

  d. That a schedule of organized and progressive work processes to be performed on the job shall have been prepared. Each such written agreement shall contain the name of the student-learner and shall be signed by the employer and the school coordinator or principal. Copies of each agreement shall be kept on file by both the school and the employer. This exemption for the employment of student-learners may be revoked in any individual situation where it is found that reasonable precautions have not been observed for the safety of minors employed thereunder.

A high school graduate may be employed in an occupation in which he has completed training as provided in this paragraph as a student-learner even though he is not 18 years of age.

CVOE personnel must have current knowledge of laws and regulations which affect the employment of minors. Some of the more important considerations have been presented in this section. Individuals responsible for initiating CVOE programs should contact the nearest office of the Wage and Hour and Public Contracts Division of the United States Department of Labor, and the respective state department of labor to obtain current information.

United States Department of Labor offices are located in the following cities:

| | |
|---|---|
| Alabama: | Birmingham, Mobile, Montgomery |
| Alaska: | Anchorage |
| Arizona: | Phoenix |
| Arkansas: | Little Rock |
| California: | Hollywood, Long Beach, Los Angeles, Oakland, Sacramento, San Francisco, Whittier. |
| Colorado: | Denver |
| Connecticut: | Hartford |
| Delaware: | Wilmington |
| District of Columbia: | College Park |
| Florida: | Jacksonville, Miami, North Miami, Tampa |
| Georgia: | Atlanta, Columbus, Hapeville, Savannah |
| Hawaii: | Honolulu |
| Idaho: | Boise |
| Illinois | Chicago, Springfield |
| Indiana: | Indianapolis, South Bend |
| Iowa: | Des Moines |
| Kansas: | Wichita |

| | |
|---|---|
| Kentucky: | Lexington, Louisville |
| Louisiana: | Baton Rouge, New Orleans, Shreveport |
| Maine: | Portland |
| Maryland: | Baltimore, College Park |
| Massachusetts: | Boston, Springfield |
| Michigan: | Detroit, Grand Rapids |
| Minnesota: | Minneapolis |
| Mississippi: | Jackson |
| Missouri. | Kansas City, St. Louis |
| Montana: | Great Falls |
| Nebraska: | Omaha |
| Nevada: | Reno |
| New Hampshire: | Manchester |
| New Jersey: | Newark, Paterson, Trenton |
| New Mexico: | Albuquerque |
| New York: | Bronx, Brooklyn, Buffalo, Hempstead, New York, Syracuse |
| North Carolina: | Charlotte, Greensboro, Raleigh |
| North Dakota: | Bismarck |
| Ohio: | Cincinnati, Cleveland, Columbus |
| Oklahoma: | Oklahoma City, Tulsa |
| Oregon: | Portland |
| Pennsylvania: | Harrisburg, McKeesport, Philadelphia, Pittsburgh, Wilkes-Barre |
| Rhode Island: | Providence |
| South Carolina: | Columbia |
| South Dakota: | Sioux Falls |
| Tennessee: | Knoxville, Memphis, Nashville |
| Texas: | Corpus Christi, Dallas, El Paso, Fort Worth, Harlingen, Houston, San Antonio, Waco |
| Utah: | Salt Lake City |
| Vermont: | Burlington |
| Virginia: | Richmond, Roanoke |
| Washington: | Seattle |
| West Virginia: | Charleston, Clarksburg |
| Wisconsin: | Madison, Milwaukee |
| Wyoming: | Casper, Cheyenne |
| Puerto Rico: | Hato Rey, Mayaguez, Santurce |
| Canal Zone | |
| Virgin Islands: | Santurce, Puerto Rico |
| American Samoa: | Eniwetok Atoll, Guam, Johnston Island, Kwajalein Atoll, Wake Island |

## OTHER CONSIDERATIONS

### Social Security

The Federal Social Security Act provides (1) economic security for individuals after they have reached a certain age and (2) survivor's insurance for the worker's dependents. Students enrolled in CVOE programs must have a social security card prior to employment. The Social Security Act is administered by the Bureau of Old-Age and Survivor's Insurance. The nearest Social Security office will willingly provide all information relative to obtaining a social security card, benefits, etc.

### Unemployment Insurance

So long as they are part-time employees, CVOE students are not eligible for unemployment benefits. An individual is considered to be ineligible if he is:

1. In regular attendance during the daytime in an in-situation of learning and performs services as a part-time worker during all or part of the school year or regular vacation period;
2. Working under a post-high school work-study program;
3. Working in an approved cooperative work-study program that is operated and supervised by a local board of education.

More relevant and timely information may be acquired from the nearest office of the State Employment Service or from the Bureau of Employment Security, United States Department of Labor, Washington, D.C. 20025.

The applicability of workmen's compensation and disability insurance to CVOE students should be investigated by the LEA via the local Workmen's Compensation Board office.

### Union Membership

LEA's should relate to union leadership, the better to assure ingress to occupations. Union contracts usually contain provisions regarding the who, when, and how of union membership. If a union contract constrains a CVOE program, the LEA's official representative should work with the union in an effort to establish provisions in the contract for CVOE students. CVOE students are usually classified as preapprentice workers in skilled occupations. (See Chapter 8 re advisory committees)

## Insurance

SEA's and LEA's have many different policies and procedures concerning liability of student workers. This matter should be investigated thoroughly by CVOE program planners. Since cooperative work experience is part of the LEA's regular academic program, the LEA's liability insurance should apply to the CVOE student. But, LEA and employer liability should be investigated and defined in each, local instance.

## FINANCIAL CONSTRAINTS

Money supply is a major constraint on development of new educational programs. To stimulate development of experimental programs, the federal government has enacted several pieces of legislation which provide funds for CVOE. Federal grants are available for post-secondary CVOE programs through the provisions of title IV, Part D, of the Higher Education Act of 1975 (as amended). These Higher Education Act funds may be awarded to an LEA in the form of grants directly from the federal level for the purpose of planning, establishing, expanding, and carrying out CVOE programs. Information relative to these grants may be obtained from the Commissioner of Education. The major funds for CVOE are administered by SEA's. Thus, CVOE personnel should maintain close liaison with SEA personnel, the better to maximize local benefits.

Because federal and state funding provisions reflect assessments of societal needs and economic and political conditions, they are subject to change, serious reductions, and elimination. Therefore, LEA personnel should be prepared to defend CVOE. There are two major legs to such arguments. (1) Under most federal programs, state monies more than match federal dollars, and local monies more than match federal *and* state dollars. Local monies are nearly always very important to CVOE. (2) CVOE is educationally and economically sound—and more so than traditional programs. LEA's are supposed to serve clientele interests rather than institutional purposes. If CVOE satisfies clientele needs, it should be funded—if need be at the expense of less important programs. (See Chapter 7 re budget allocations.)

### Summary

Success of CVOE programs depends on support of various publics, e.g., students, faculty, administrators, governing boards, labor, and private and public employers. These publics and various constraints complicate CVOE planning.

The LEA which does not recognize and accommodate real world constraints while planning CVOE programs will fail. The cooperative approach to providing relevant educational experiences interfaces on several fronts with forces which "in-house" vocational programs do not encounter. CVOE program planners must be cognizant of such forces and use them to advantage. Very few constraints are serious barriers to program success, i.e., gateways to viable programming are nearly always clearly evident.

### Activities

1. Make a list of the various publics on which the success of a CVOE program is contingent. Tell why each can influence CVOE success in three sentences or less. Refer to real world situations if you can.
2. Make a list of twelve constraints on CVOE.
3. Write a two-page paper describing ways to alleviate the constraints you identified in Activity 2.
4. Contact the local State Employment office and make a list of its services which might benefit CVOE students.
5. Write letters to the federal bureaus and agencies identified in this chapter, requesting information which would be useful to CVOE program planners.
6. Obtain and study the text of the 17 hazardous occupations orders and write a paragraph on the meaning of the term "incidental to a student's training."
7. Write a rationale for experiential learning.
8. List current federal and state acts which might provide funds for CVOE in your LEA.

# Chapter 4

# Determining Needs for CVOE

Historically, the first step in the development of cooperative vocational/occupational education (CVOE) programs has been to conduct community surveys to ascertain demands for workers in specific occupational areas and to locate training stations which might be utilized in the experimental portion of cooperative programs. In a review of state manuals for cooperative education, Efralim Farahbokhshira (16), p. 2890-A, found that the most common cooperative program development model was: (1) survey community, (2) select coordinator, (3) select advisory committee, (4) publicize the program, (5) select training stations, (6) select students for participation, and (7) make provisions for evaluation. Emphasizing concern for assessing occupational needs of a community, Mason and Haines (41), p. 185, listed three steps which should be accomplished in determining feasibility of cooperative programs: (1) ascertaining the need for trained manpower in the community, (2) determining opportunities for part-time employment, and (3) identifying changes in the community which affect employment opportunities.

Recent events and contemporary literature of cooperative education appear to signal a departure from the practice of beginning with community needs assessment. The departure may be no more than a short-lived position on a "chicken or egg" issue. Hopefully, it will be long-lived. It emphasizes the importance of ascertaining needs and aspirations of students, as a first step.

The basic operational pattern of CVOE assumes match between career aspirations of students and manpower demands of communities. Thus, it is assumed that communities can and should provide diversities of experiences which are congruent with varied career goals of student clientele.[1]

This chapter deals with concerns, methods, and procedures which are important to LEA's involved in CVOE program planning processes. Consideration is given to needs and aspirations of student clientele, manpower opportunities and demands of the local community, and contributions of existing institutional programs. The reader is encouraged to

---

[1]The degree to which jobs should be adapted to people and the degree to which people should adapt to jobs are obviously questions which can never be resolved on other than limited scale.

appreciate that the activities and procedures described are typically accomplished in concert with a steering committee. (See Chapter 6.)

Some of the outcomes of reading this chapter are:

1. Realization that CVOE program designs should be based on relevant empirical data.
2. Knowledges and skills necessary to conduct of local surveys.
3. Understanding of secondary sources of data useful in program planning.
4. Cognizance of procedures for ascertaining occupational needs and aspirations of student clientele.
5. Understanding of diverse civic, social service, and government agencies.

## DETERMINING STUDENT NEEDS AND ASPIRATIONS

Increasingly, young people and displaced workers are pressured to make judicious occupational choices. Successful CVOE programs assume that employment needs and aspirations may be fulfilled by placing students in jobs which are directly related to occupational interests. CVOE program planners must not diminish the importance of occupational choice. The simple question, "What type of work do you want to do?" seems almost unanswerable. It necessitates choosing from among more than 30,000 occupations currently engaged in by American workers.[2]

Program planning is not an end; it is a means to the end of employability of given students. The end of all CVOE programs should be to serve unique career needs of a particular student clientele. For purposes of gathering data for effective programmatic decision-making, planners should realize that inputs of three distinct populations are valuable: (1) students who have withdrawn, dropped out, or graduated; (2) students who are currently enrolled; and (3) prospective students.

### Past Students

Student clientele which have been served by LEA's consist of three specific groups, i.e. (1) withdrawals, (2) dropouts, and (3) graduates. Each LEA has some withdrawals and dropouts. These groups can provide information relative to types of cooperative programs implemented. Some students withdraw from educational institutions via established procedures and some students take leave without notification. For clarity it is

---

[2]For more thorough treatment of occupational choice see, for example, Bailey and Stadt (4),

well to refer to all students who discontinue attendance prior to program completion as early leavers and to differentiate between withdrawals and dropouts.[3] Students who follow normal institutional termination procedures are withdrawals, and those who leave without contacting appropriate officials are dropouts.

Standardized procedures should be established to gather information from students who withdraw prior to program completion. Procedures should include an exit interview conducted by a member of the career counseling staff. Among many things, the interview should ascertain (1) why the student is leaving the LEA and (2) whether the student would have remained if an appropriate CVOE program had been available.

These two questions provide information useful to CVOE program planners. Many LEA's have established procedures for exit interviews with students who are withdrawing or transferring. The person(s) designated to plan CVOE programs should make certain that these questions are incorporated in the established process. One of the values of utilizing normal exit procedures to obtain information is that data may be obtained from students leaving both occupational and nonoccupational programs.

LEA's which are striving to meet changing occupational education needs of student clientele should obtain much more information from early leavers. For example, it is well to know the number or percentage:

1. Withdrawing from each curricular area.
2. Accepting full-time employment.
3. Withdrawing because of financial constraints.
4. Withdrawing because of academic problems.
5. Planning to enter military service.
6. Withdrawing because of personal and/or family problems.
7. Who feel that no program relates to personal career objectives.
8. Who feel that training offered is inappropriate.

Much can be learned from early leavers. Most public LEA's claim to maintain an open door policy. By collecting, analyzing, and acting on data obtained from early leavers, an LEA can help to assure that the *open door* policy does not become a *trapdoor* experience for many. Obviously, data from withdrawals should be collected continually.

There has been a concerted effort in education to reduce seemingly high dropout rates. This effort is founded upon the widespread belief that young and/or unskilled are easy victims of downshifts in economic activity. Dropouts are plagued by high unemployment and low income. Because many of them have had first-hand experiences at job seeking, dropouts can provide information useful to CVOE program planners.

[3]It is assumed that professionals, cognizant of educational values to be gained from experiences in the community, do not attach negative connotations to the "dropout" classification.

Several steps are essential to surveys of dropouts. First, program planners must make every effort to obtain a complete list of individuals previously, but not presently, enrolled. The list should include early leavers not officially withdrawn. Counseling and admissions and records offices are the major sources of information for such a list. The list should contain name, last known address, possible alternate address, and name and address of a relative or guardian.

Next, the CVOE planner should determine the objective of the survey, and develop items for the survey instrument. Information should be obtained in at least three areas. The first area should deal with name, address, and employment history since leaving the LEA. The second area of the survey instrument should deal with factors which contributed to the student's leaving. This might be a checklist of reasons why students terminate (Fig. 4-1).

---

**Checklist of Student's Reasons for Leaving Employment**

1._____I had financial difficulties.
2._____I was unable to obtain transportation.
3._____Courses were too difficult.
4._____I entered military service.
5._____Courses did not relate to my career goal.
6._____I accepted full time employment.
7._____I had to quit for health reasons.
8._____Other. (Please specify.)

---

Fig. 4-1.   Sample checklist of student's reasons for leaving employment.

The third area of the instrument should ascertain types of programs which might have been more meaningful to the dropout. These are best identified by asking the leavers to indicate what occupation the student wishes to enter, what occupation the student might have prepared for in an LEA program.

Finally, a cover letter for the survey instrument should be developed (Fig. 4-2). Even the most carefully developed survey instrument may not achieve the purposes for which it is intended. Therefore, a field test should be conducted. Before an LEA invests mailing and handling expenses, the planner should assure that the survey instrument will accomplish what it is intended to accomplish. A field test involves selecting a small sample of the population to be studied and administering the survey instrument. Results from the small sample are examined to see whether questions were understood, whether information was provided fully, and whether information is adequate to decision-making needs.

(Letterhead of LEA)

Dear Sir:

The___(name of LEA)___ is continually striving to develop occupational programs which meet the needs of students. You can contribute valuable information to the program development process. Please take a few minutes to complete the enclosed survey instrument and mail it in the envelope provided.

We solicit your frank and honest opinion. Be assured that your contribution will be held in strict confidence.

Thank you for helping us in this manner.

Sincerely,

_____
(signature)

_____
(title)

**Fig. 4-2.  Sample cover letter for survey instrument.**

Followup studies of early leavers have traditionally resulted in low rates of return. The CVOE program planner should strive for the highest possible rate of return. To this end, an attempt should be made to:

1. Keep the questionnaire as short as possible.
2. Ask only questions which are relevant to survey objectives.
3. Refrain from asking for information which can be acquired from other sources such as cumulative records and the LEA's placement office.
4. Require as little work as possible of respondents.
5. Abide by proven principles of item and questionnaire format.
6. Use high-quality reproduction processes for the survey instrument, covering letter, and reminders.
7. Convince respondents of the importance of the activity.
8. Do at least one reminder mailing to nonrespondents.

It is well for CVOE program planners to be familiar with the literature of survey research. Texts by Wentling and Lawson (83), Rummel (67), and Brockstrom and Hurch (7) are especially useful. These texts deal with the following steps in the basic survey process.

1. Formulating a committee to assist with the survey.
2. Identifying the population to be surveyed.
3. Determining objectives of the survey.

   4. Listing activities to be completed during conduct of the survey, and
      preferably assigning committee members specific responsibilities
      and establishing time limits.
   5. Developing instrument items which will accomplish objectives.
   6. Developing a cover letter.
   7. Field testing the instrument.
   8. Correcting deficiencies identified via the field test.
   9. Duplicating the survey instrument.
   10. Developing a plan for controlling mailing and returns.
   11. Mailing the cover letter, survey instrument, and return envelope to
      each person in the test population.
   12. Sending reminder cards (preferably after one week).
   13. Sending followup letters and survey instruments.
   14. Tabulating results.
   15. Preparing a report of findings.
   16. Disseminating the report and proposing decisions and actions.

Students who have successfully completed LEA programs are another
excellent source of information for CVOE planners. The typical practice
is to conduct followup studies of vocational/occupational program completers one, three, and five years after leaving.[4] If CVOE program planners are associated with an LEA with established followup procedures,
their work will be significantly reduced.

The primary purpose of the followup survey is to ascertain the employment status of program completers. Whether the graduate is (1) working in
the occupation or occupational cluster for which he/she was prepared or in
a related occupation, (2) working in an occupation unrelated to previous
training, or (3) unemployed is the primary concern of followup studies.
Usually, surveys also attempt to assess relevance of program components
to employment requirements. Obviously, these types of information bear
upon decisions regarding additions to, modifications on, and deletions of
CVOE program components. Program planners who are associated with
LEA's which do not conduct periodic followup studies should use the
previously presented procedure for conducting surveys. See Chapter 17,
Evaluation, for more detailed treatment of student and employer followup
for ongoing CVOE programs.


**Presently Enrolled Students**

   Initial CVOE successes or failures depend in large part upon consideration of occupational needs and aspirations of enrolled students. Types of

---

[4]The authors are skeptical of five-year followup surveys. Program components should have changed by
then and data would be spurious.

CVOE programs implemented should depend upon career interests and other characteristics of students to be served. The enrolled population should be informed before it is surveyed. Several methods may be used to inform students about purposes and operation of CVOE programs. One is to schedule an assembly for explaining the cooperative concept and program elements. Several techniques have proved useful for such assemblies:

1. State CVOE consultants participate in presentations.
2. Teacher-coordinators from other LEA's make presentations.
3. Films and/or slides which depict cooperative program components augment presentations.
4. Students enrolled in and/or graduated from CVOE programs participate in presentations.

At the end of an assembly program, students may be given opportunity to complete a survey instrument and leave it with the CVOE planner. The instrument should request information which will help to define needs for CVOE programs and to determine types of cooperative programs which should be implemented. Questionnaire items should deal with student's:

1. Name, age, address, and current educational experience.
2. Career desires and projections.
3. Educational plan.
4. Financial needs.
5. Past and present work experience.
6. Desire to participate in a CVOE program.

If an assembly program is not feasible, students may be contacted through other means during homerooms or regular class sessions. In some LEA's, a mail survey will be most effective. Needs and interests of student clientele are among the most important types of information for CVOE program planners.

As Chapter 6 indicates, the CVOE program need not, and should probably not, be a teacher-coordinator who is expected to conduct a program in the near future. The traditional model of CVOE program development called for appointment of a teacher-coordinator early in the program planning process. Because types of cooperative programs implemented should depend upon needs and interests of students, it is well for staffing to occur after data have been collected and program types have been determined. That is, teacher-coordinators should not be hired to sell given programs. Rather, they should be hired to conduct programs which reflect student and labor market needs. Types of CVOE programs to be implemented should determine types of personnel to be employed.

**Future Students**

CVOE programs are developed to meet present and projected student needs. Data from enrolled students provide information relative to appropriate types of CVOE program for the short term. Data from people who may be enrolled several years hence provide some information relative to types of CVOE programs for the longer term. Information from prospective student clientele helps planners avoid program obsolescence.

Variables such as level on the educational ladder, size of the LEA's service area, variety of potential programs, and variety of LEA's lower on the educational ladder will influence the system for obtaining information from potential students. Program planners must decide whether a survey will be necessary to obtain necessary data.

It is possible that secondary data sources can provide the information. Most LEA's maintain records and make reports regarding characteristics of students and services. Some of the kinds of data available from secondary sources are:

1. Names, etc., of early leavers.
2. Names, etc., of people enrolled in various programs.
3. Current and projected enrollment statistics.
4. Reports of followup studies.
5. Published test profiles on selected students.
6. Lists of students who have expressed interest in selected careers or programs.

If it is decided that a survey is necessary, the following areas of concern should be incorporated in the questionnaire:

1. Name, age, and educational level of the prospective students.
2. Educational/occupational aspirations.
3. Employment history.
4. Occupational interest.

It is important to appreciate that maturity of prospective students influences both validity and reliability of surveys. Some students do not have good foundations of information on which to base responses. Quality of occupational awareness programs in elementary schools and other educational and cultural variables affect how people respond to survey items. Program planners should be cognizant of such conditions and utilize results of surveys judiciously.

Inputs from presently enrolled students, early leavers, and program completers establish one data base for programmatic decisions. Another data base for CVOE program implementation is manpower demands of the community. It should be emphasized that this and other activities

associated with planning CVOE programs may be completed simultaneously by several subcommittees of a steering committee. (See Chapter 6.)

## FORECASTING AREA MANPOWER NEEDS

The previous section provided information regarding assessment of
occupational needs and aspirations of student clientele. When students'
needs and aspirations can be matched with employment opportunities in
the community, conditions are favorable for implementing a CVOE prog-
ram(s).

Program planners must have an employment profile for the local community to determine feasibility of CVOE programs. The major features of
an employment profile are descriptions of selected types of occupations in
the community, and information concerning openings in those occupations.

Several factors must be considered by program planners as they devise
a system for determining an employment profile of a community. A large
community with many establishments may require an extensive survey. A
smaller community may require only a few interviews with employers.
Civic clubs, chambers of commerce, regional planning commissions,
government agencies, and other organizations should be visited before a
decision is reached on methods to be utilized in manpower studies. LEA's
are relative newcomers to the task of determining job opportunities in the
communities. Program planners should contact other agencies to find out
what is known relative to "work" in the community. What is known about
a community's occupational profile can be contrasted with what program
planners need to know and the difference can be defined as the remaining
study problem.

Some of the more important types of data needed for CVOE program
design are:

1. Number employed in occupations in the community.
2. Short- and long-term demand projections in various occupational
   categories and clusters.
3. Learning experiences which might be provided by business, industrial, government, and other enterprises.
4. Size and location of establishments.
5. Special employment restrictions of certain employers.
6. Projections regarding reductions, expansions, and additions to establishments in the employment community.

The manpower survey is a very useful instrument in vocational/
occupational program development. Many LEA's make periodic assessments of employment conditions. Therefore, program planners should

examine results of past efforts to conduct manpower studies. The basic purpose of the CVOE survey is to ascertain whether a community can, or cannot, provide sufficient and diverse job opportunities, in keeping with occupational needs and interests of an LEA's student clientele.

Secondary information sources may be useful in planning for CVOE. *The Occupational Outlook Handbook*, published every two years by the Bureau of Labor Statistics, provides information relative to job opportunities in selected occupational areas. Other publications which may be useful are the *Dictionary of Occupational Titles* and the annual *Manpower Report of the President*. These publications present national trends. Local occupational outlooks are, of course, more important to the success, or failure, of CVOE programs.

Characteristics of the local community should determine the activities to be performed in a manpower survey. A general system for ascertaining manpower profiles in local communities will be presented. Local CVOE program planners should modify this procedure in accord with local conditions.

First steps in ascertaining a manpower profile should entail study of available secondary sources of manpower data for the community. Several organizations are likely to have conducted investigations of local employment conditions. Some of these are:

1. Labor unions.
2. State Employment Service.
3. Chamber of Commerce.
4. State educational associations.
5. Other local educational agencies
6. Area planning commissions.
7. Utility companies.
8. Municipal government units.
9. Retailer's associations.
10. Manufacturer's associations.
11. Community action agencies.
12. Bureau of Labor Statistics.
13. National, state, and local planning groups.
14. Local civic organizations.

After planners have identified possible sources of manpower information, they should be contacted in person, on the telephone, or by letter.

Information from agencies in the community may be sufficient for program planning. In many instances, a community manpower supply/demand study will have to be completed. Because various institutions prepare individuals for gainful employment, both supply of and demand for trained personnel must be considered.

A list should be developed of all establishments in the community which employ workers in categories which are being considered for CVOE. The telephone directory is usually the best place to start this process. Planners also need to list agencies which are engaged in training for respective categories of occupations. The following form is useful for developing lists of manpower users and manpower developers (Fig. 4-3):

## Employing Establishments and Training Agencies

| Number Identified | Name & Address of Business or Agency | Type of Organization | Selected for Survey |
|---|---|---|---|
|  |  |  |  |

Fig. 4-3.   List of employing establishments and training agencies.

This form may be used to identify the total population of establishments and training agencies and institutions within the community. Organizations listed in column two should be designated numerically in column one. It is well to use separate numbering systems for employers and training establishments. (Some do both.) Employers might be numbered sequentially according to number of employees in selected categories. These numbers will be useful in large communities where the local planner may want to survey only a sample of establishments. (See Fig. 4-3.)

Column three may be used to designate the type of organization identified. Categories should depend upon characteristics of the employment community and CVOE programs under consideration. Column four may be used to indicate which organizations will be included in the survey. These may be selected randomly or by a design which assures a sample of establishments by size, type, and other variables which may be essential to learning experiences.

The manpower supply/demand survey (Fig. 4-4) should be conducted by a subcommittee of the steering committee. The individual(s) designated as CVOE program planner(s) should direct the survey. The planner

(Address of LEA)

Dear Mr._____:

This is to confirm our conversation of_____ (date)

Because occupational programs must meet present and projected manpower demands, we are studying the feasibility of a cooperative vocational/occupational education program. We would appreciate any information you can share with us regarding occupational and economic conditions in the community. Your organization has been extremely helpful to us in times past, and we can make good use of additional information on employment conditions which you can share with the_____ (Name of LEA)_____. (Identify type of information mentioned during verbal contact.)

Note: Consider cosignature of steering committee member.

Sincerely,

_____
(signature)

_____
(title)

**Fig. 4-4.   Sample letter for requesting manpower information.**

should meet with the subcommittee to develop a list of activities to be completed during the course of the survey. During this initial meeting, deadlines should be established for each phase of the survey, and sub-committee members should be assigned specific responsibilities (Fig. 4-5). The previously developed listing of establishments and training organizations should be examined by the subcommittee. Committee members should make additions to and/or deletions from the list and should have a voice in selecting establishments to survey. (See Fig. 4-3) A format similar to the form in Fig. 4-5 may be used for scheduling activities.

Several techniques may be utilized to gather necessary data. Three of the most common are (1) personal interview, (2) telephone interview, and (3) mail survey. Each has particular advantages and disadvantages. The technique(s) selected should depend on local conditions. Answers to the following questions should influence survey techniques.

1. How much money is available to complete the survey?
2. How much time is available?
3. What human resources are available?
4. How many organizations must be surveyed?
5. What is the size of the employment community?

**Survey Activities Schedule**

| Activities | Estimated Time for Completion | Personnel Assigned | Deadline for Completion |
|---|---|---|---|
| 1. | | | |
| 2. | | | |
| 3. | | | |
| 4. | | | |
| 5. | | | |
| 6. | | | |
| | | | |
| N | | | |

Fig. 4-5.   Schedule for survey activities.

In addition to the manpower data, valuable public relations and information sharing benefits accrue from face-to-face and telephone contacts. Therefore, personal contacts should be used insofar as possible.

Planners should work with the subcommittee of the steering committee to determine what types of information need to be collected. Usually, two different survey instruments should be developed. One will be used to ascertain labor market demand and the other will be used to define training efforts in the community. CVOE program planners should keep in mind that some private and public employers are also extensively involved in training.

Many LEA's utilize the community survey to (1) communicate the values of CVOE to the community, (2) ascertain the number of employers who would be willing to serve as training sponsors, and (3) identify possible training stations. This practice is of questionable value. The primary and almost sole purpose of the manpower survey should be to determine the supply of and demand for trained personnel. Selling the concept of CVOE should be left to CVOE personnel who may be appointed if survey results warrant. The purpose of the survey should be to determine whether or not the community has need for, and will support, a CVOE program(s).

A comprehensive manpower survey may become very involved and complicated if program planners lose sight of objectives. Three basic questions need to be answered by such surveys.

1. Does the community have an employment base which can support CVOE?

2. Are insufficient numbers of people currently prepared for respective occupations?
3. In what occupational areas are needs for trained personnel greatest?

Answers to the first two questions indicate go or no-go on CVOE program implementation. Answers to the third question indicate which types of CVOE program(s) should be pursued.

Interviews or questionnaires should determine the following from employers.

1. Number of personnel employed, full- and part-time.
2. Types of jobs, especially those appropriate to vocational/ occupational education.
3. Training opportunities available.
4. Anticipated manpower increases or decreases by job title.
5. Educational requirements of various jobs.

Interviews or questionnaires should determine the following from training establishments.

1. Number of graduates by occupational area.
2. Number of students enrolled in various programs.
3. Status of plans to implement new programs.

Comparison of manpower supply and demand survey data should indicate whether a community can support a CVOE program(s).

### Summary

Two basic conditions are essential to the support of CVOE programs. (1) student needs and (2) manpower demands. When needs and aspirations of student clientele have approximate match with manpower demands of the community, conditions are favorable for implementation of CVOE. Numerical and descriptive information about students and the employment community provide data for judicious decisions regarding types of CVOE programs at the local level.

### Activities

1. Design the format and develop the content of a two-page survey instrument which could be utilized to survey an LEA's dropout population.
2. Develop a list of names and addresses of all civic and service organization in a local community. Develop a list of all government organizations (local, state, and federal) which may provide valuable data for CVOE program planners.

3. Visit an LEA to determine procedures a CVOE program planner would have to follow to obtain names and addresses of early school leavers.

4. Develop covering letters for dropout, program completer, and manpower demand survey instruments.

5. Visit an LEA to examine followup study practices. Write a one- to two-page paper, evaluating the utility of findings for program planning and redesign.

6. Visit a local office of the state employment service and/or regional manpower office to ascertain types of available information which might be useful to CVOE program planners.

7. Develop a plan for completing a manpower demand survey, containing a list of *all* activities to be accomplished and time provided for each activity.

8. Develop a similar plan for ascertaining student occupational needs and aspirations.

9. Contact an LEA to examine available manpower data and means of obtaining same.

10. Draft a letter to a United States Department of Labor regional office, asking for manpower data for your community.

# Chapter 5

# Determining CVOE
# Program Types

The preceding chapter dealt with processes involved in establishing empirical data bases for programmatic decisions. Results of community and student surveys, described in Chapter 4, should be used to determine types of cooperative vocational/occupational education (CVOE) program's to be implemented in local educational agencies (LEA's).

Hasty implementation has resulted in many ill-conceived CVOE programs. Careful planning and time for developing understanding and supportive publics are essential to processes which establish occupational programs which will serve (1) occupational needs of various clientele and (2) manpower needs of nearby and larger communities.

This chapter describes programmatic decision-making processes. Some of the outcomes of reading this chapter are:

1. Understand factors involved in determining form and format of CVOE programs.
2. Greater awareness of alternative decisions regarding types of CVOE programs.
3. Understanding of various publics which may be served by CVOE.
4. Understanding of the concepts that students should not be molded to "fit" existing CVOE programs but, that programs should be developed to "fit" student needs and manpower demands.

### DECISIONS ACROSS AND WITHIN OCCUPATIONAL CLUSTERS

Results of student and community surveys provide bases for decisions regarding types of CVOE programs. Data should facilitate answers to two basic questions.

1. Which occupations or occupational clusters provide greatest opportunities for employment?

2. Which occupations or occupational clusters are of greatest interest to students?

Answers to these two questions should be juxtaposed with constraints identified in Chapter 3, to provide foundation for deciding upon types of CVOE programs for LEA's. Knowledge of student needs, manpower demands, and real world constraints is necessary to assessments of the appropriateness of programs in (1) the occupational clusters described in chapter two, i.e., applied biological and agricultural; business, marketing, and management; health; industrial-oriented; and personal and public service; and (2) the many specialty areas which have been the concern of CVOE.

Prior to passage of the Vocational Education Act of 1963, vocational education consisted of a rather limited number of specific programs. Program areas were conducted according to specific program guidelines in most states. Guidelines for administration and supervision of cooperative programs *specified* occupations in which students could be placed, characteristics of students to be served, qualifications of teachers and other personnel, and program content and format. The primary concern was to maintain program integrity. *The* program was predominant. Thus, *the* mission of vocational educators was to sell *the* program to communities and students. By the 1950's, the force of change in the labor market was so enormous, that traditional programs, obviously, could not meet increasingly diverse demands.

**Strategic and/or Tactical Models**

CVOE is viewed from at least two perspectives. (1) It is perceived by some vocational educators as a method for providing all vocational skills, attitudes, and competencies which an individual needs to enter a particular occupation. This view of cooperative education may be called *strategic* as contrasted from *tactical*. Operationally, the strategic model appears as follows: (1) A student indicates that he is interested in becoming an auto mechanic. CVOE personnel find employment in the community for the student in the auto mechanic occupations cluster. (3) Together with the employer, a teacher-coordinator analyzes the auto mechanic cluster to ascertain what the student must be able to do and what he must know to function as an auto mechanic. (4) The employer indicates which competencies the student can learn on the job and the LEA assumes responsibility for developing competencies which cannot be acquired at the training station. The total training experience is cooperative. The student spends a portion of his learning time on the job, developing necessary competencies, and a portion of his time at the LEA, taking prescribed general education courses and a CVOE related class in which he learns technical and general information related to auto mechanics. Professionals who prefer the strategic model of CVOE submit that on-the-job training takes the place of laboratory facilities in the LEA.

Educators who prefer the tactical model of CVOE perceive the cooperative education experience as a culminating activity, i.e., occurring at the end (or near the end) of a "regular" sequential program of vocational studies. Operationally, the tactical model appears as follows: (1) The student enrolls in an LEA and indicates that he is interested in becoming an auto mechanic. (2) The student is enrolled in auto mechanics laboratory classes and required and elective courses. (3) Near the end of his program of studies, he is placed at an appropriate training station and enrolled in a related class. He applies skills developed in laboratory classes and develops competencies which could not be learned in laboratory courses. Although there is not sufficient empirical evidence to substantiate the superiority of one model over the other, it appears that the tactical model is more effective because it combines laboratory and CVOE methods of competency development.

In most LEA's the tactical model cannot be used exclusively because laboratories cannot be provided for all occupations identified in manpower and student need surveys. Even in small communities, it is apparent that people enter a wide range of occupations as they leave full-time schooling. To serve student training needs and manpower demands, many LEA's must develop both tactical and strategic CVOE models. Even though the tactical approach, i.e., combining laboratory and on-the-job learning experiences, is best for some occupations, an LEA has to function on the principle that some occupational training is better than no occupational training at all. Strategic CVOE programs have to be developed if the LEA does not have a sequential program in an occupational cluster which surveys show to be important to students and employers. Sometimes it is appropriate to begin efforts in an occupational cluster with the strategic model and develop a tactical model(s) as resources permit. The rule-of-thumb is that CVOE programs should capstone existing occupational programs, that is, extend in-house programs into the community. But, if an LEA is unable to offer occupational programs for certain identified needs, one or more strategic programs should be developed.

### Program Types

Decisions regarding types of CVOE program's in LEA's should be based primarily upon data which describe characteristics of local clientele. Some of the variables to be considered when determining types of CVOE programs are students':

1. level of career development,
2. chronological age,
3. educational level,
4. occupational interests,
5. occupational aptitude.

It is important to understand that CVOE programs should be tailor-made to meet occupational development needs of students. For example, there may be greater need for an exploratory than for a preparatory program. Decisions of this type can be made only after careful study of local conditions.

One of the occupational classification systems identified earlier in this text was (1) applied biological and agricultural, (2) business, marketing, and management, (3) health, (4) industrial-oriented, and (5) personal and public service occupations. An example will demonstrate some of the kinds of alternatives regarding program types. Assume that surveys indicate large student and manpower demand for applied biological and agricultural programs, especially for training clusters such as agrimechanics, agribusiness, and horticulture. Given evidence of demand, an LEA can consider several alternatives. Decisions regarding alternatives should depend primarily upon conditions unique to the LEA. The first alternative is whether to provide cooperative experiences via tactical or strategic models.

1. A capstone or tactical CVOE program could be conducted if the LEA is offering preparatory courses in all the identified agricultural areas of student and manpower demand. The work experience portion of the program could be scheduled so that more students could be accommodated in agricultural programs. This should reduce certain manpower shortages. Capstone, cooperative experiences should also be expected to improve placement and followup functions of the LEA's agricultural programs. Most post-secondary programs should be tactical; depth of specialization is best assured by the tactical model.
2. A strategic CVOE program could be conducted in one (or more) of the identified areas. This would be a viable alternative if the LEA did not have in-house programs in the identified areas and did not have means or inclination to develop one or more programs. A strategic program might (a) utilize external resources, such as training stations, as the primary source of nearly all skills and knowledges and (b) conduct a related class to provide general and technical related occupational information.

Ongoing programs in clusters other than applied biological and agricultural occupations might be expanded and/or redirected to meet student needs in agricultural occupations. The following examples describe two alternatives concerning occupational clusters.

1. *An automotive technology* program could be expanded to include some components of agrimechanics. Much of the technical information in typical automotive programs is relevant to agrimechanics. Principles of internal combustion engines, power transmission, electrical systems, and many other topics are relevant to both automotive and agricultural mechanics. Following preparation-level courses which deal with such areas of knowledge, cooperative education experiences could provide remaining entry skills for several kinds of mechanics.

2. Similarly, *a distributive education* program or a *business education* program could be modified to accommodate some components of agribusiness. This approach might entail addition of a course or several courses directly concerned with agribusiness. But, some savings would be realized by courses common to several occupational clusters. Such courses might include data processing, accounting, salesmanship, distribution, management, and economics.

Strategic programs are especially useful when an LEA wishes to add services for a small number of students and has ongoing, closely related programs, when an LEA has few students interested in and small demand for divergent occupations, or when special needs students are expected to enter part-time employment with minimal lead time, e.g., WECEP and early school leaver programs.

The above examples are illustrative of only some of the kinds of alternatives which should be considered. Local opportunities and institutional constraints should be the primary considerations in decisions regarding how many CVOE programs should be conducted for which occupations or occupational clusters. There should be no attempt to mirror other LEA's or to accommodate available teachers or the wares of educational suppliers. Form should follow function and available means. Tactical and/or strategic programs should maximize the match between interests and manpower demands. Common orientation and preparatory-level, in-house courses and, in some instances, strategic CVOE programs should be utilized to increase scope of occupational clusters beyond what can be offered in tactical programs alone.

## DECISIONS ALONG THE EDUCATIONAL LADDER

Historically, CVOE programs have served high school seniors and post-secondary students. Recently, small numbers of 14- and 15-year-olds have been benefited.

**Midteens and CVOE**

A significant number of students in the early teen years look forward to the day when they exceed compulsory attendance age. Many of the young are alienated from traditional forms of education. As was indicated in Chapter 2, one program for serving midteens is referred to as the Work Experience and Career Exploration Program (WECEP). WECEP programs resulted from an agreement between the Department of Labor and Health Education and Welfare, which relaxed (with proper supervision) barriers to employment of individuals under 16 years of age. A number of studies have been conducted to assess the benefits of WECEP. The typical procedure of such studies is as follows. First, counselors and other personnel identify potential participants on criteria such as failing grades, poor attendance, assertion of desire to quit school, and potential for or history of being adjudicated. Then one-half of those identified are randomly assigned to WECEP cooperative programs and the others are allowed to continue in "regular" educational programs. Finally, at various intervals, experimental and control groups are compared on work performance and educational development. Weisman (82) conducted a study of a number of WECEP programs. WECEP students demonstrated improved attendance patterns, significant educational progress, and decreased dropout rates.

Through data collection techniques described in Chapter 4, LEA's should determine whether CVOE may be used to provide occupational exploration and preparation-level experiences to students who are less than 16 years old. The strategic cooperative education model should be provided for midteens who can benefit from new understandings of the relationship of school and productive society. Special steps must be taken to assure legality and to provide close supervision of participants in such programs.

**Late Teens and CVOE**

The great majority of students participating in CVOE programs are secondary school students 16 years of age and older. Most CVOE programs are conducted at the high school level. (But, the number of programs at both high school and post-secondary levels is increasing very rapidly.) The following discussion treats issues which are related to determining types of secondary CVOE programs.

Small LEA's in communities with limited employment opportunities should consider implementation of interrelated CVOE programs, the better to serve diverse occupational interests of students. Contrastingly, large LEA's should consider implementation of a number of specialized CVOE programs, the better to accommodate manageable-size groups of students with similar goals. Specialized programs may be either tactical or strategic. But, large LEA's should conduct at least several technical programs, i.e., sequences of courses, beginning in grade nine or ten and culminating in cooperative experiences.

Although the purpose of most CVOE programs at the secondary level should be to develop entry-level occupational skills, programs which achieve other purposes should be considered. Even in LEA's with articulated career, vocational, and occupational education programs, occupational orientation and exploration objectives cannot be fully achieved by all students by grade eleven or twelve. Many students can benefit from occupational orientation and/or exploration standpoints, if they are afforded CVOE experiences for these as contrasted to preparatory-level purposes. For example, students who expect to pursue careers in medicine and law would do well to work in entry-level occupations in various establishments where those professions are practiced. Many "college prep" students would benefit from well-structured and supervised experiences which assure that they learn about people, places, and things in their areas of interest. Similarly, students who intend to pursue vocational or occupational programs in high school and/or college would benefit from cooperative education experiences which occur prior to specialization and increase understandings which are necessary to decisions such as choice of clusters or specialties and selection from among preparatory programs, e.g., secondary or post-secondary LEA's should consider short term and summer CVOE programs to provide occupational orientation and/or preparation for a great variety of students—the better to complement elementary school occupational awareness and junior high school occupational orientation programs and the better to dispel myths which might be fostered by visual media such as television serials.

As has been indicated above, in LEA's with diverse student needs, adequate manpower demands, and large enrollments, CVOE programs should be established in specific occupations or occupational clusters. It is unusually well to assure diversity by offering at least one program in each of several categories across the spectrum of occupations. A good plan might be to (1) offer at least one program in each of six categories of occupations: applied biological and agricultural; business and marketing management; health ; industrial-oriented; personal service; and public service and (2) to add programs when enrollment and manpower demand in a given category support even greater specificity. CVOE programs in specified occupational areas have major advantages. For example, CVOE personnel have professional preparation *and* work experience directly related to the occupations in which students are working. Thus, training plans and other essentials are expertly done. Related classes can also deal more directly with job tasks. Such advantages must not be overemphasized because CVOE assumes that supervisors contribute job knowledge, skills, and attitudes in major measure. The supervisor on the job is "the downtown teacher."

### Adults and CVOE

It is wrong to assume that all clientele served by community colleges, technical institutes, Comprehensive Employment and Training Act programs, and other post-secondary programs are firmly commited to particular occupational specialties. It is possible to say, with some degree of certainty, that student clientele served by such institutions are older than clientele served by secondary schools; but, assumptions beyond that level of sophistication are difficult to substantiate.

Decisions regarding types of CVOE programs to implement in post- and extra-secondary institutions should be founded on the same kinds of data as at other levels of education, i.e., the occupational training needs of student clientele and manpower needs of the community.[1] In public LEA's, if studies indicate that large numbers of students desire training for a specific occupational area, it is often best to develop CVOE programs accordingly.

By far, most CVOE programs conducted by community colleges and technical institutes are of the capstone or tactical type. Typically, in this type of program, participants are enrolled in sequences of classroom and laboratory courses and then in cooperative experiences.

In some LEA's, conditions may suggest consideration of other types of CVOE programs, e.g., programs which meet needs of special target groups. One such program which is gaining in popularity is the early school leaver (ESL) cooperative program. ESL programs are designed to serve high school dropouts via on-the-job and classroom experiences. ESL students usually work in occupations related to career aspirations for one-half day and attend the LEA the other one-half day. The in-house part of the program should be very individualized. Students should have opportunity to (1) complete preparation for and pass the General Educational Development (GED) examination, (2) take special courses for high school credit and graduation, (3) enroll in occupational courses directly related to career goals, or (4) enroll in special courses chosen because of some other identified deficiency.

Even though ESL programs serve student clientele which many would classify as secondary, growing numbers of professionals advocate that they be implemented at the college level for at least two reasons: First,

---

[1] In many instances, *community* may mean employers in selected industries in many regions of the nation or even beyond.

college-level institutions provide environments significantly different from environments in which ESL participants met with failure. Second, community colleges and equivalent institutions are able to serve early leavers from several LEA's with diversified options.

In *Cooperative Education in Community Colleges,* Heermann (20), pp. 21-27, proposed a "cooperative community college" which incorporates the cooperative plan of educational delivery for virtually every program offered. Heermann developed the concept of seven distinct program clusters in which the community college's student clientele could be placed. These were designed to serve students (1) with a " . . . clearly defined career objective in a middle-management, technical or semi-professional occupational area," (2) " . . . not decided on a particular occupational area," (3) with "a well defined career objective which embraces a professional occupational responsibility," (4) with a current, full-time job and desire for upgrading or advancement, (5) with a desire to "explore science, humanities, and social science areas for personal fulfillment," (6) without clearly identified educational, personal, or career objectives and with a desire for counseling re a program of studies which facilitates examination of interests and relationships with surroundings, and (7) with a " . . . desire to develop basic skills in mathematics and communications before selecting" one of the other program clusters.

The model proposed by Heermann assumes that work is valuable in the educational development of an individual. The present authors agree; but, they distinguish between cooperative programs which provide general educational development experiences from those which make "an individual more employable in one group of occupations than in another" [Evans, (15), p. 1 ]. Cooperative programs which enable one to function more efficiently and effectively in one occupation than in all other occupations are the overriding concern of this book.

## DECISIONS ACROSS ABILITY AND INTEREST GROUPS

CVOE programs are beneficial to students with diverse mental abilities. Various experiential programs benefit the full range of ability from mentally handicapped to gifted. In the past, personnel in LEA's have tried to be highly selective when choosing participants for CVOE. Part of the rationale for selecting was the desire of administrators and coodinators to place only students who would "properly" represent the LEA. This practice was highly desirable from a restricted institutional perspective. However, the cream-skimming process had the effect of providing cooperative experiences only for students who needed it least, i.e., for people who would, in the main, become contributing citizens no matter what school program they pursued as seniors.

In several states vocational/occupational education leaders have helped LEA's develop special CVOE programs which serve students who do not "qualify" for "regular" cooperative programs. Where they have been fostered, many special programs have been implemented and have enjoyed good enrollment. In case after case, the notion that only "better" students should be selected for participation in CVOE has been refuted. For example, in Illinois, where there are approximately 1,400 CVOE programs at the secondary level, nearly one out of every four programs serves those whom many would classify as nontraditional cooperative students.

It is important to know the characteristics of the student clientele served by an LEA before developing various types of CVOE programs. Planners should use group and individual profiles on the following variables:

1. mental ability,
2. vocational aspirations,
3. educational development,
4. career and occupational development,
5. work experience,
6. personality characteristics, and
7. physical handicaps.

Profiles may indicate that special populations should be served. For example, studies may disclose physically and/or mentally handicapped people who can best be served by sheltered work shop experiences prior to entry-level employment in the community, sponsored by and supervised by the LEA.

Because it is virtually impossible for a public LEA to offer occupational programs which meet the career needs of all clientele, profiles are likely to suggest development and implementation of CVOE programs which increase occupational options. In doing so, the LEA should not be restricted to types of CVOE programs conducted previously by other institutions. Rather, the LEA should implement programs in accord with identified career development needs of its enrolled and potential student clientele.

### Summary

Decisions regarding implementation of various types of CVOE programs should be based upon two kinds of data, i.e. (1) needs and aspirations of student clientele, and (2) manpower demands of the local community. Decisions should not be controlled by or limited to CVOE programs which have worked in the past. Development should be forward-looking. Projections regarding employment and clientele should determine program types.

The following factors should affect determinations re types of CVOE programs to implement in an LEA.

1. Planners should consider the vocational program offerings of all LEA's along the educational ladder. Articulation among various LEA's should be fostered. Transition from one educational level to the next should be smooth. Unnecessary duplication of effort can best be avoided in early planning stages.
2. CVOE programs should be developed and implemented to meet present and projected manpower training needs of enterprises in the community. The tradition of CVOE program types should not govern programmatic decisions.
3. The fact that various CVOE programs have satisfied training needs along broad ability and interest spectrums should be appreciated by planners.
4. CVOE programs should interface with existing vocational programs whenever possible. But, absence of an in-house occupational program in a given occupation or occupational cluster should not preclude development of a strategic CVOE program.
5. Individual CVOE programs may be established to serve one, several, or many occupational areas simultaneously. Local program planners should attempt to establish specialized CVOE programs whenever feasible; however, programs which serve diverse occupational needs should be established when specialized CVOE programs are not feasible.
6. CVOE programs should be developed primarily for preparing individuals to enter (and progress in) occupations. But, career awareness, occupational orientation, and exploration can also be fostered by CVOE.

### Activities

1. Compare and contrast advantages and disadvantages of strategic and tactical CVOE models in a five-page paper.
2. Define three CVOE models which might prepare students for several occupational clusters.
3. Compare and contrast advantages and disadvantages of incorporating cooperative education experiences in sequential programs which have been restricted to the classroom/laboratory model.
4. List and describe four new and innovative types of CVOE programs.
5. Arrange a visit to an innovative CVOE program. Write a three-page or shorter report, describing why and how it was implemented.
6. Describe a CVOE program which might be implemented to meet special needs of mentally handicapped aged 15-30.

7. Define the characteristics of clientele which should be understood by program planners. Indicate how each might be measured by LEA personnel.

# Development and Implementation of Cooperative Vocational/Occupational Education (CVOE) Programs

# Chapter 6

# Working With a Steering Committee

In Chapter 5, decisions concerning types of cooperative education for given Local Education Agencies (LEA's) were dealt with. This chapter deals with the work of a steering committee in initial phases of the development of cooperative programs, regardless of program breadth, program level, or clientele served. Because cooperative vocational/occupational education (CVOE) relies very heavily upon functioning advisory committees, public relations, training stations, and other linkages with the community, it is essential that early phases of program development involve representatives from several segments of the community.

Some of the outcomes of reading this chapter are increased readiness to:

1. Begin the program implementation process by studying institutional and community characteristics and establishing a steering committee.
2. Conduct a steering committee meeting.
3. Monitor and assist the work of subcommittees between meetings.
4. Conduct a second steering committee meeting.
5. Draft agenda, questionnaires, proposals, a report of findings, and recommendations, and various letters relevant to a steering committee's efforts.

## MANAGING INITIAL PHASES OF PROGRAM DEVELOPMENT

There are several tested methods for implementing cooperative education programs. Each requires adequate lead time and a major portion of the time of a qualified teacher-coordinator. Because details of initial development determine what will occur when students appear for classroom and training station experiences, it is essential that a qualified person have time and material resources to do first things right.

People who have witnessed the development of cooperative programs in various situations are quick to agree that lead time should be at least one year. Anything less than a year results in "crash" programming. Professionals and governing boards who think this is overstated need only consider what must be accomplished before students appear for the first session of a related class to understand that one year is adequate and not more than ample.[1] Subsequent portions of this chapter emphasize that certain things take time and can be done properly by a qualified person with time to manage them.

Like most staffing matters, this management problem can be solved either by assigning an organization member to the task or by appointing a new person. Three kinds of people may be considered for assignment from within. (1) A director of vocational education or a dean of occupational education might be assigned half-time to the tasks of working with a steering committee and/or program planning until a teacher-coordinator is assigned from within or appointed from without. (2) A successful teacher-coordinator from another occupational cluster might by assigned. (3) A teacher from the occupation or occupational cluster for which a cooperative program is being developed might be assigned. In given situations, work loads and individual characteristics provide bases for decision. Each alternative has advantages, e.g., the latter approach provides a teacher the opportunity to consider becoming a teacher-coordinator and the teacher's superiors opportunity to consider his/her qualifications for the emerging position.

A new person may be employed at the beginning of the year and assigned to half-time teaching and half-time planning with a steering committee. This approach assumes that a program will be instituted and that qualifications of a teacher-coordinator can be known quite early in the process. It has the disadvantage of not involving steering committee members in selection of a teacher-coordinator. Although a committee cannot be responsible for staff selection, representation of a steering committee should be involved in the interview process if possible.

A combination approach is often best in light of staff time commitments and financial considerations. Many successful programs have been implemented by the following approach:

1. An existing staff member serves as chairman of a steering committee which works for three to six months on a number of matters, includ-

---

[1] It seems that modern, fast-living America is reluctant to provide resources for adequate preparation of the workers whose products and services it desires. Many of the very people who are proud to provide adequately for the preparation of so-called professionals are averse to preparing tradesmen, mechanics, and others at public expense. One year's lead time for a cooperative education program is meager compared to the time and expense of implementing a school of veterinary medicine or dentistry. Yet, the quality of automotive mechanics may have more immediate impact on human livelihood.

ing criteria for and selection of a teacher-coordinator and perhaps other staff members.

2. A teacher-coordinator, appointed from within or without, and a steering committee work on additional matters for several weeks or months, including appointment of a permanent advisory committee.
3. The teacher-coordinator finalizes preparations for the first term, with some help from the advisory committee.


### FIRST THINGS FIRST

As soon as responsibility for working with a steering committee is assigned to an existing employee or a new appointee, that individual should do four things in close time proximity.

#### Meet State Agency People

The individual should meet appropriate people in the state education agency or agencies. This is usually best done together with an officer of the institution who has worked with agency personnel. In the case of a secondary school, the individual should meet people at two or more levels in the state vocational education agency and spend an hour or more with the specialist(s) on cooperative education for the span of occupations to which the program under consideration might lead. In the case of a public technical institute or community college, the individual should meet occupational education experts in the respective state agency and in the agency responsible for vocational education funding. (Where his professional counterparts are to be found varies from state to state.) In the case of a private institution, the individual should meet his professional counterparts and the person(s) who is responsible for approving programs in private institutions which participate or have students who participate under various funding opportunities, e.g., financial aids. In any of these cases, the purpose of the mission should be to:

1. Establish contact and extend professional courtesies.
2. Secure current manuals, rules and regulations, legal restrictions and requirements, guildlines, etc., pertinent to the program under consideration.
3. Obtain support of agency personnel at least in word and preferably in consulting time, for program development and evaluation.

In the case of programs which might lead to occupations which involve state licensure, the individual should also contact a counterpart(s) in the licensing agency. The purposes of this mission will vary from occupation to occupation and will be obvious to the individual teacher-coordinator. In many instances the licensing agency will have stop-and-go authority over program development and initiation and will have to approve documents, facilities, personnel appointments, etc.

### Study the Institution

The individual should make a thorough study of the institution and its prior experience relevant to the program under consideration. Some of the kinds of things the individual should study were dealt with in Chapters 3-5. These include structure of the institution, programs, courses, etc.; studies of graduated and enrolled students; area manpower studies; existing linkages with the employment community; and previous decisions regarding vocational or occupational education and especially cooperative education. Study of these things should entail (a) discussions with various people within the institution and in the community and (b) reading any and all documents which pertain to the matter, e.g., governing board minutes, survey results, department goals statements, staff and student handbooks, class schedules.

### Learn About the Community

The individual should make several kinds of efforts to learn about the community via reading. This may be difficult in very small communities, but some effort should be made in even the very smallest. Minutes of institution general advisory counsel meetings, accrediting agency reports, local newspapers, Bureau of Census, surveys of the community which might have been done prior to bond issues or referenda, state employment agency reports, chamber of commerce documents, want ads, literature of major employers, descriptions of government employers—these and many other sources tell things about a community which a teacher-coordinator must know to be fully effective in one of the most important roles in community education. Documents need not be read thoroughly in every instance. But, they should be more than scanned for understanding the quality and quantity of people, employers, community agencies of various kinds, and especially community leaders.

### Establish a Steering Committee

The individual should prepare a plan for establishing and chairing a steering committee. The plan should describe purposes, probable duration, and makeup of the committee. In most LEA's the plan will have to be approved by several levels of administration and perhaps by the governing board. The purposes of a steering committee are (1) *to advise* the institution whether to proceed or not to proceed with the implementation of a program[2] *and* (2) if the recommendation is to proceed, *to have input* to definition of program parameters and goals, of staff needs, of facilities needs, and of a plan of action, beginning with the appointment of an advisory committee. The duration of a steering committee is typically six to eighteen months. A diversified occupations program might be implemented with an even shorter period of input from a steering committee and a licensed practical nursing program or a very unusual program, such as a mining technician program designed to serve several states, might require a longer period.

A steering committee should be broadly representative. But, membership should be restricted to manageable size. The following should be represented.

From the Community:

1. Employer associations
2. Several kinds of employers
3. Chamber of Commerce
4. Employee groups
5. Labor councils
6. State and private employment agencies and military recruiters
7. Service clubs, affirmative action groups, and religious organizations
8. Media personnel

From the Institution:

1. The chief administrative officer
2. One or two levels of vocational or occupational education administration
3. Teachers most closely concerned with the program
4. Student personnel and counseling people
5. Students who might enroll in the program
6. Teacher, student, and parent groups

The individual should have discussions with superiors to decide upon a list of people who will be invited to serve on the steering committee and a list of alternatives. Special attention should be given to several of the categories. It is especially important to invite employers and employees from a variety of establishments. The span of occupations and community characteristics will suggest what dimensions to consider. Some general

---

[2]This word, *advise,* cannot be overemphasized. Committee members, LEA personnel, and governing board members should be reminded from time-to time that steering and permanent advisory committee are not responsible for decisions; they only give well-founded advice regarding decisions.

dimensions are: private/public, large/small, nearby/distant, and all-purpose/specialized. In many instances it is appropriate to consider representation from suppliers to employing enterprises, because they employ similar people in sales and service capacities. Representation can often be broadened by inviting people who are prominent in more than one segment of the community, e.g., a private employment agency officer who is a leader in one or more civic groups. It should be made obvious that such persons represent more than one constituency. The list of people to be invited should include one person from nearly all of the above categories and several from the employer and employee categories. The number should not vary greatly from twenty.

The chief administrative officer should invite people to serve on the committee. He should judge whether to make the first contact by telephone or letter. In any case, significance of the matter should be indicated by a letter which describes the purpose, probable duration, and contribution in terms of meeting time and other commitments. When an individual declines an invitation, the chief administrator should invite an alternate. Sometimes, he should confer with the individual who will be working with the committee to decide on alternates.

When all have agreed to serve, the chief administrative officer should send a second letter which expresses appreciation of willingness to serve and announces the first meeting time and place. This mailing should include a list of steering committee members and their affiliation and an agenda.

### FIRST STEERING COMMITTEE MEETING: STUDY AND PLANNING

The first steering committee meeting should include at least the following agenda items.

#### Welcome, Thank-You, and Introduction of Members

The chief administrative officer or the administrator of vocational or occupational programs should introduce people, indicating their affiliation or the community segment(s) they represent.

#### Orientation to Cooperative Education and Committee Functions

Institution personnel should plan to share responsibility for this agenda item. If no one on the staff has had teacher-coordinator experience, it might be well to invite a state agency or university expert to describe the kind of cooperative program which is under consideration and serve as a resource person during the rest of the meeting. A professionally prepared film and/or printed materials may also be used to develop basic understanding of cooperative education essentials. Exploration of committee functions should stress the importance of information and the meaning of *advise*.

### Information Which Suggests Consideration of the Program

The individual who will be working with the steering committee, i.e., the chairman, should share information which contributed to the decision to establish the committee. This includes needs assessments (see Chapter 4), descriptions of existing and emerging institutional programs (see Chapter 5), and information the individual has acquired from various other sources (see previous portions of this chapter).

### Tasks To Be Accomplished by the Committee

Obviously, the work of steering committees will vary a great deal, depending upon circumstances. The following are minimal and typical of tasks which *ad hoc* committees can do with small time commitments.

1. *Survey Employment Community.* Before it can recommend that a program be instituted and define program goals and parameters, a committee must know the current and projected employment markets for part-time and "permanent" job placements of student learners and graduates. The following form is representative of information which may be collected by mail or interview surveys (Fig. 6-1). In some

## Survey Form for Establishing Employer Participation in Cooperative Education

1. Name of Establishment  _____

2. Address  _____

3. Nature of Enterprise  _____

4. Number of Employees  _____

      Part-time _____

      Full-time _____

      Office and Clinical Employees _____

      Production Employees _____

      Sales and Service Employees _____

      Other _____

Fig. 6-1. Sample survey form for establishing employer participation in cooperative education. (Cont'd on next page).

5. Does employment increase during a particular time of the year? __
   If so, when? _____
   For what occupations? _____
6. Possible training stations.
   a. Would your establishment provide part-time employment for cooperative education students when possible? _____
   b. If yes, what type?

      Office and Clerical _____

      Production _____

      Sales and Service _____

      Other _____
7. Possible Contributions
   a. Would your establishment provide resource persons for special presentations to students? _____
   b. If yes, what type?

      In School _____

      In Your Establishment _____
   c. Might your establishment contribute material to the program from time to time? _____
   d. If yes, what materials? _____
   e. Would your enterprise like to be represented on a citizen committee which gives advice regarding the conduct of the cooperative education program? _____
      If yes, who might serve? _____

_____          _____
(name)                                    (name)


_____          _____
(title)                                   (title)

Fig. 6-1.   Sample survey form for establishing employer participation in cooperative education.

situations it would be well to forego questions re resource persons and contributions of materials and supplies until a later time. (See Chapter 7.) The covering letter illustrates some of the things which might be included in a mail survey (Fig. 6-2). Note that the form and/or letter

**Sample Covering Letter of Survey for Establishing Employer Partici-
pation in Cooperative Education**

Dr. James Murphy, D.D.S.
1100 Remington Street
New Haven Connecticut 06792
Dear Dr. Murphy:

The Slippery Elm Technical Institute is studying the feasibility of
establishing a Cooperative Occupational Education Program. Cooperative Education is a program which involves study in school, part-time
paid work at a training station in the community, and a training plan
which is designed by a teacher coordinator and the student-learner's
job supervisor. The proposed program would involve approximately
_____ and _____ students, working approximately
_____ hours per week.

This program would require the support of various segments of the
community. We are conducting a survey to ascertain how many
employers might support the program by providing part-time, paid
employment for students and/or resource persons and/or advisory
committee membership. Please complete the enclosed form and return
it in the envelope provided.

Please call if either of us can help. Thank you for your cooperation.

Sincerely,

Herman Seitz
President (502) 634-8791

Fred Welham
Executive Director
Chamber of Commerce (502) 634-8687

**Fig. 6-2.   Sample covering letter for survey form for establishing employer participation in
cooperative education.**

and/or face-to-face interview should be designed for the specific program. For example, items concerning kinds of employees should be
designed to gather necessary information and no more.
2. *Survey Potential Students.* Similarly, a steering committee must have
information about career and educational interests of potential students. The following forms illustrate what might be discovered relevant to high school and post-high school programs (Figs. 6-3 and 6-4).
Properly modified, these forms could be used to survey students

**Survey Form (High School) for Establishing Student Participation in Cooperative Education**

**Personal**                                    Date_____

　　Name _____

　　Address _____

　　_____ Telephone _____

　　Grade level_____Register Room _____

**Educational Plans**

　　High School Major in _____

　　Interested in

　　　　Applied Biological Occupations _____

　　　　Agricultural Occupations_____

　　　　Distributive Occupations_____

　　　　Home Economics Related Occupations_____

　　　　Industrial Occupations_____

　　　　Office Occupations_____

　　　　Secretarial Occupations_____

　　　　Other_____

　　　　Attending Community College

　　　　　　yes_____        no_____              maybe_____

major_____

　　　　Attending Technical Institute

　　　　　　yes_____ no_____ maybe_____ major_____

　　　　Attending University

yes_____    no_____    maybe_____    major_____

**Employment Experience and Plans**

　　Previously Employed

　　　　Name of Employer _____

　　　　Responsibilities _____

　　　　_____

　　　　Name of Employer _____

　　　　Responsibilities _____

　　　　_____

　　Presently Employed

　　　　Name of Employer _____

　　　　Responsibilities _____

　　　　_____

　　Plan to be Employed

　　　　Occupation _____

　　　　Place of Employment _____

**Fig. 6-3.** Sample survey form (high school) for establishing student participation in cooperative education.

## Survey Form (Post High School) for Establishing Student Participation in Cooperative Education

**Personal**                                             Date_____

  Name _____

  Address _____

  _____

  Telephone _____

  High School Attended _____

  Graduation Date Month_____ Year _____

  High School Major _____

**Educational Plans**

  Interested in



(program or programs being offered by institution entered here)

  Plan to attend university yes_____ no_____

  Possible Major _____

**Employment Experience and Plans**

  Previously Employed

    Name of Employer _____

    Responsibilities _____

    _____

    Name of Employer _____

    Responsibilities _____

    _____

  Presently Employed

    Name of Employer _____

    Responsibilities _____

    _____

  Plan to be Employed

    Occupation _____

    Place of Employment _____

**Fig. 6-4.  Sample survey form (post high school) for establishing student participation in cooperative education.**

already designated as majors or students enrolled in the LEA, but undecided, or students in "feeder" institutions, or potential students already employed or unemployed or underemployed. What group or groups should be surveyed varies from specialty to specialty and depends further upon such things as span of occupations.

3. *Define Program Goals and Parameters*. This and the next two tasks should be done near the end of the steering committee's tenure. This task might best be accomplished by having a small group prepare a proposal for the committee's consideration. This and the next two tasks should be undertaken only if it is clear that the committee will recommend that a program be implemented. Goal statements should define the type of program(s) to be established and time frames for several steps in the implementation. Parameters should include number of students to be served, span of relevant occupation(s), approximate number, types, and location of establishments where work stations might be established, hours or work, academic credit, and tentative plans for evaluation.

4. *Define Staffing Needs*. Staffing needs depend upon the program parameters. Even if needs seem obvious to some educators, community members should have opportunity to learn SEA and LEA requirements and to contribute to definition of number and type of positions. Later, some community members—perhaps some of those who will serve on a permanent advisory committee—should interview candidates.

5. *Define Facilities Needs*. Obviously, facilities requirements vary a great deal from program to program. This is especially true of training stations. But, in-school facilities needs vary from a regular classroom and career information materials for a diversified program for disadvantaged learners to several classrooms and laboratories for programs such as some health occupations or marketing programs. The committee will be able to specify number and types of training stations, pending firm information about students. The teacher-coordinator will be responsible for matching students and training stations—and much more. The committee should also be expected to describe in-school facilities needs in general terms. One of the early tasks of the teacher-coordinator will be to detail and pursue plans for providing adequate in-school space, equipment, and materials. (See Chapter 7.)

In given situations, the steering committee may have other tasks. These will depend upon such things as history of cooperative education in the community and nature of other LEA's in the area. One set of tasks relevant to many kinds of programs which a steering committee may help to accomplish are approvals from SEA's, LEA's, licensing bodies, and labor associations. The committee may wish to make initial public relations efforts, e.g., to influence reluctant employers, to soften resistive approval agencies, to encourage taxpayer and direct contributor support of the program(s).

**Division of Labor**

One of the final agenda items for the first steering committee meeting should result in homework for almost everyone on the committee. A typical assignment of duties might be as follows.

1. *Survey Employment Community.* A neutral community representative with resources and contacts might assume responsibility for this survey. A representative of the chamber of commerce or state employment office might conduct a mail survey with input to questionnaire design from the steering committee chairman and the vocational director or occupational dean. Or, he might conduct the survey via personal interviews together with the steering committee chairman or other school personnel. Having a community member conduct the survey and collate the findings adds credibility to the committee's work.

2. *Survey Potential Students.* It would be well for the committee member from the LEA's student personnel or guidance unit to assume responsibility for this survey. Such units have usually had similar experiences and have resources such as addresses and secretarial services. A student representative, the director or dean, and a teacher from the relevant occupational area should work cooperatively on the survey instrument design.

3. *Define Program Goals and Parameters.* A group of not more than six—say three from the community and three from the LEA—might agree to prepare a proposal for the total group's consideration prior to and during a second steering committee meeting. This group might include an employer, an employee, and a community agency representative and an administrator, a teacher and a counselor. This group should meet after findings of the two surveys have been collated. The group should prepare statements similar to the goal and definition statements in Figs. 6-5 and 6-6.

4. *Define Staffing Needs.* The director or dean might offer to work with an employer and an employee to prepare a job(s) announcement which accommodates SEA and LEA constraints and recommendations from "the field." The announcement should be discussed by the total committee. One of the functions of this and interview and appointment procedures is to assure that teacher-coordinators are acceptable to both management and labor.

5. *Define Facilities Needs.* A plan for housing the in-school part of the program and descriptions of necessary training stations might also be prepared for reaction at a subsequent steering committee meeting. The committee chairman and one or two people from the relevant employment sector could prepare a general statement, including classroom space, laboratory space, and probably major pieces of instructional

## Goal and Definition Statement (High School)

Program Goal: To place twenty health care aides in hospitals, clinics, nursing homes, and community health agencies by mid-November.
  a. Appoint teacher-coordinator during Spring Semester.
  b. Allocate classroom and laboratory space for the Fall Semester by end of Spring Semester. Modify space during Summer.
  c. Order equipment and supplies by April 1.
  d. Establish Work Stations during summer.
  e. Plan related-class experiences during summer.
  f. Start related class and begin cooperative placements early in Fall semester.

Program Parameters:
  Numbers: 20
  Occupations: Health Care Aides, i.e., any paid non-licensed occupation involving patient contact.
  Establishments:  2 hospitals
                   3 clinics
                   3 nursing homes
                   2 county health departments
  Hours: Work afternoons, typically 12:30—4:30, and/or weekends. Related class one period per day.
  Credit: 2 Carnegie units for related class and cooperative experience
  Evaluation: see SEA manual re local evaluation

**Fig. 6-5. Sample goal and definition statement (high school).**

and laboratory equipment and costs. If supplies are expected to entail prohibitive expense or if live work, e.g., on automobiles or dental hygiene clients, is likely to be performed in-school, the committee might propose methods for securing same at minimum expense or scheduling difficulties, e.g., weld on scrap which is later returned for resalvage, or do tonsorial work on students for supply costs only. (See Chapter 8.)

### BETWEEN MEETINGS

As several of the above sections indicate, the steering committee chairman must be available to help various individuals and groups with assigned tasks. He/she will need to provide professional expertise, know-how regarding the LEA, and secretarial and clerical assistance as needed. Small groups should be welcomed to use LEA facilities for

**Goal and Definition Statement (Post High School)**

Program Goal: To place twelve coal mine technicians in strip and shaft mines during Spring semester two years hence.

- a. Get approvals of State Department of Mines and United Mine Workers (UMW) by June 1.
- b. Appoint one teacher for next school year by June 1
  Appoint second teacher for subsequent school year.
- c. Allocate classroom and office space for next school year.
- d. Modify and expand and re-equip physics and chemistry laboratories for next school year.
- e. Allocate and equip special laboratory for subsequent school year.
- f. Order equipment and supplies by April 1 each year.
- g. Acquire and prepare curriculum materials during next summer and subsequently.
- h. Establish work stations during Spring semester next year.

Program Parameters:

Numbers: 12 per year
Occupations: repairman trainee
repairman
supervisor trainee
supervisor
Establishments: 4 shaft mines
3 strip mines
Hours: Work 8 hours per day February 1 to May 1
Related class January 10 to 31 and May 1 to May 15 and two hours one evening per week February 1 to May 1.
Credit: 14 semester hours
Evaluation:

- (a) Advisory Committee evaluation as first class finishes cooperative experience.
- (b) State Bureau of Mines during second class's cooperative experiences.
- (c) Regional accreditation visit when appropriate to total institution.
- (d) Locally directed evaluation according to design prepared by institutional staff during second year.

**Fig. 6-6.   Sample goal and definition statement (post high school).**

meetings and the chairman should attend as many of their work sessions as possible—many times as an observer being careful not to dominate discussions or decisions. When survey data are ready she/he should assure that efforts to prepare statements re goals, staffing, and facilities are begun—assuming the data suggest "go." If needs be, the chairman should call an extra total group meeting. In any event, after tentative goals, staffing, and facilities statements have been drafted, he/she should present them to the chief administrative officer together with a suggested agenda and time for a second steering committee meeting.

### SECOND STEERING COMMITTEE MEETING: DECISIONS

Prior to the second steering committee meeting, members should receive the following:

1. An agenda
2. Report of the Survey of the Employment Community
3. Report of the Survey of Potential Students
4. Proposed Program Goals and Parameters
5. Proposed Staffing Plan
6. Proposed Facilities Plan
7. Items Relevant to Other Tasks the Committee May have Undertaken
8. Proposed Plan for Subsequent Action

The meeting should be a series of decisions, beginning with the basic go/no-go decision. This decision should be made after discussion of employment and student surveys (2-3 above). If the decision is go, the bulk of meeting time should be devoted to discussion of proposals re goals, parameters, staffing, and facilities. Community people should be encouraged to contribute ideas freely because this is the basic reason for having a steering committee. All committee members should be reminded that not all advice can be utilized—if for no other reason than fiscal limitations.

Proposals (4-6 above) might be approved in turn or in concert. If proposals require major modifications, it might be well to suggest that the proposals be redrafted and distributed to members for final comment and return. The more likely result will be minor modifications to one or more of the proposals and approval. Another result might be approval with the understanding that certain changes will be made by institution personnel.

The proposed plan for subsequent action (7 above) may be as simple as a statement from an administrative officer, outlining future events such as appointment of a program advisory committee, seeking approval from the governing board and/or SEA's, provisions for staff and facilities, and establishment of training stations in the community in accord with student members and needs. The roles which various steering committee members might serve in the future, e.g., accommodating students at training stations, public relations, terms on the advisory committee, contributions of materials, should be stressed. Several of the LEA officers should express gratitude for the efforts of community people and stress the facts that not all input can be used but that all is appreciated. The chief administrative officer should indicate that he will be thanking the community members in writing and that each will receive a copy of the completed steering committee report and recommendations.

### Summary

The steering committee technique has been very effective at all levels of CVOE and in a great many specialties. In most situations, a carefully selected combination of community and LEA people can accomplish necessary tasks via two meetings with "homework" in between. Steering committee findings and recommendations should serve as bases for subsequent planning and implementation.

### Activities

1. Prepare a calendar of events for establishing and working with a steering committee. Include at least ten events and give the month during which the event should occur.
2. Draft a letter which a chief administrative officer might use to invite steering committee members.
3. Prepare agenda for a first and for a second steering committee meeting.
4. Prepare a list of information items which might be shared at a first steering committee meeting.
5. Draft a letter for thanking steering committee members.

# Chapter 7

# Providing Internal Resources

This chapter and the next deal with resources for cooperative vocational education (CVOE). This chapter treats allocation of internal resources and the next describes methods for utilizing community resources via vehicles such as advisory committees. Because CVOE is one of several primary interfaces with the community, it is paramount that adequate provisions be made for staffing, housing, equipping, conducting, and renewing programs.

Some of the outcomes of reading this chapter are:

1. Understanding the role and function of four types of CVOE personnel.
2. Ability to define qualifications for CVOE personnel.
3. Understanding variables which impinge upon work loads of CVOE personnel.
4. Understanding variables which affect facilities needs of CVOE.
5. Understanding special budget requirements of CVOE.

## TYPES OF CVOE STAFF

That a program is only as good as the staff which conducts it is trite and patently true. Adequate staffing for CVOE may be achieved via well-tested techniques. Superior staffing may be achieved via judicious application of combinations of techniques to local conditions. Four kinds of staff may be considered. These are supervisor, teacher-coordinator, full-time coordinator, and related-subjects teacher.

### Supervisor of CVOE

If there are more than three or four teacher-coordinators and/or full-time coordinators in an LEA, it is well to consider appointing (from within or without) a supervisor for all CVOE. In large vocational/occupational education units, internal efficiency and external effectiveness may be enhanced by vesting total CVOE program responsibilities in one individual. The supervisor should report to the director or dean of vocational/occupational education on a par with heads of units such as business, health, and industrial occupations. Unless CVOE programs are very diverse and numerous, the position should be defined as fifty percent of a full-time load. The other half of the supervisor's position may entail one of several assignments. (The supervisor should not be the director or dean; the combination involves too many external contacts.) In a community college, one individual might supervise both CVOE and cooperative experiences for university parallel students. This is rarely the case, but advisable for LEA's which place nonvocational students in temporary jobs. In typical instances, supervisors of CVOE are assigned a half-time teaching load—perhaps, but not necessarily, in one of the kinds of assignments described below.

A supervisor can increase internal efficiency by assuring consistent policies, procedures, services, and activities among occupational areas. Such matters as selecting students, relationships with other units such as guidance and financial aids, and resource allocations can be more equitable and judicious if a well-qualified individual is held accountable for them. Such things as a system-wide awards banquet can be properly planned and managed by a supervisor.

The supervisor is certain to have staff responsibilities and may have line responsibilities. In most LEA's, the major portion of her/his work will be as a staff officer. This work will entail such functions as planning, scheduling, budgeting, and procurement. Teachers in respective occupational departments should report to their unit heads and not to the supervisor. Indeed, unit heads may serve as teacher-coordinators and be guided by, but not answerable to, the CVOE supervisor.

Teacher-coordinators for interrelated programs, for special needs programs such as Work Experience Career Exploration Program (WECEP), and for non-CVOE college cooperative programs should report to the supervisor. That is, the supervisor should serve as a line officer, i.e., as the supervisor of teacher-coordinators who are not members of an occupational department. The supervisor might also be made responsible for EMH teacher-coordinators. But, in many instances, such persons should report to a special education department head.

A supervisor can improve external effectiveness by shepherding the interface with employers and community agencies such as placement services. Especially when a single establishment employs students from diverse programs, it is well for one individual to be the major contact and be fully aware of all traffic with the establishment. This is not to say that respective teacher-coordinators or full-time coordinators should not coordinate students in the respective establishment just as they do in other establishments. Rather, the supervisor should function as a control and information center. For example, he/she should be expected to ease the efforts of such establishments by relaying messages, scheduling coordination visits to minimize disruption of work, and request contributions of materials and personnel time via one contact person—according to the wishes of the establishment. Employers and placement agencies deserve the efficiencies of one major contact point with an LEA.

### Teacher-Coordinator

Most professionals in cooperative education are teacher-coordinators. That is, they teach related classes and coordinate student-learners at training stations in the community. Huffman (23), p. 16, maintains that "the key person in a cooperative program is the coordinator." He suggests that the teacher-coordinator should be (1) trained in coordination techniques, (2) experienced in an occupational area, and (3) professionally prepared to meet relevant certification requirements. ". . . the success of the cooperative program hinges on the skill and professionalism of the teacher-coordinator [Huffman, (23), p. 17 ]." Ashman and Klaurens (3), p. 28, noted that the important considerations in educating the teacher-coordinator were: (1) human awareness; (2) counseling responsibilities; and (3) school-community relations.

The Tennessee handbook (73), p. 2, lists the following qualifications for coordinators: (1) a minimum of a bachelor's degree from an accredited college or university in the vocational field or subject area to be taught; (2) a valid teacher's certificate; and (3) employment, or other experiences, in the area of specialty to add depth and meaning to instruction.

Most states require that teacher-coordinators have employment experience outside education. However, in a study which compared the effect of occupational experience of teacher-coordinators upon student competencies developed within the cooperative program, Olsen (56) found no significant difference in student placement or progress between programs coordinated by teachers who did, and did not, have work experience.

In Smith's (70) study, North Carolina coordinators ranked ten qualifications as most important: (1) ability to get along with people; (2) good judgment; (3) initiative; (4) ability to organize and carry out plans; (5) awareness of the duties of a teacher-coordinator; (6) desire to improve the program; (7) ability to work harmoniously with all people associated with the cooperative program; (8) leadership ability; (9) a college degree; and (10) two years work experience.

Mason and Haines (41), p. 124, suggest that a teacher-coordinator must be:

(1) a *teacher* who must be among the best; (2) a *public relations man* who may come in contact with more important taxpayers and voters than the superin-

tendent; (3) a *counselor* who deals first hand with educational, social, and personal problems; (4) a *successful employee* who knows a trade and the language of that trade; (5) an *administrator* who keeps reports and records and arranges the schedules of others; (6) an *evaluator* who engages not only in classroom measurement but also in measurement of the students on-the-job and of the contributions of his program.

As reported in the Minnesota Guide for Cooperative Vocational Education (44), p. 79, participants in the National Conference on Cooperative Vocational Education listed the following essential competencies, understandings, and personal qualifications for teacher-coordinators.

### Essential Competencies of Teacher-Coordinators

1. Ability to communicate effectively with students, employers, labor groups, parents, and school personnel
2. Ability to provide the students with guidance and inspiration as they are helped to establish solid vocational foundations
3. Ability to select and use appropriate learning materials and methods for effective teaching
4. Ability to coordinate the youth organization program
5. Ability to prepare appropriate reports
6. Ability to integrate school, work, and club learning experiences
7. Ability to utilize appropriate public relations devices and media
8. Ability to help students make personal adjustments
9. Ability to teach related classes
10. Ability to perform evaluation and followup activities
11. Ability to keep up-to-date on business trends and developments
12. Ability to help training sponsors plan and organize individual instruction to be provided students

### Essential Understandings for Teacher-Coordinators

1. Understanding of the requirements, demands, and atmosphere of the work situation of the students
2. Understanding of the business point-of-view as well as the needs of the particular students
3. Understanding of Federal and State laws relating to vocational education and employment

### Essential Personal Qualifications

1. Sufficient occupational experience to earn and maintain the respect of the students, employers, school personnel, and community and to perform the essential duties and responsibilities of an occupation in the teaching field.
2. Warmth and commitment to helping youth make the transition from school to the world of work. (Especially strong commitments are required of personnel who work with disadvantaged students.)

3. Public relations qualifications
   a. Enthusiasm
   b. Attractive appearance
   c. Ability to sell ideas (pp. 79-80)

The Minnesota Guide for Cooperative Vocational Education (44) pp. 92-94, lists ten major duties and numerous tasks which are performed by teacher-coordinators.

1. Guidance and selection of students
   Describing the program to students
   Working with guidance personnel
   Providing occupational information
   Counseling students about entering the program
   Gathering information on students
   Programming and scheduling
   Helping enrollees with career planning
2. Placing students in training jobs
   Enlisting participation of cooperating employers
   Selecting suitable training stations for each student
   Orienting employers, training supervisors, and coworkers
   Preparing students for job interviews
   Placing students on the job
3. Assisting students in adjusting to their work environment
   Helping students on their jobs
   Dealing with job problems
   Planning personal development with training supervisors and students
   Evaluating job progress
4. Improving training done on the job
   Establishing responsibilities on the job
   Developing training plans
   Consulting and assisting training supervisors
   Maintaining training emphasis
5. Correlating classroom instruction with on-the-job training
   Determining needed instruction
   Assembling instructional materials
   Preparing for instruction
   Teaching classes
   Directing individual projects and study
   Obtaining assistance from other teachers
   Advising training supervisors concerning applications of classroom instruction to be made on the job
   Evaluating learning outcomes
6. Assisting students in making personal adjustments
   Aiding students in correcting poor personal habits
   Counseling students with personal and socioeconomic problems

Assisting students with educational problems

Resolving behavioral problems

7. Directing vocational youth organizations

Advising youth group

Guiding students in organization of activities

Participating in group activities

8. Providing services to graduates and adults

Providing guidance and placement services for graduates

Participating in the planning and operation of adult education programs

9. Administration activities

Planning program objectives

Research and planning—surveys

Organizing and working with advisory committee

Planning curriculums

Communicating school policy

Preparing reports

Budgeting and purchasing

Participating in professional meetings

Consulting with manpower agencies such as employment services and CAMPS

10. Maintaining good public relations

Planning the publicity program

Preparing printed publicity

Constructing displays and exhibits

Contacting news media

Maintaining communication with faculty, parents, community, employers, school administrators, and student body

A very comprehensive listing of performance requirements for the teacher-coordinator was presented by Cotrell (13). He listed 385 performance activities associated with the duties and responsibilities of the coordinator. These were classified under: (1) program planning, development, and evaluation; (2) instructional planning; (3) execution of instruction; (4) evaluation of instruction; (5) management; (6) guidance; (7) school-community relations; (8) student youth organizations; (9) professional development; and (10) coordination activities.

The 53 performance activities of the *program planning, development, and evaluation* portion of the teacher-coordinator's job may be classified under the following functions: (1) organizing and utilizing a steering committee; (2) conducting a community survey; (3) conducting a student survey; (4) planning and organizing an advisory committee; (5) analyzing occupations for standards of performance; (6) developing goals and objectives of the program; (7) preparing budgetary plans; (8) developing and maintaining a student placement and followup system; and (9) developing a comprehensive system of program evaluation.

The 26 performance activities of the *instructional planning* portion may be classified under the following functions: (1) reviewing and organizing general program objectives and student performance goals; (2) identifying and developing instructional units based on these goals and objectives; (3) correlating classroom instruction with laboratory experiences; (4) evaluating instructional effectiveness; and (5) writing programmed instruction units.

The 62 performance activities of the *execution of instruction* portion may be classified under the following functions: (1) utilizing various instructional methods and techniques to meet the goals and objectives of the program participants; (2) maintain bulletin boards and exhibits; (3) conducting field trips; (4) utilizing audiovisual equipment; and (5) developing information, operation, and job assignment sheets.

The 32 performance activities of the *evaluation of instruction* portion may be classified under the following functions: (1) establishing performance criteria based on objectives and goals; (2) formulating a system of grading consistent with the educational institution; (3) appraising and evaluating the student's classroom and on-the-job performance; (4) formulating, administering, and analyzing evaluation instrument; (5) assessing the effectiveness of instruction; (6) incorporating student and employer input in the evaluation process; and (7) incorporating a system of self- and supervisory evaluation.

The 38 performance activities of the *management* portion may be classified under the following functions: (1) requisitioning and maintaining supplies, tools, equipment, and instructional materials necessary to carry out the instructional program; (2) developing an operational budget; (3) maintaining a reference library of books and periodic literature; (4) maintaining the acceptable behavior of students in the related classroom, and on the job; (5) organizing related-subjects classroom facilities for maximum instructional efficiency and effectiveness; (6) ensuring compliance of safety requirements for the employment of student-learners; and (7) organizing and maintaining a filing system for records, reports, objectives, policies, and instructional materials.

The 34 performance activities of the *guidance* portion may be classified under the following functions: (1) testing students; (2) counseling students; (3) working with employment service; (4) assisting the regular guidance personnel; (5) analyzing student's performance, background, and records; (6) selecting students for the cooperative program; (7) placing students in occupational areas that closely relate to their career objectives; and (8) conducting home visitations.

The 31 performance activities of the *school-community relations* portion may be classified under the following functions: (1) developing and implementing a public relations plan for the cooperative program; (2) developing and presenting informational programs for the school and community; (3) conducting and analyzing surveys and studies relating to the needs and opinions of the people of the community; (4) utilizing the advisory committee; (5) sponsoring student, parent, and employer activities; (6) joining and assisting community, social, and service organizations; (7) maintaining satisfactory relations with faculty, administration, students, employers, and other members of the community; and (8) providing consultant services to local business and industrial establishments.

The 30 performance activities of the *student vocational organization* portion may be classified under the following eight categories: (1) organizing the club; (2) promoting the club; (3) operating the club; (4) assisting the student leadership of the youth organization; (5) providing advice and direction for the club; (6) supervising all activities of the organization; (7) affiliating the local chapter of the organization with the state and national structure; and (8) correlating the activities of the youth organization with the objectives of the cooperative program.

The 31 performance activities of the *professional development* portion may be classified under the following functions: (1) affiliating with professional organizations; (2) conducting research related to the cooperative program; (3) writing for professional publications; (4) cooperating with, and assisting, fellow educators; (5) participating regularly in in-service training programs; (6) working wtih student-teachers; (7) maintaining and upgrading professional qualifications and certifications; and (8) keeping up to date with the new developments within the profession.

The 46 performance activities of the *coordination* portion may be classified under the following functions: (1) selecting student-learners; (2) informing student-learners; (3) testing student-learners; (4) identifying and selecting training stations; (5) placing student-learners in appropriate training stations; (6) evaluating training stations; (7) visiting training stations; (8) informing administration of the progress of the cooperative program; (9) correlating the classroom instruction with the activities of the job; (10) assessing student progress on the job; (11) providing instruction for the supervisors of the students on the job; and (12) evaluating the effectiveness of the training provided by the training station.

### Full-time Coordinator

Full-time coordinators do not teach related-subjects classes. They perform all of the duties and tasks of teacher-coordinators, excepting actual teaching of related classes. They must be able to determine what related instructional programs are most suited to respective students and to work with related-class and related-subjects teachers to assure that student-learners have appropriate in-school experiences.

### Related-Subjects Teacher

When it seems appropriate to assign one or more staff members to full-time coordination, there will, of course, be vocational/occupational teachers who do not coordinate. In the literature of cooperative education, such teachers are called related-subjects teachers. Often when an occupational area has several teachers, one or two do all of the coordination and the others manage classroom and laboratory experiences. Related-subjects teachers must correlate classroom instruction with on-the-job experiences together with the coordinator. The major duties of the related-subjects teacher are planning and developing instructional units, managing classroom and laboratory experiences via various and secondary methods and techniques, guiding individual learning, and evaluating outcomes to modify both student and teacher behavior.

### QUALIFICATIONS OF CVOE STAFF

There is widespread agreement that CVOE staff qualifications may be categorized as occupational experience, occupational study, courses in education, courses in vocational/occupational education, and personal characteristics. An LEA should establish criteria in each of these categories, taking into consideration such things as (a) requirements of SEA's, (b) general requirements of the LEA, (c) features of the respective cooperative program, such as diversity of occupations to be learned and characteristics of students and firms, (d) the LEA's affirmative action program, and (e) licensing agency and professional association stipulations.

### Occupational Experience

It is often essential to assure that CVOE staff meet a designated minimum work experience requirement. Many SEA's specify minimum experience in a rather narrowly defined occupation for secondary and post-secondary vocational/occupational education personnel of various types. Most state requirements are within the range of 2000 to 8000 hours (one to four years) of experience. A few states have minimum requirements for private technical school teachers. Some states certify graduates of selected teacher education programs, which include shorter periods of supervised work experience.

Licensing agencies in some states specify requirements for occupational teachers. These must be adhered to by any institution which gives training in the respective fields. For example, many states license teachers of cosmetology, requiring work and schooling beyond regular licensure. Similar stipulations are made in some states for teachers of nursing and some other health occupations.

Obviously, it behooves LEA's to discover constraints which are imposed by licensing agencies within their respective states. If graduates are likely to apply for licensure in other states, it may be well to ascertain stipulations re teaching personnel, at least in the neighboring state(s). In general, it is essential to employ CVOE staff who have achieved what vocational educators refer to as "journeyman" status or beyond. If for no other reason than the public relations benefits and status which accrue to a program whose representatives are well qualified, it is essential to employ people who are respected and accepted by their occupational counterparts in the community.

More important in many respects than amount of work experience are the level, variety, and recency of experiences. Part-time employment in only one establishment and long before assuming teaching duties might satisfy a minimum time requirement. But, it would likely not qualify a teacher for coordinating students who rotate through a variety of training stations in a modern establishment.

1. *Level of Experience.* Because CVOE personnel must be able to analyze jobs and occupations and to direct the work of others, supervisory-level experience is especially valuable. Supervisory experience is not essential in all cooperative programs, especially not in programs such as WECEP. But, it is well for program leaders and coordinators of programs, such as licensed practical nursing and mechanical engineering technician to have had supervisory experience, which involved scheduling and on-the-job training responsibilities akin to those of the training station supervisors. Obviously, it is well for teachers to have higher-level and broader knowledge and skill than their students. Few coordinators can be expert and experienced at all of the tasks which each student-learner confronts, But, most coordinators should have functioned successfully at the student's responsibility level or above.

2. *Variety of Experience.* The qualification must be defined for various programs. Of course, variety of experience has a special relationship to WECEP, interrelated, and DO programs. It is also relevant to any program which places student-learners and graduates in a variety of establishments—say in large automobile dealerships, chain store repair centers, small garages, and specialty shops, such as transmission

shops. The variety of experience of personnel should approximate the experiences students will confront.

3. *Recency of Experience*. This qualification needs little explanation. It is difficult to satisfy. Some would-be teacher-coordinators get "rusty" while they acquire degrees. Some related-subjects teachers meet minimum qualifications for CVOE, without substantial, recent occupational experience. It is also possible for practicing teacher-coordinators to get "rusty." It behooves LEA's to address special attention to the matter of support and benefits for coordinators who update occupational experience through summer work, sabbaticals, etc.

**Occupational Study**

Some SEA's specify minimum credits in college or equivalent courses for CVOE personnel in at least some fields. Minimums are nearly always less than twenty semester hours and most states provide for approval of equivalent experience in occupations which are taught in special schools such as in the military or of work experience alone in emerging occupations, which have not been of concern to schools and colleges. Drafters of the Minnesota guide (44), p.97, were wise to mention "technical courses directly related to an occupational field, such . . . as economics, industrial relations, occupational sociolgy, and vocational psychology . . . for all occupational fields. LEA's should use judgment to align occupational study qualifications with what the better and best prepared practitioners in an occupational area are expected to have by prominent employers. LEA's should also be careful to evaluate the source of occupational course work. Especially in occupational areas which have no specialized accrediting body, the quality of preparatory programs varies greatly. Depth of occupational study should correlate to program purpose and should be greater for personnel in post-secondary CVOE.

**Courses in Education**

SEA's specify requirements for credentials at various levels. Some do not stipulate requirements for post-secondary personnel. In any case, it is well to assure that CVOE staff have had formal coursework in adolescent and adult psychology, school/college and community, and educational psychology with emphasis on modes of learning.

**Courses in Vocational/Occupational Education**

Nearly all states require specified course work for personnel in reimbursed programs at all levels. Some stipulate a few courses for personnel in private schools and colleges which participate under various student benefit programs. CVOE personnel are usually required to have the same courses as teachers plus one or two specialized courses. A list of typical courses is:

1. Principles of Vocational/Occupational Education
2. Occupational Analysis and Curriculum Building
3. Occupational Teaching Methods
4. Vocational Guidance
5. Organization and Administration of Vocational/Occupational Education
6. Cooperative Education Techniques
7. Evaluation
8. Student Teaching

These and specialized methods courses vary by title, credit hours, and number of courses. But, the range is, typically, quite like the above.

### Personal Characteristics

Qualifications under this heading must be defined so that they do not discriminate against people who are capable of conducting successful CVOE programs. In general, it is characteristics of leadership, which CVOE personnel should display. Some leadership characteristics which are obviously appropriate to CVOE are:

1. Dependable and Reliable
2. Good at Human Relations
3. Good at Communications
4. Innovative and Creative
5. Good at Judgment and Decision
6. Neat Appearance and Orderly Manner
7. Responsible and Self-Disciplined[1]

CVOE personnel must foster and coordinate productive efforts of several kinds of people in several kinds of organizations. This is leadership and some are better at it than others. Therefore, demonstrated potential to lead is a qualification for CVOE personnel.

## DETERMINING WORK LOAD

CVOE personnel cannot be "loaded" on the same basis as classroom or classroom-laboratory teachers. It is widely agreed that secondary-level

---

[1]For a more thorough treatment of leadership styles and patterns, see Stadt, et.al., (72), pp. 47-74.

CVOE personnel should spend a minimum of one-half hour per week per student in coordination of on-the-job experiences.

### Teacher-Coordinator Weekly Load

Typical weekly work loads for teacher-coordinators with twenty-four cooperative education students approximate the following.

$$
\begin{aligned}
\text{3 hours of related classes x 5 days} &= \text{15 hours} \\
\text{1 preparation and individual} & \\
\text{counseling period x 5 days} &= \text{5 hours} \\
\text{½ hour x 24 student-learners} &= \text{12 hours} \\
\text{Total} &= \text{32 hours/week}
\end{aligned}
$$

This compares closely to the typical teaching load of six class periods or approximately thirty contact hours per week. Where contact hours are appreciably less, such as under professional contracts in some community colleges, preparation and on-the-job coordination for approximately twenty-four students should be considered to be more than half a work load. Put another way, in some LEA's, teacher-coordinators should be assigned only two related clases.

### Full-Time Coordinator Weekly Load

The full-time coordinator can properly coordinate twice as many student-learners. Typical weekly loads for full-time coordinators with forty-eight students approximate the following:

$$
\begin{aligned}
\text{2 hours of individual counseling} & \\
\text{and preparation x 5 days} &= \text{10 hours} \\
\text{½ hour x 48 student-learners} &= \text{24 hours} \\
\text{Total} &= \text{34 hours/week}
\end{aligned}
$$

### Variables Which Affect Loads

It must be emphasized that these examples are only descriptive of model situations. Several variables require judgment in typical situations: (1) Coordination may be less time consuming if *more than one or two student–learners* are placed in an establishment. For example, a health occupations coordinator who visits only three or four establishments might properly be expected to coordinate more students or teach an additional related class. Yet, in a large establishment, such as university campus, students might be dispersed geographically and across job categories and thus may require more, rather than less, coordination time. (2) Coordination time can be greatly affected by *geography*. Consider, for example, a situation wherein nearly all work stations are in a community twenty miles from the campus. Assuming that within that community, students are not widely dispersed, the coordinator should be allotted one hour per day travel time in the load formula. (3) *Maturity of student* affects coordination time. WECEP students might require more visits and more time per visit, especially during the first several weeks on the job. (4) *Maturity of employer* affects coordination time in the same way. New employers should be visited more frequently, the better to avoid problems and give assurances. Some employers may always require more tender loving care than others.

The matter of coordination time is very important to CVOE. LEA leadership must be aware of variables which affect this essential resource. CVOE must be individualized and best quality. Programs which are only better or good jeopardize all parties to the contract. Quality cannot, for long, be sacrificed in the interest of quantity. Those who allocate resources must understand that the innate system of checks and balances, i.e., advisory committees, student clubs, employer followup, etc., sound the death knell of poor-quality programs and serve to perpetuate and improve high-quality programs which are equitably supported.

## SOURCES OF CVOE STAFF

There are two primary sources of CVOE staff (Fig. 7-1). In the interest of fairness and to assure that the best possible staff is employed, both sources should be utilized to identify potential employees. (Unless it is given that a person already employed must be reassigned because of overstaffing.) The two sources are teacher education centers and vocational/occupational teachers within the LEA. Teacher placement offices should be apprised of positions for both new and experienced personnel. Qualified persons already in the LEA should be encouraged to apply. Cooperative education is, in many LEA's, an attractive higher status assignment—much like counseling and administration.

There is a third source, i.e., people working in an occupation relevant to the program for which a position has been created. Generally, it is well for such people to pursue vocational/occupational teacher education programs and related class teaching prior to serving as teacher-coordinators or full-time coordinators. That is, generally, coordinators should be among the more experienced of an LEA's staff. Nevertheless, it is sometimes appropriate to employ a teacher-coordinator directly from the world of work, e.g., for a new post-secondary program for an emerging occupation for which there is no relevant baccalaureate program and no available,

## CVOE Staff Complement and Organization

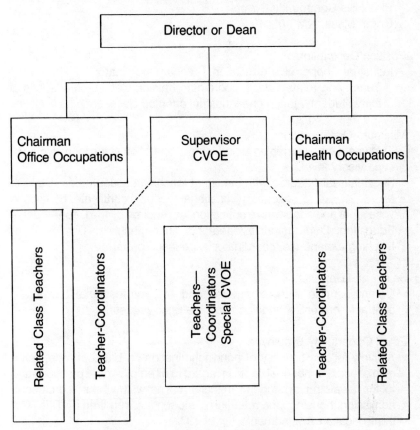

Fig. 7-1.   Sample CVOE staff complement and organization.

experienced teacher. Positions should be made known to placement agencies and individuals via formal announcements (Fig. 7-2).

### Interviewing and Evaluating Applicants

Applicants should be evaluated against specified qualifications and ranked in order of preference. This might be done by assigning weights to the qualifications and arriving at a point score for each applicant. Depending upon LEA procedures, one or more of the high-ranking applicants should be invited for interviews.

The standard LEA interview schedule and procedures should be followed and expanded so that some of the community representatives on a

## Position Announcement for Cooperative Education Program

Pine Hills Community School
Grand Mesa, NM 00001

Position Description:
Industrial Cooperative Education Teacher-Coordinator
Teach one related class, coordinate training station experiences of
thirty students, teach one industrial oriented class, such as drafting.

Minimum Qualifications:
Two years employment in an industrial occupation at the journeyman or
supervisory level.
Baccalaureate degree with industrial teaching concentration. State of
_____ secondary vocational teaching certificate, courses in
vocational and cooperative education, as required by the Department of
Education. Demonstrated leadership characteristics. Two years of
teaching experience, coordinator experience preferred.

Salary and Benefits:
Commensurate with experience and AFT professional bargaining
contract—current schedules available upon request.

Equal Opportunity Employer:
Actively follows a policy of nondiscrimination on basis of race, color,
religion, sex, or national origin in regard to all employment practices and
to the awarding of student financial aid as well as the recruitment,
admission, housing, and retention of students as required by Title IX of
the Education Amendments Act of 1972.

Apply to:
Dr. Siegfreid Mathias
Director of Vocational Education
Pine Hills Community School
Grand Mesa, NM 00001

Provide:
Credentials and/or Resume
References

Deadline for Application:

Fig. 7-2.    Sample position announcement for a teacher-coordinator.

steering committee or advisory committee may interview the candidate(s). This may be accomplished by an extended schedule of one to-one interviews or by a social event, such as a coffee at the Chamber of Commerce offices. In any event community representatives should have input to the hire/not-hire decision. Input may be via evaluation forms or conversations. Community representatives should know that their advice re selection and decision is well taken.

## PROVIDING FACILITIES

The provision of offices, classroom/laboratories, auxiliary space, equipment, and furniture for CVOE is a local matter, depending very much upon characteristics of specific programs.[2] The intent here is not to deal with classroom and laboratory design for all related classes in sequential programs. The concern is (1) to list principles which apply to facilities for CVOE-related classes which are corequisites to on-the-job experiences and facilities which are essential to business-like coordination, (2) to discuss acquisition of free and inexpensive materials and supplies, and (3) to describe two typical kinds of facilities.

### Principles for Providing Physical Resources

1. Cooperative vocational/occupational education classrooms and laboratories should be designed and equipped to facilitate learning knowledges, skills, and attitudes relevant to respective occupations.
2. Classrooms should have movable individual tables and chairs which may be arranged for large and small group discussions and for individual instruction and study.
3. All CVOE classrooms should have storage space which permits each student to secure independent study materials and projects.
4. Adequate space and equipment for storing and using reference books, periodicals, and other learning materials should be provided.
5. The coordinator should have an office(s), adjoining the classroom and equipped with a telephone, filing cabinets, bookshelves, and work stations for himself/herself and a secretary.
6. Model stores, offices, shops, laboratories, and other simulated work stations are highly recommended.
7. It is usually desirable to have all classrooms, laboratories, offices, and storerooms for CVOE in the same general location within the LEA.
8. Special instructional equipment is needed for each occupational field.

---

[2]See also the section in Chapter 12 regarding the Related Class and Facilities.

### Typical CVOE Facilities

The provision of CVOE facilities for secondary school health occupations programs is illustrative of the above principles. Although some programs make very effective use of classrooms and learning laboratories in health care agencies which happen to conduct other instructional programs, most have to utilize a patient-care classroom/laboratory in the LEA. Such a laboratory need not be elaborate. It should contain several hospital units and related equipment and supplies so that students may learn basic patient-care, bedside procedures, sanitation practices, etc., before assignment to a training station.

The one CVOE program for which descriptions of facilities have become rather standardized in the literature is distributive education. The handbook for secondary distributive education programs in Tennessee (11) illustrates a typical facility (Fig. 7-3).

## ADEQUATE BUDGETING FOR CVOE

Just as it is impossible to prescribe facilities and equipment for CVOE, it is also impossible to project budget items without a great deal of information re an LEA and its ongoing and projected program(s). The following are budget line items which require special provision beyond what might be budgeted for the rest of vocational/occupational education. Most are self-explanatory. Others may be provided through several means, which are described.

1. *Secretary salary or wages.* Ideally, several CVOE programs should have a full-time, permanent secretary. Another plan is to share a secretary with one or more of the vocational/occupational departments or the director/dean. Another technique which may be considered is establishing training stations for office occupations students. A less-desirable alternative is utilizing 00 students during simulated office or even study hall or free periods. Of course, some of these solutions may be used in combination.

2. *Extra pay for coordinators.* One major city pays teacher-coordinators a twenty-percent premium in accord with a professional contract. In LEA's which operate on a nine-month academic year, coordinators should be employed for at least ten months so that related-class and on-the job experiences may begin immediately in the new term. In LEA's which operate throughout the year, it is likely that all CVOE personnel should be employed for eleven or twelve months. (Many employers of CVOE students prefer year-round operation.) New programs should be begun by teacher-coor-

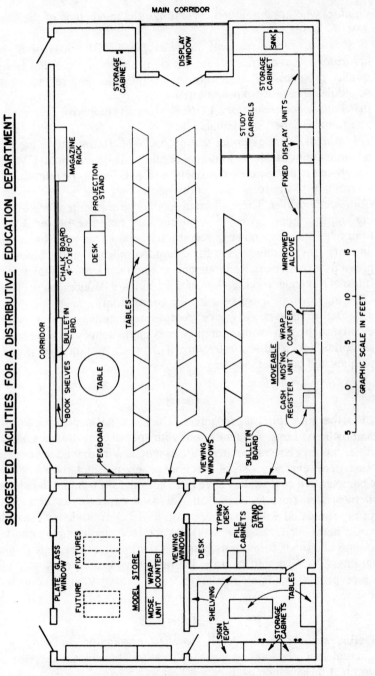

Fig. 7-3.    Suggested facilities for a Distributive Education department.

dinators who are employed several months in advance of the first day of classes.

3. *Equipment, furniture, and supplies for CVOE classroom(s)/ laboratory(s) and offices.* (See previous section.) Note that best-quality programs utilize equipment maintenance and replacement schedules. These are expensive items.

4. *Instructional materials for CVOE.* Textbooks, audiovisual materials and rentals, paper, incidentals, etc.

5. *Telephone(s).* It is essential that each CVOE staff member have a telephone for outside and internal contacts. It is well for all CVOE telephones to be on a common line(s) so that calls may be referred by a secretary to the respective coordinator.

6. *Coordinator travel.* Three alternatives may be considered for assuming transportation costs. (a) Coordinators may use personal automobiles and keep mileage records for reimbursement. (b) Coordinators may be reimbursed for estimated mileage on the basis of previous experience. Reimbursement should be at or above the Internal Revenue Service allowance for mileage deductions. (c) The LEA may own or lease vehicles for coordinators.

7. *Meeting expenses.* Advisory committee meetings and special events, such as an awards banquet, may entail items such as special janitorial fees, food and refreshments, travel, speakers' fees, and plaques and commemoratives.

### Summary

CVOE requires internal resources which are not necessary to other educational programs. Adequate staff with special competencies, special facilities, and special budget items are essential. Whether added expense for such items exceeds costs of in-school programs is not known because few comparative cost studies have been conducted on sound data bases. That these items are far less than would be expenses for conducting carefully simulated work experiences in an LEA is obvious. That such expense items are far and away offset by effects upon employability of graduates and other community benefit is demonstrated by a great many programs. CVOE should be provided resources as are programs which prepare professionals in medicine, law, dentistry, and veterinary medicine.

### Activities

1. Define supervisor of CVOE, teacher-coordinator, full-time coordinator, and related-class teacher. Show relationships. Compare and contrast tasks which each entails.

2. Draft a position announcement for a supervisor of CVOE. For a full-time coordinator. For a related-class teacher, including a statement re opportunity for advancement.
3. Visit an ongoing program. Interview CVOE personnel regarding adequacy of facilities. Write a short paper, indicating good features and recommendations for providing more adequate facilities. (See Chapter 17.)
4. Prepare a proposed budget for introducing a new CVOE program. Indicate which items of expense would be incurred without CVOE, the better to stress added cost as contrasted to total cost.

Chapter  *8*

# Utilizing External Resources

As the previous chapter deals with providing internal resources, this chapter deals with utilizing external resources in behalf of cooperative vocational/occupational education (CVOE). While the previous chapter emphasized the importance of staffing, this chapter emphasizes working with advisory committees.

The major external resource utilized by CVOE is, of course, training stations in the community. Training stations are treated in Chapters 10 and 13. The keys to identifying and utilizing external resources are general, departmental, and program advisory committees. Advisory committees contribute to all aspects of CVOE. What committees and other community resources can do to assist student clubs, guidance functions, public relations efforts, and evaluation are treated in respective chapters. In addition to lengthy treatment of advisory committees, this chapter deals with facilities and equipment; free and inexpensive materials and supplies; and speakers, resource persons, and field trips which are related to, but not limited to, advisory committee efforts. Since these matters involve contacts in the community, utilization of external resources should be undertaken with at least knowledge of, if not involvement of, the advisory committee members.

Some of the outcomes of reading this chapter are:

1. Understanding the functions of several types of advisory councils and committees.
2. Understanding how committees are organized.
3. Ability to utilize committees effectively and efficiently.
4. Ability to plan committee activities in accord with CVOE program progress.
5. Ability to enlist community members in the procurement of free or inexpensive equipment, materials, and supplies.
6. Ability to incorporate speakers, resource persons, and field trips in CVOE learnings.

145

## WORKING WITH ADVISORY COMMITTEES

Vocational/occupational educators have long maintained that programs are destined to obsolescence, unless they are altered in accord with changes occurring in the world of work. Vocational/occupational education must have direct lines of communication with various and sundry segments of productive society if it is to maximize services to the work force. In modern times, educators have been pressured to serve larger publics by providing programs which fit the needs of both target groups and employers. Matching people to jobs is better done by bringing the two as close as possible during preparatory-level education. The single most successful vehicle for combining efforts of LEA's and productive society is the advisory committee. Properly used, this vehicle is a great asset to training programs. Approximately forty state plans for vocational/ occupational education stipulate utilization of local advisory committees. Nearly all the others recommend that LEA's use such groups. Many SEA's provide manuals for working with committees. Most state CVOE manuals contain similar information. The New Mexico cooperative education guide (50), p. 2, lists five basic reasons for advisory committees:

1. They provide advice that is not easily obtainable elsewhere.
2. They have important public relations potential.
3. They offer support and advice on policies from a layman's point of view.
4. They can actively aid in the placement of graduates.
5. They assist in keeping educational programs up-to-date.

### Advisory Committee Defined

An advisory committee is a group composed primarily of persons from outside the education profession, chosen from segments of the community, state, or nation to advise educators regarding one or more educational programs. The advisory committee is usually formally organized and appointed by proper authority for a definite term. Committees may be appointed and established on national, state, regional, or local levels to advise those who are responsible for planning, implementing, and maintaining vocational and technical education programs. [Illinois (26), p. 1]. Advisory committees establish and maintain important avenues of two-way communication between an educational agency and its public, which are paramount, especially to CVOE.

### National and State Councils

It is widely agreed that national- and and state-level advisory groups shall be called *councils* and that local groups shall be called committees.

Before creating local advisory committees for CVOE, it is well to have basic understanding of national and state councils.

In modern times, three groups with government authority have given advice to the nation's leadership and to vocational and occupational educators. The first of these was the Presidents' Panel of Consultants on Vocational Education, appointed by President John F. Kennedy on February 20, 1961. The Panel conducted studies, commissioned other studies, and held conferences. Its full report was titled *Education for a Changing World of Work*. This document provided a framework for the Vocational Education Act of 1963. [American Vocational Association (2), p. 11]. This act established two advisory groups. One was the National Advisory Committee, consisting of three government and twelve lay members. This group was to advise the Commissioner of Education re programing for and administration of vocational education. The second was The National Advisory Council on Vocational Education which was to evaluate programs and report at least every five years to the Secretary of Health, Education, and Welfare (HEW). (The act also required SEA's and LEA's to establish avenues which provided regular advice and counsel from people knowledgeable of the labor market.) The Council was appointed on November 22, 1966 and reported on December 11, 1967. With some modification, many of the recommendations contained in its report were incorporated in the Vocational Education Amendments of 1968.

This act provided for a permanent National Advisory Council on Vocational Education. This council has had great impact upon subsequent legislation and has issued a number of sweeping and cogent reports of findings and recommendations on vocational education and guidance. Twenty-one members are appointed by the President. The Council advises the Commissioner of Education regarding legislation, submits annual reports and recommendations to the Secretary of Health, Education, and Welfare (HEW) for transmittal to Congress, and conducts independent evaluations of programs in the states.

VEA 68 also mandated state advisory councils.

1. Any State which desires to receive a grant under this title for any fiscal year shall establish a State Advisory Council, which shall be appointed by the Governor, or in case of States in which the State board are elected, by such board, and which shall—
   (A) Include as members a person or persons—
      (i)    familiar with the vocational needs and the problems of management and labor in the State, and a person or persons representing State industrial and economic development agencies,
      (ii)   representative of community and junior colleges and other institutions of higher education, area vocational schools,

technical institutes, and post-secondary or adult education agencies or institutions, which may provide programs of vocational or technical education and training,

(iii)   familiar with the administration of State and local vocational education programs, and a person or persons having special knowledge, experience, or qualifications with respect to vocational education and who are not involved in the administration of State or local vocational education programs,

(iv)   familiar with programs of technical and vocational education, including programs in comprehensive secondary schools,

(v)   representative of local educational agencies, and a person or persons who are representative of school boards,

(vi)   representative of manpower and vocational education agencies in the State, including a person or persons from the Comprehensive Area Manpower Planning System of the State,

(vii)   representing school systems with large concentrations of academically, socially, economically, and culturally disadvantaged students,

(viii)   having special knowledge, experience, or qualifications, with respect to the special educational needs of physically or mentally handicapped persons, and

(ix)   representative of the general public, including a person or persons representative of and knowledgeable about the poor and disadvantaged, who are not qualified for membership under any of the preceding clauses of this paragraph;

(B)   Advise the State board on the development of and policy matters arising in the administration of the State plan submitted pursuant to paragraphs (4) and (5) of section 123 (a);

(C)   Evaluate vocational education programs, services, and activities assisted under this title, and publish and distribute the results thereof; and

(D)   Prepare and submit through the State board to the Commissioner and to the National Council an annual evelution report, accompanied by such additional comments of the State board as the State board deems appropriate, which (i) evaluates the effectiveness of vocational education programs, services, and activities carried out in the year under review in meeting the program objectives set forth in the long-range program plan and the annual program plan provided for in paragraphs (4) and (5) of section 123 (a), and (ii) recommends such changes in such programs, services, and activities as may be warranted by the evaluations.

2.   Not less than ninety days prior to the beginning of any fiscal year ending after June 30, 1969, in which a State desires to receive a grant under this title, that State shall certify the establishment of, and membership of, its State Advisory Council to the Commissioner.

3. Each State Advisory Council shall meet within thirty days after certification has been accepted by the Commissioner and select from among its membership a chairman. The time, place, and manner of meeting shall be as provided by the rules of the State Advisory Council, except that such rules must provide for not less than one public meeting each year at which the public is given opportunity to express views concerning vocational education.

4. State Advisory Councils are authorized to obtain the services of such professional, technical, and clerical personnel as may be necessary to enable them to carry out their functions under this title and to contract for such services as may be necessary to enable them to carry out their evaluation functions.

5. From the sums appropriated pursuant to section 102 (c) for any fiscal year, the Commissioner is authorized (in accordance wtih regulations) to pay to each State Advisory Council an amount equal to the reasonable amounts expended by it in carrying out its functions under this title in such fiscal year, except that the amount available for such purpose shall be equal to 1 per centum of the State's allotment under section 103, but such amount shall not exceed $150,000 and shall not be less than $50,000.

State Councils have been variously effective in evaluation and advice giving. The story of how various states have complied and how their councils function is not readily available. For some of the story see Burt (9).

### Types of Advisory Committees

In addition to steering committees or ad hoc committees, which were the subject of Chapter 6, there are at least three kinds of local advisory committees for vocational/occupational education. These vary primarily in scope of advice giving and in breadth of representation. [1]

*General advisory committees* are concerned with development and conduct of all of the programs offered by the LEA. Membership is representative of the range of occupations served by the institution's vocational/occupational programs. Some of the members may represent departmental or program committees and serve liaison roles within the structure of committees. The general advisory committee performs many of the functions of departmental or program committees but on a broader scale or in more general ways. The American Vocational Association (2), p. 13, put the matter succinctly.

"They identify the needs of individual and community; help access labor market requirements; contribute to the establishment and maintenance of

[1] Advisory committee members should be helped to understand the work of the state and national advisory councils. Members should know that they serve on a network of advisors which is answerable at the cabinet level.

realistic and practical programs; participate in developing community understanding and support; aid in building the prestige of and respect for the entire program of occupational education; and, are concerned with long-range goals.''

General advisory committees have been effective under two arrangements. Some have served as control or governing agents for all other committees. Others have served primarily as coordinating units quite apart from departmental or program committees, excepting for a few functions, such as sponsorship of an annual awards and recognition banquet for all CVOE students and employers in an LEA. Often, when the general advisory committee serves as a governing agent, other committees are called subcommittees.

When an LEA has several attendance centers, e.g., a multicampus community college or a number of high schools within a sector of a large-city school system, committees should be organized so that they parallel the administrative structure of vocational/occupational education. That is, the official linkage for each committee should be to an administrator—general advisory committee linked to the total program administrator and departmental or program committees linked to administrators at those levels. Sometimes it is appropriate to have one program committee for two or three campuses, e.g., an office occupations committee for programs in two high schools which serve essentially the same labor market.

*Departmental advisory committees* serve one vocational/occupational unit in an LEA. Many agriculture departments in schools and colleges have one committee which serves several programs. This arrangement is judicious when teachers serve more than one program and/or when the number of employers which should be represented on committees is small. For example, a community college conducting licensed practical nursing, operating room technician, and medical laboratory programs in a community with less than ten health care enterprises might have one health occupations committee which serves all health programs. From time-to-time, subcommittees might perform tasks peculiar to one program, e.g., helping with preparations for an accreditation team visit. Similarly, many high school business departments have one advisory committee rather than separate committees for office occupations and distributive education.

*Program Advisory Committees* are concerned with a specific occupation or a small cluster of occupations. Many industrial educators have heretofore called program committees *craft committees*. The American Vocational Association (2), p. 14, calls them *specific occupations* committees. As contrasted to a departmental committee, program committees in an industrial education department would serve programs such as welding, building technology, electronics technology, or commercial art.

A special kind of craft committee is seldom mentioned in contemporary literature. The *joint apprenticeship committee* has more authority than other committees. It is usually organized by the Bureau of Apprenticeship and Training of the United States Department of Labor and develops and conducts industrial apprenticeship programs in a craft such as commercial electricial, carpenter, or patternmaker. According to Stadt and Jensen (71), p.7, joint apprenticeship committee performs the following administrative functions.

1. Develops suitable training standards for the craft.
2. Reviews applications and selects apprentices.
3. Prepares apprentice training agreements.
4. Registers apprentices with the United States Bureau of Apprenticeship and Training.
5. Supervises on-the-job training of apprentices.

It performs the following advisory functions [Stadt and Jensen (71), p. 7 ].

1. Assists school administrators in determining related instruction.
2. Advises school administrators regarding instructional materials.
3. Recommends skilled craftsmen as prospective teachers.

Joint apprenticeship committees are nearly alway composed of equal numbers of employers and employee representatives. Obviously, they provide assistance to the adult and continuing education functions of an LEA.

### Structure of Committees

It is the view of the authors that an LEA's committee structure should mirror the CVOE structure. Since cooperative education is essential to best-quality vocational/occupational education, programs should culminate in cooperative education experiences. Cooperative education cannot excel for long unless each program, or at least each department such as business, has an advisory committee. Thus, the authors recommend a structure (a) beginning with a general advisory committee, reporting and making recommendations to the director/dean of vocational/occupational education, (b) and having departmental and/or program committees, in accord with the structure of CVOE programs and reporting and making recommendations to the respective program leaders. (See Chapter 5 regarding structure of CVOE programs.)

### Advisory Committee Authority

Advisory committees are formed to assist development, implementation, operation, and evaluation of programs by offering advice, suggestions, and recommendations, and by providing certain resources. As early as possible, each committee member should come to understand that such contributions are invaluable and that committees and individual members have no legal authority. The administrators should use diplomacy when inviting and orienting committee members to assure that the full meaning of "advise" is internalized. It is well to stress two facts when developing this understanding. (1) Advisory committees are contrasted to governing boards. Committees give advice and contribute various resources, and governing boards have legal authority and responsibilities for finances and governance. (2) Not all advice given by committees can be utilized. Advice must be given freely, but expense and staff limitations prevent full realization of all the potential of all suggestions.

### Functions of Committees

The literature is replete with lists of functions for advisory committees. Several of these are quoted below. The reader is encouraged to note similarities and differences.

The Illinois Cooperative Health Occupations manual (29), p.3, lists ten ways in which a committee may assist an LEA.

1. Communicating the values of Cooperative Vocational Education to the community.
2. Preparing training sponsors to be effective in on-the-job instruction.
3. Identifying suitable training stations.
4. Evaluating the effectiveness of Cooperative Vocational Education programs.
5. Serving as a liaison group between the school and the business community.
6. Providing instructional help through resource speakers, trade materials, and occupational information.
7. Assisting in determining the criteria for measuring job performance of the student at the traiing station.
8. Providing public relations at the local level
9. Assisting in solving problems regarding the program that develop (sic) at the local level (i.e. student-learner wages, safety).
10. Projecting manpower needs in occupational fields.

The Texas home economics handbook (74), p. 15, lists eleven suggested duties of an advisory committee.

1. Aid in publicizing and promoting the program in the community.

2. Identify areas into which cooperative home economics can expand.
3. Help to determine criteria for the selection of training stations.
4. Review training plans.
5. Sign all training plans (Chairman).
6. Recommend a minimum wage for the purpose of preventing exploitation of students.
7. Provide supplementary instructional materials when available.
8. Assist with the evaluation of the program.
9. Advise as needed in relation to program objectives, course content, and the competences expected in the occupations, which the training is being offered.
10. Advise on criteria for the selection or recruitment of trainees.
11. Help obtain information regaring job opportunities in the occupational areas included in the cooperative program.

The Virginia office occupations guide (80), pp. 36-38, lists twelve suggested functions and many more subfunctions.

1. To advise and assist office education staffs in determining initial employment opportunities in the school service area. To assist in making job opportunity surveys.
2. To assist in determining the kind and amount of training needed.
   a. To help determine whether minimum training only sufficient to qualify for initial employment should be given or whether initial training plus some additional training to qualify for promotion should be given.
   b. To help determine whether training should be restricted to one phase of business, such as stenography or bookkeeping, or whether more than one phase of business should be included.
   c. To determine whether training should include part-time work training.
3. To assist in determining the training needs of out-of-school youth and adult workers.
   a. To find the number and kind of adult business workers within the community and the approximate annual rate of turnover.
   b. To find out the causes of dismissals and layoffs.
   c. To find out to what degree employees were properly prepared by school training for jobs in which they are now engaged.
4. To give advice on curriculum and course content.
   a. To act as a consultant to local school authorities in revising curriculums and course content in the light of the findings in the local school service area.
   b. To advise the school as to the short, intensive, specific courses needed to meet a definite training need recognized by either or both employee and employer, such as a course on federal or state income taxes for the bookkeeper or the layman, particularly for adult training.

5. To assist in maintaining and achieving better selection and placement of trainees.
   a. To give advice on the number that should be trained for specific jobs, the qualifications of the employees as to age, sex, personality, interest, ability, knowledge of general subjects (non business subjects, such as English), and skill in technical subjects.
   b. to give information concerning the leading characteristics employees should possess for particular jobs.

6. To assist in setting up standards for and selection of training stations for students participating in cooperative part-time work training programs.
   a. To help determine whether the organization considered for student placement is progressive and forward looking.
   b. To help determine whether the organization considered for student placement is interested in young people, whether it is public spirited and desires to help the public school in training young people.
   c. To help determine whether work standards within the organization are satisfactory to give the student opportunity to learn acceptable methods and procedures and whether the work is of sufficient variety and importance to give the student broad training.
   d. To help determine whether the physical surroundings are satisfactory, sanitary, and clean.
   e. To help determine whether the business or employer has the respect and goodwill of the people of the community.
   f. To find out if the company is willing to pay wages comparable to that of other beginners performing similar duties.
   g. To find out if there is a manager, a supervisor, or an experienced employee within the organization who would and could take an interest in the student and give him the right kind and amount of instruction for "breaking in" on the job.

7. To assist in obtaining part-time employment for cooperative students.

8. To assist the school in selecting and obtaining the services of department supervisors, junior executives, managers, and other outstanding office workers to conduct classes for adults.

9. To advise and assist in making follow-up studies of graduates to find out the kinds of businesses in which they have secured employment and to help determine the extent to which their school training prepared them for satisfactory employment and promotion.

10. To advise and assist in making job analyses of the principle occupations within the school service area to determine vocational training needs and standards.
    a. To advise in the selection of the personnel for special temporary occupational committees to help make job analyses and to develop training materials, outlines, and standards for specific occupations within the community.
    b. To help select a special occupational committee to give advice in

setting up a course in a particular field, such as accounting, to meet the local situation. In such a case, it is advisable to establish a special committee on training in accounting, comprised of representatives of bookkeepers and accountants and their employers. (This committee will help school people in analyzing the extent of training needs in setting up an outline for a training program for such workers, in selecting a competent teacher, and in arranging the time and place for such a class on adult education.)

11. To assist the school personnel in promoting business education and to interpret the program and its needs to the community.
    a. To work with the school in arranging field trips for business students to offices, stores, and manufacturing organizations.
    b. To work with the school in organizing student clubs and arranging extracurricular activities of a business nature.
    c. To advise and help in arranging for appropriate contests, displays of work, community demonstrations, and open house.
    d. To help secure from other businessmen and women of the community suitable awards, prizes, and recognition.
    e. To interpret to the school administrators, school board, taxpayers, and the public in general the business training needs of the beginning worker and of employed workers in the community.
12. To advise and help in securing summer employment for business teachers. Such employment contributes to their occupational competency by affording them opportunities for keeping their knowledge, skills, and methods in line with constantly changing business methods and good business practice.

In a study of the advisory committees utilized by distributive education programs in Tennessee, Poe (61), pp. 81-86, conducted an extensive review of literature relating to advisory committees for the purpose of developing a comprehensive list of functions associated with cooperative education advisory committees. The following functions were found by Poe to be representative of the opinions of leaders in vocational-technical education: (1) determine community training needs; (2) conduct community surveys; (3) assist the teacher-coordinator; (4) publicize the cooperative education program; (5) introduce the coordinator to influential people in the community; (6) assist the coordinator with the instructional program; (7) provide assistance with youth club activities; (8) provide guest speakers for the instructional program; (9) assist in organizing the employer appreciation banquet; (10) help establish program standards; (11) assist the coordinator in training station selection; (12) provide career guidance for student learners; (13) help organize the adult education program; and (14) evaluate the program.

The New Mexico cooperative education manual (50), p. 3, lists twelve committee functions.

1. Assist in making a community survey to determine the need for the program.
2. Advise as to general training policies.
3. Advise on qualification of teachers.
4. Assist in ascertaining student selection criteria.
5. Assist in planning the course outlines and review course of studies.
6. Assist in placement of students.
7. Advise as to adequacy and appropriateness of facilities and equipment.
8. Assist teachers in relating their instruction to the needs of the community.
9. Review and recommend approval of cooperative training plans and training agreements.
10. Recommend wage scales for various occupations.
11. Recommend criteria for the evaluation of programs.
12. Assist in development of a good public relations program.

The Vermont cooperative education manual (79), p. 26, lists ten suggested advisory committee duties.

1. Aid in publicizing and promoting cooperative vocational education programs in the community.
2. Identify areas in which cooperative vocational education programs can be expanded.
3. Help to determine criteria for the selection of training stations.
4. Review training plans.
5. Assist with the evaluation of the program.
6. Advise on program objectives and course content and provide information on job opportunities in the occupational areas included in the cooperative vocational education program.
7. Assist in obtaining jobs for graduates who have successfully completed their training.
8. Help organize community surveys by determining the data to be gathered, by supporting the need for the survey, and by helping evaluate the data.
9. Help to acquaint other citizens with the needs of the school.
10. Serve as a liaison group to help cooperative vocational education students who are interested in seeking post-secondary, college, or university education to make the transition.

Perhaps the most carefully developed list of things an advisory committee can do is found in the Illinois bulletin "Advisory Council Member" (25).

### HELP FOR TEACHERS AND ADMINISTRATORS

- Assisting school administrators and instructors in establishing a philosophy of career education

- Assisting in the preparation of measurable objectives for career programs and courses
- Maintaining all advisory council activity on an advisory status only, but at the same time realize the school needs your assistance to insure community relevance to local educational careers
- Assisting in establishing career education programs and advising on the use of proper criteria of evaluation
- Extending your expertise for clinics, in-service workshops, seminars and training programs to school career education faculty
- Assisting in establishing teacher qualifications for specific career occupation teaching
- Identifying substitute or resource instructors from the community to assist regular teachers in the classroom and/or teach in specialized program areas both day and evening
- Assisting in preparing job descriptions on which course content may be used
- Suggesting general occupational abilities necessary for a graduate of an occupational area to have in order to compete in the community job market
- Providing criteria for awards and prizes to outstanding students
- Identifying potential training stations for the placement of students in cooperative education programs
- Arranging meetings to establish cooperative relationships between the schools and industry (also parents in high school or elementary schools

## STUDENT CAREER SELECTION, PLACEMENT AND EVALUATION

- Assisting in public relations procedures both externally and internally to encourage young people to consider vocational and technical education to include:

  assisting in the formulation of a speaker's bureau to make speeches to civic clubs, career day meetings, etc.

  assisting in establishment of peocedures for approaching parents to provide vocational and/or technical information

  providing ideas for taking steps to acquaint younger students and teachers in lower grades with the programs

  considering ideas for a system of visits to vocational center area schools to acquaint them with the programs available to them

  assisting in procedures for approaching and providing information for guidance counselors who help encourage students into the programs

- Assisting in the establishment of criteria and qualifications necessary for students to apply for admission to the vocational-technical programs, including use and interpretation of aptitude tests for student self analysis
- Providing information concerning desirable aptitudes, education and

experience preferred for entry-level jobs and in the area of higher job level specialization requiring advanced training

- Arranging plant and/or field visits for students and instructors (also parents in high school or elementary) that are interesting and educational, and which in some instances may serve as classroom instruction as relevant to work experience information
- Providing specialized vocational literature to teachers, counselors, parents and students; such as occupational folders, brochures, pamphlets,
- Assisting the instructors in the formation of accurate, realistic specialized instructional products for group and individualized instruction
- Assisting in the development and obtaining of qualification, certification and licensing tests, including apprenticeship requirements to be used for initial employment of graduates
- Participating in and helping to interpret surveys of local industry manpower needs, job availability, anticipated employment in the community and identification of employment areas
- Assisting in placement of students in part- and full-time employment and advise in job placement of career program graduates
- Assisting in establishing certain vocational technical programs as recognized sources for craft apprenticeships
- Assisting with procedures for continuous evaluation of the programs and follow-up evaluation of graduates for program accountability which spotlights the value of the program or programs to the community and its employment needs

## EDUCATIONAL PROGRAMS

### PERTAINING TO CAREER INFORMATION AND COMMUNITY-PARENT INVOLVEMENT

- Evaluating and issuing supporting recommendations on budgetary requests, physical conditions, adequacy of equipment and supplies, laboratory shops, classrooms, etc.
- Assisting in the development and periodic evaluation of course content to assure its being up to date in meeting the changing skill and knowledge needs of the community, and employment area for industry and business
- Obtaining needed school equipment and supplies on loan, as gifts, or at special prices
- Assisting in the establishment of standards of proficiency to be met by students and helping with job analysis and task analysis in specialized areas
- Assisting in the development of school procedures concerning the kinds and volume of production work or "live jobs" to be produced by

students so that this work will be of instructional value in the educational program

- Establishing and helping to maintain a library of specialized visual aids, magazines, and books concerning industry and business in conjunction with the school library
- Assisting in the development of special educational and training programs for disadvantaged and handicapped students conducted with funds made available by the Manpower Development and Training Act, the Economic Opportunity Act, etc., in accordance with the needs of the community and representatives of the administrative agency
- Assisting in the development of evening school skill improvement and technical courses for employed personnel on the continuing adult level
- Assisting in the development of apprenticeship and on-the-job training related courses, in accordance with recommendations of local craft representatives and their specialized requirements
- Arranging plant or field trip visits for teachers to upgrade their teaching background in particular occupational areas
- Providing, whenever possible, training resources, i.e., raw materials, finished products, equipment, charts, posters, etc., for exhibit and instructional purposes in classrooms and shops
- Assisting in making cost studies for specialized programs and courses
- Assisting in establishing sequence of courses for proper student development in order that graduates will have proper training in job cluster areas to compete in the job market
- Seeking the cooperation, when needed, from other agencies for career education

## PUBLIC RELATIONS

- Supporting career education in its direct relationship to the activities of local and state school officials, boards and legislative groups
- Helping to obtain speakers to address trade and civic groups, school banquets and assembly programs which concern the development of career programs
- Assisting in arranging for publicity subject to school review, by using their contacts with news media—such as newspapers, trade magazines, radio and television stations—that would not otherwise be available to the school
- Participating in radio and T.V. programs designed to sell career education to the public
- Participating in an "open house" for students, parents and other adults in the community
- Inviting teachers, counselors, administrators and students to visit various plants and businesses
- Advising employees and their families concerning school programs by posting information on bulletin boards, news stories in company publi-

cations and enclosures in pay envelopes with approval of top management

- Assisting through donations and help to arrange for funds to advertise and advance specific school career education and training programs
- Supporting through attendance educational workshops and conferences that advance career education
- Assisting in evaluating the public relations policies and actions of the school in respect to the community and the overall career programs

## APPLICABLE TO AREA VOCATIONAL CENTERS

- Aiding Area Vocational Centers in studies of area school curriculums to determine needed specialized programs that augment member school programs
- Studying and advising on the proper representation for the advisory council from each area school community
- Helping develop a communication method to report on Area Vocational Center activities and progress to each member school and community
- Aiding in supplying specialized knowledge for site selection, necessary equipment and facility requirements for Area Vocational Center
- Assisting in development of sequential curriculum for area schools that will help provide a complete training program between all schools, including the Area Vocational Center
- Assisting in development of sequential curriculum for area schools that will help provide a complete training program between all schools, including the Area Vocational Center
- Giving specialized vocational assistance in planning interaction between teachers in specific occupational fields in area schools and an Area Vocational Center

## ADVISORY COUNCIL OPERATIONS

- Assisting in setting up and implementing a set of rules and bylaws to insure an active permanent advisory council
- Support through regular attendance at meetings and encourage total attendance of fellow members, to insure a well-represented and effective council

## STUDENT RECOGNITION

- Providing scholarships and other financial assistance for outstanding graduates who wish to continue their career educational training
- Providing recognition through prizes, awards and publicity for outstanding students, as approved by appropriate regulatory agencies
- Providing recognition for outstanding leadership, and encouraging greater involvement.

### Selection of Advisory Committee Members

Selection of committee members should be done according to design. Characteristics of committee members and representations of various community and professional segments should be decided upon before making appointments.

The size of the committee should also be fixed, before prospective members are contacted. A steering committee (see Chapter 6) may have made this and related determinations. Usually committees have not less than seven nor more than twelve members. Governing boards nearly always consist of five or seven voting members to minimize the votes and to assure manageability and full communication within the group. It is well to restrict membership to fifteen or less — a larger group is almost certain to demonstrate the management principle that a committee is no excuse for progress.

Individuals should display the following:

1. *Competence* in the specialty being represented. Respect and confidence of his associates and counterparts in the community.
2. *Interest and willingness* to support the program in several ways.
3. *Adequate time* to attend committee meetings, subcommittee meetings, and special events.
4. *Intelligence, social vision, and other leadership characteristics* which make favorable impressions upon young workers and enlist efforts of others.
5. *Civic mindedness* and ability to restrain personal politics and motivations in the interest of developing a competent labor force.

The following community and professional segments should be represented.

1. Management from various segments of the relevant private and/or public employment sector. People influential in management groups, such as Chamber of Commerce, members of civic or professional clubs, and supervisors of student-learners should be represented.
2. Employees and labor group representatives from various segments of the relevent employment sector.
3. Student-learners and recent graduates. In secondary schools, parents might also be represented.
4. Public and private employment agency officers.
5. The LEA administraton.
6. The LEA student services unit.
7. Teacher-coordinators in the program.

The teacher-coordinator and the administrator who is responsible for the program should prepare a list of potential committee members and alternatives for the approval of one or more levels of administration and perhaps the governing board (Fig. 8-1). People who have served on steering committees or other advisory groups should be considered. The director/dean and his/her superior should decide who will interview and invite committee members from the community. Normally, the director/dean will be well suited for this task because of understandings established via steering committee and other associations.

Interviews should provide prospective members information regarding need for their services, functions, and time commitments, length of term, need for balance on the committee, and importance of representing broad community concerns and specific student needs rather than personal or single-employer interests. Near the end of an interview both parties should agree on one of three alternatives. (1) That the interviewee will serve, (2) that the interviewee prefers to be asked to serve at a later time, (3) that the interviewee cannot serve for any of many good reasons. If an interviewee offers to encourage a subordinate to serve, the interviewer should accept the suggestion if it has been previously decided that the

**Interview Form for Prospective Advisory Committee Member**

Name _____

Employer or Affiliation _____

Position _____

Address _____Telephone_____

Home Address _____

Approximate Number of Employees:  Men_____Women_____

Representation on other advisory committees.

Yes _____

Best Meeting Time                         Preferred Days of Week

    Breakfast _____        _____

    Lunch _____        _____

    Afternoon _____        _____

    Evening _____        _____

Special Concerns, Interests, Comments.

_____

_____

_____

_____

Fig. 8-1. Sample interview form for prospective advisory committee members.

interviewee's affiliation—employer, union, club, whatever—must be represented. If such is not the case, the interviewee should be told that the committee is composed of individuals who have been carefully selected according to standard criteria and that his segment of the community will very likely be represented another time through normal rotation.

Appointment should be formalized by the chief administrative officer. An appointment letter should include term of office and what-happens-next information. (Fig. 8-2).

## Advisory Committee Member Letter of Appointment

(School letterhead)

(Date)


Dr. Jacob Schultz
Murray Convalescent Home
Broad and Main Streets
Nevada City, Oklahoma 00003


Dear Dr. Schultz:

We were very pleased to learn of your willingness to serve as a member of our General Advisory Committee. Your term will be from _____to_____.

Much of the success of vocational/occupational education has been due to the efforts of advisory committee members. Through the enthusiasm and interest of citizens such as you it is possible for this institution to provide citizens of (name of community) educational opportunities which will be of great benefit to students and employers alike.

We thank you for your consideration and are certain that you will find your association with our programs both pleasant and rewarding.

You will be hearing from (name here), director/dean of vocational/occupational education, concerning time and place of the next meeting.

Sincerely,

_____

(name)


_____

(title)

**Fig. 8-2.   Sample letter of appointment of advisory committee member.**

### Organization of Committees

Most committees function with a chairman and a secretary. It is widely maintained that the chairman should be a community member and that the secretary should be from the institution. It is well to select the chairman by vote of the full committee. The chairman should have conference leadership experience. The secretary of general advisory committees should be the dean/director of vocational/occupational education. The secretary of departmental committees should be the department head. And, the secretary of a program or craft committee should be the program leader.

When a committee is formed, a plan for replacing members should be decided upon. Normally, the following will satisfy the various kinds of members and the committee's purpose. (1) Institution members serve by virtue of position. (2) Student representative serves one-year term and is elected by students in relevant program(s) or clubs. (3) Community members serve two- or three-year terms and one-half or one-third complete terms each year. (Community members "draw straws" when committee is formed to determine which ones have short and long terms.) Many successful committees do not replace members on regular schedules. Members are replaced only as they change jobs and/or request to leave the committee and usually are replaced by representatives from the same segment of the community. This plan works well when it is obvious that certain key positions in the employment community should be continuously represented. The replacement plan works well and is essential when there are more employers than can be represented directly at one time.

### Care and Feeding of Committees

The following are do's, must's, and courtesies which will help to assure that committee members have positive attitudes and make valuable contributions.

1. Notify members two weeks or more in advance of meetings and other events.
2. Plan agenda for meetings well in advance and mail with related materials for arrival at least three days before meetings. Make telephone reminders a few hours (during the working day) before a meeting.
3. Explain committee functions, institutional needs, and member strengths at annual organizational meeting and review same at special events such as awards and recognition banquets.
4. Create a relaxed atmosphere in which all kinds of representatives have opportunities to speak and feel compelled to contribute to discussions and decisions.

5. Guard against domination by an individual or by a community segment.
6. Emphasize positives at the expense of negatives.
7. Move through agenda in businesslike fashion, giving time for all to comment and coming to clear closure on each matter (Fig. 8-3). Limit meetings to two hours. Close meeting by reviewing decisions and agreed upon "homework" assignments of various members. Don't waste time loitering. Plan for gracious and snappy finishes.

## Agenda for an Established Advisory Committee Meeting

1. Call to order
2. Consideration of minutes
3. Old business
4. Comments from chief administrative officer and director/dean
5. Report of teacher-coordinator(s) on program activities, especially student progress at training stations
6. New business and plan of action
   a. Public relations program
   b. Expansion of work experiences
   c. Awards banquet planning
7. Decision or reminder regarding next meeting
8. Chairman's recap and adjournment

Fig. 8-3.    Typical agenda for an established advisory committee meeting.

8. Make repeated expressions of gratitude for committee member contributions, never taking credit for accomplishments without recognizing community imputs. Emphasize plural and passive pronouns, e.g., we, us, ours.
9. Pay special attention to the chairman's needs for information, documents, and support during meetings.
10. Have the secretary take notes and prepare minutes for the chairman's perusal and later distribution.
11. Ask repeatedly for comments, suggestions, negative and positive criticisms, views from the field, etc.
12. Exercise common courtesies and observe the group's wishes regarding meeting times, meals, refreshments, etc.
13. Consider other than routine meetings. Occasional public meetings to get reactions of interested citizens on particular issues and problems may serve a general advisory committee's concerns. Subcommittee meetings may save time and effort for all. Invite

guests for consultations as needed. View similar CVOE programs for renewed planning and program evaluation.

### Plan of Action

The committee chairman and secretary should draft a tentative action plan on an annual or term basis. The plan should include functions, things to be accomplished, dates, and some indication of who is to do what. This plan will suggest things for meeting agenda and for things which institutional personnel and community representatives must accomplish between meetings. One form for these plans is shown in Fig. 8-4. Committees would usually accomplish more things than are listed in the sample action plan.

### Recognition of Committee Members

Because committee members serve without compensation and at some expense to themselves and their employers, they should be recognized in one or more ways. Advisory committee names and affiliation should be listed in catalogs, bulletins, etc. Public relations efforts should feature committee work and names from time to time. Certificates of appreciation should be printed or engraved and presented publicly—such as at a year-end awards and recognition banquet. (See Chapter 16, Public Relations.) Letters of appreciation should be sent annually by the chief administrative officer to members and their superiors if they wish (Fig. 8-5). Members should receive special invitations to selected special events of the LEA. At appropriate times, they should be introduced and recognized for service to the institution. They should be afforded parking permits, reserved seats, and other niceties which recognize their importance.

## FACILITIES AND EQUIPMENT

It is essential to define learning experiences (see Chapter 12); identify needed learning areas and pieces of equipment; and select free, inexpensive, and commercial sources in that order. Given knowledge of facilities and equipment needs, an advisory committee or subcommittee may be utilized to identify (1) which facilities in the community may be available for student groups and which must be provided by the LEA, and (2) which major items of equipment must be procured commercially or via contributions.

Several examples indicate what kinds of facilities in the community may be used for what otherwise would be in-school learning. Some employers have "classrooms in the factory." Such facilities may serve well to orient CVOE students to policies and procedures before they assume training stations. Such facilities might also be used for job and career information, for demonstrations on special pieces of equipment, and for other learnings for all students in a program.

Some employers may have unutilized or underutilized facilities which may be loaned or, more typically, leased (often for a nominal fee) so that the LEA assumes liability. Thus, an LEA might use an otherwise idle service station, hospital wing, warehouse section, marginal acreage, or storefront to conduct related classes and especially orientation sessions immediately prior to training stations experiences.

It is often well to have a subcommittee of a program advisory committee serve as an equipment committee. An equipment committee can serve two basic functions. (1) The first is to solicit free or inexpensive contributions of equipment. With information from a steering committee survey (see Chapter 6 ), from a special survey of employers, or from knowledge of work places, committee members are sometimes able to identify pieces of equipment which are no longer useful to employers but are appropriate to the learning situation. Some items are sometimes donated gratis, sometimes donated with expenses, such as moving, accruing to the LEA, and sometimes loaned for extensive periods to the LEA. An equipment committee and individual members can also help commercial suppliers to appreciate the value of making contributions to educational enterprises. One of the authors recalls several instances wherein major food processing firms which purchased large numbers of delivery trucks, influenced two of the big-three automotive companies to contribute several thousands of dollars annually to an LEA's supply fund. Although major cash contributions may be rare, contributions from equipment suppliers are rather common in food service, vehicular machanics, and some medically related programs. Some LEA's have been so successful at relationships with equipment suppliers that an equipment committee is needed to screen offers of contributions or loans and decline many of them as graciously as possible. Equipment committee members can also help to assure that appropriate items are purchased at very competitive prices. Solicitation of contributions and/or low prices are often best made via advisory committees. Such solicitations should be made with approval of administrators and perhaps the respective governing board. (2) An equipment committee should also be involved at several stages of major purchases. As indicated above, advisory committee members should have a voice in defining major pieces of laboratory equipment. Often, equipment subcommittee members should be asked for help in preparing specifications and for pursuing regulation bid and requisition procedures. Advisors represent some of the largest taxpayers in the community and

## Plan Of Action for Advisory Committee

| Function & Actions to be Accomplished | who | |
|---|---|---|
| **1. Occupational Survey** | | |
| a. Review content and format of old instrument | Chairman Secretary and Chamber of Commerce Representative | December 15 |
| b. Apply instrument to ten participating and five new employers | Each community representative makes three visits with secretary | January 30 |
| **2. Program and Course Components** | | |
| a. Review Junior high school exploration and guidance program | One employer and one employee representative | Team review November 10-11 |
| b. Annual welding program review | All members | Final meeting before awards banquet |
| c. Special review of units in junior-level course | One employer and one employee representative | February 20 for distribution prior to Winter committee meeting |
| **3. Placement** | | |
| a. Writing letters of recommendations for permanent placement files | All members as requested by students | Ten days after request from student |
| b. Establishing special coop placement for Spring term | Chairman and secretary | December 10 |
| c. Increase from 15 to 23 placements for next fall | Secretary and other coordinators | June |

Fig. 8-4. Sample action plan for advisory committee. (Cont'd on next page.)

| | | |
|---|---|---|
| 4. Public Relations | | |
| a. Speak before civic clubs | Chief administrative officer honor current request, any member | October 13 (noon) anytime (slide available) |
| b. Redo program brochure: Contribute pictures and edit copy | Any member submit pictures, chairman | January 27 |
| c. Plan awards and recognition banquet and news releases | Chairman, secretary, student representative | March 16 for distribution prior to Spring committee meeting |
| 5. External Resourses | | |
| a. Survey potential contributors of scrap for sample welding | One employer representative and one coordinator | April |
| b. Secure free charts and illustrations from commercial suppliers | Chairman and secretary | As soon as meetings with sales managers can be arranged |
| 6. Evaluation | | |
| a. Followup of last year's graduates | Teacher-coordinator | March |
| b. Follow up of their employers | Teacher-coordinator | March |
| c. Use of annual program checklist | Subcommittee of five to be named at Winter meeting | March |
| d. Recommendations for improvement | Same subcommittee and review by entire committee | March draft and spring meeting action |

Fig. 8-4.  Sample action plan for advisory committee.

## Letter of Appreciation for Committee Member

(School letterhead)

(Date)

Dr. Jacob Schultz
Murray Convalescent Home
Broad and Main Streets
Nevada City, Oklahoma 00063

Dear Dr. Schultz:

I should like to express appreciation for myself and the District for your participation on the _____ Advisory Committee. You have Contributed greatly to the development of this program and to an improved manpower resource in our community.

We look forward to recognizing you at the awards and recognition banquet and to working with you on matters of common concern in the future.

Sincerely,

_____
(name)

_____
(title)

**Fig. 8-5.  Sample letter of appreciation for a committee member.**

have special expertise—two good reasons for involving them in equipment procurement.

All too few public education enterprises make good use of opportunities to get equipment from federal and state surplus properties agencies. The writers are familiar with a high school heavy equipment operation and maintenance program which is better equipped than commercial schools of on-road and off-road equipment operation and heavy-duty and diesel mechanics—virtually all via inexpensive surplus property and contributions from commercial enterprises. Administrators should pursue opportunites to partially equip both classrooms and laboratories with surplus property which satisfy predetermined selection criteria. Used equipment should also be considered. Trade papers and metropolitan telephone directories list used equipment suppliers in many industries. Enterprises such as farm implement and automotive dealerships, body and fender shops, and office equipment suppliers are also good sources of inexpensive or free demonstration units.

### FREE AND INEXPENSIVE MATERIALS AND SUPPLIES

For nearly all occupational areas, there are sources of free or inexpensive instructional materials and supplies. Resourceful CVOE personnel maximize learning by utilizing such resources. Teachers should consult standard reference works to acquire or borrow career information brochures, films, etc. Many materials for human relations, safety, and other important areas of learning may be procured through similar means. Some employers can also contribute or loan such materials or can help the LEA obtain such materials from parent corporations or higher levels of government.

Laboratory supplies are a different and potentially extremely expensive matter in many CVOE fields. Resourceful CVOE personnel often reduce supply costs through association with employers and supply companies. Teachers should work via advisory committees to identify probable sources of supplies. Examples from the author's observations illustrate what can be accomplished. It is rather common for metals processing and welding programs to obtain metal for casting, machining, and welding practice from industrial establishments; use it for as long as they like, and then return it (scraps and all) for salvage. The American Institute of Baking in Chicago annually uses more than $70,000 worth of contributed ingredients. Public LEA programs which serve national or international employment communities could do more to obtain similar contributions from major suppliers. The authors recall a post-secondary equipment parts warehousing and distribution program which "contracted" to warehouse parts for ten-year-old and older equipment and "pull" the few orders which came to the part distribution enterprise. Thus, students had a large parts inventory and complete sets of manuals for use in a very realistic learning laboratory.

Many CVOE programs utilize materials which commercial enterprises cannot use or sell because of overruns, bad accounts, business failures, or obsolescence. Personnel must "keep their nose to the ground" and encourage advisers to do likewise for opportunities to procure appropriate supplies inexpensively. Often, firms are willing to donate such materials because benefits to students (and indirectly the firm) far outweigh salvage values. Indeed, contributions are often forthcoming because the LEA is willing to transport surpluses and save the firm transportation and/or storage costs.

## SPEAKERS, RESOURCE PERSONS, AND FIELD TRIPS

Utilization of these external resources can spice related classes. To be effective, these techniques must be used according to designs which are based in student needs and training plans.

### Speaker's Bureaus

It is not always well to establish an elaborate system for utilizing speakers in vocational/occupational education alone. Sometimes it is better to establish a speaker's bureau managed by a larger LEA or community agency in the area. If a speaker's bureau is to be established it should (1) have information on LEA people who are willing to make presentations in the community and (2) have information on community members who are willing to make presentations in the LEA or at their job sites for students and staff (see next two sections). The sample form illustrates information which should be catalogued. (Fig. 8-6).

### Form for Member of a Speaker's Bureau

Name _____

Job Title  _____

Employer or Affiliation _____

Address _____

Telephone  Work_____Home _____

   To Whom Should Request Be Made _____

   Address _____ Telephone _____

A. **Presentations in the Community**
   List topics you might treat          1 _____
   in talks before committee            2 _____
   groups                               3 _____

B. **Presentations in the (name of LEA here)**
   List topics you might treat          1 _____
   in career or occupational            2 _____
   classes.                             3 _____

C. **Presentations at your Place of Work**
   List topics you might treat          1 _____
   if a career or occupational          2 _____
   education class visited your         3 _____
   place of work.

Fig. 8-6.  Typical form for a member of a speaker's bureau.

A form for a speaker's bureau should not be distributed widely. It should be distributed under a covering letter to people in the LEA. This letter should state relevant institution policies re such things as released time and remuneration. People in the community who might contribute to the LEA's programs should be contacted via advisory committees, governing board members, teacher-coordinators, counselors, and others who (1) relate to people in one-to-one situations and (2) can explain what kinds of things might be listed in parts "B" and "C." Staff members should be reminded from time-to-time to ask potential resource persons and field-trip hosts to complete a form.

A speaker's bureau should be managed by a central officer. A well qualified secretary who is familiar with the community can handle nearly all transactions. The kinds of transactions are (a) entering and cross-referencing new forms, (b) helping LEA personnel enter the system with predetermined presentation or field-trip topics and select one or more potential presenters or hosts, and (c) helping community members who request information re potential speakers.

A brochure indicating kinds of topics, appropriate groups, and procedures for making requests should be distributed internally and to various publics.

### Resource Persons

As the following purposes for utilizing resource persons in CVOE indicate, experts of various kinds may contribute to all levels of career, vocational, and occupational information.

1. To provide career information relevant to local labor market conditions.
2. To provide current job expertise.
3. To provide banking and other personal finance expertise.
4. To provide information re job requirements and placement.
5. To provide information re community service agencies.
6. To reinforce previous learnings.

Resource persons may be obtained via several means. A well-eveloped speaker's bureau (see previous section) may lead to one or more appropriate presenters. Advisory committee contacts and/or contacts at training stations may result in good matches with particular learning purposes. Other contacts in the community, such as club membership and personal shopping can also lead to ideas for improving learning via guest presenters. It is important to observe several principles when utilizing resource persons. (See Chapter 12.)

**Field Trips**

It is many times better to transport students to the job sites of resource persons. In addition to the purposes listed for resource persons, field trips can provide first-hand knowledge of working conditions, demonstrations of commercial and industrial-scale equipment, and observations of and brief interviews with a variety of employees.

It is important to practice the principles of four-step teaching when utilizing trips to employment sites: (See Chapter 12 for more thorough treatment of four-step teaching.)

1. Preparation
   a) Teacher preparation
      (1) Visit the site.
      (2) Outline items to be observed and described.
      (3) Estimate times and plan for parking, meals, safety, etc, as needed.
      (4) Get necessary institutional and/or parental approvals.
      (5) Provide for transportation.
   b) Orient Students
      (1) Discuss purposes.
      (2) Outline key observations and questions.
      (3) Provide pretrip reading.
      (4) Define appropriate dress, behavior, whatever.
2. Presentation
   a) Arrive on time.
   b) Show interest and abide by wishes and directives of host(s) and guide(s).
   c) Attempt to procure printed materials, samples, etc., for class review and discussion and for future classes.
   d) Abide by safety rules and common sense re courtesy and neatness.
3. Application
   a) Use at least one half of a class period to review major objectives and learnings and answer questions.
   b) Relate subsequent learnings to field trip experiences.
   c) Involve students in drafting of appreciation letter.
   d) Display printed materials, samples, etc.
4. Testing
   a) Assess student opinion re value of the trip.
   b) Prepare a written evaluation for your superior, indicating worth as contrasted to expense and to other trips which might serve similar purposes.
   c) Involve student leaders in the evaluation report.

There are many more kinds of field trips than most teachers and students appreciate. In addition to differences in purpose, trips should vary in terms of whether an entire class, small groups, or individuals are taken, how many establishments are visited, and whether they are accomplished in a few minutes, a few hours, a few days, or an extended time. Far too few vocational/occupational classes are privileged to have field experiences in related classes akin to those of foreign language, anthropology, government, archaeology, and other classes—which travel great distances for entended periods. CVOE students deserve to observe a great deal, at least in the area within which they are likely to obtain permanent employment—the better to understand what can be done careerwise.

## Summary

CVOE can be greatly enriched via judicious utilization of external resources. Foremost among these resources are community members who serve on advisory committees. In addition to participation in selection of training stations and students, contributions to student club and guidance programs, and assistance in public relations and program evaluation (which are treated in subsequent chapters) advisors can serve as keys to the utilization of other external resources. Some of these are external facilities, contributed or loaned equipment; free and inexpensive equipment, materials, and supplies; and speakers, resource persons, and field trips. Benefits from various external resources can be maximized by adherence to well established principles of planning, utilization, and evaluation.

## Activities

1. Obtain copies of several reports of the National Advisory Council on Vocational Education and/or the National Advisory Council on Career Education, and/or other national councils which are concerned with human resource development. Identify recommendations which impinge upon CVOE and indicate how.
2. Do the same with annual reports of your state's advisory council for vocational/occupational education.
3. Do the same with annual reports of your state's council(s) for manpower, human resources, or the like, if such bodies exist.
4. Obtain descriptions of all CVOE programs in a school, college, or technical insitute. Design a two-level structure of advisory committees, describing lines of communication and membership.
5. Draft several paragraphs which could be used to inform a superior

that advisory committees (a) are essential to several CVOE program components and (b) are advisory rather than administrative.

6. Study the several statements of committee functions in this chapter. Draft a composite statement, using a two-level outline and trying to accommodate all of the items of the various lists. Consider the major headings: occupational surveys, program and course components, placement, public relations, external resources, and evaluation.

7. Study the composite list you made for Activity 6 or several of the lists of functions in this chapter. Select several functions which you believe are not proper committee activities and/or which cannot be done well by committees. Write several paragraphs defending your beliefs.

8. Obtain minutes of one or more LEA advisory committees. Make a list of functions which the committee appears to be serving.

9. Write a two- to five-page paper describing potential sources of and approaches for obtaining free or inexpensive materials and supplies for your specialty within CVOE. Use standard reference works, such as film catalogs from a nearby university. Consider the several sources discussed in this chapter and add others.

10. Write a plan for establishing a speaker's bureau in a specific LEA.

11. Write a plan for using resource persons and/or field trips in a specified, semester or year-long related class.

Chapter *9*

# Student Ingression and Orientation

Much of the literature of cooperative education emphasizes the importance of careful selection and proper placement of program participants to program success. If one were to develop an hierarchy of factors which affect success of cooperative vocational occupational education (CVOE) via review of the literature alone, characteristics of the coordinator would far and away rank first. Student selection would rank second.

The student admission process, which developed in CVOE, was influenced significantly by supply and demand and had traditionally emphasized the "selection" function. Until recently, there have been far too few CVOE programs to serve an increasing student population. As would be expected, when faced with large numbers of applicants for limited numbers of CVOE programs, most LEA's admit the more capable student. Prior to recent increases in numbers of CVOE programs, it was not uncommon for two or three hundred applicants to apply to a program which could accommodate only thirty or forty students. This supply/demand situation fostered development of stringent student selection criteria. The practice of "selecting" only the "best" students for participation in CVOE grew quietly and was unchallenged for quite some time.

A followup study of one medium-size (1500 students) midwestern secondary school revealed that 85 percent of graduates of the office occupations cooperative program "went on to college." Examination of student-selection criteria utilized by the teacher-coordinator revealed that students had to earn the privilege to participate in the cooperative program by earning "B's" in typing I, typing II, and stenography I. In addition, the students had to have good attendance records, four recommendations from faculty members, good personal appearance, and numerous other desirable characteristics. The program was doing an excellent job of selecting successful students and appearing to help them become successful students. It was betting on established winners—only. Needless to say, administrators were pleased with the public relations benefits which accrued from the program. Some of the outcomes of reading this chapter are *ability to:*

1. define CVOE program purposes,
2. develop student profiles,
3. match student profiles and program purposes, and
4. work with LEA personnel to smooth ingression and orientation of students.

### DETERMINING PROGRAM PURPOSES

There are at least two divergent schools of thought regarding types of student clientele which should be served by CVOE. Proponents of one camp view students as representative of the educational institution, and feel that cooperative students should be the best possible representatives. This camp places great stock in the fact that definite public relations benefits are derived from placing only the better and best students in jobs in the local community. Proponents of the other camp believe that highly selective CVOE programs do not serve student clientele who have the most to gain from cooperative experiences.

In an analysis of some of the literature which supports the first group, Mason (40), p. 23, noted that each teacher-coordinator should develop criteria for the selection of student-learners by considering the relevance of age, skills, personality, health, school achievement, interest, aptitude, and how well the student would represent the school in the business community. This same concern is reflected by two of the findings of a study conducted by Houstman (22), p. 2251-A, of the perceptions of state supervisors and teacher educators regarding the future of vocational office education and distributive education programs. Those findings were: (1) Programs should acquire increased status, and (2) More university-bound students should be enrolled in the programs.The Tennessee handbook (73), p.43, contains the following statement re student selection.

"If the Cooperative Vocational Education Program is to achieve its vocational objective, it must not be used as a dumping ground and be crowded with misfits. Cooperative Vocational Education must be only for those who want, need, and can profit from it. The Cooperative Vocational Education Coordinator has the responsibility for the careful selection of cooperative students. Careful selection is of the utmost importance since these students will be representing the Cooperative Vocational Education Program and the school to the community. Poorly selected students will give the Cooperative Vocational Education Program a bad image and will reflect upon the total program, the school, and the coordinator.

In a study which compared selected student characteristics and cooperative programs, Ullery (75), p. 4502-A, found that students were rejected on the basis of socioeconomic level, class, race, age, sex, and dropout proneness. Ullery noted that students were rejected from special-needs cooperative programs for possessing special needs. Similarly, Bullard (8), pp.7-9, noted that educators wanted perfect students for "the taxpayers to see" in the business community. He submitted that selection procedures and criteria utilized by cooperative educators are outmoded, and tend to reject the very people who have the most to gain from the cooperative education experience.

A study conducted by Munisteria (48), p. 2630-A, added support to the belief that cooperative education is an effective vehicle for holding potential dropouts in school. In an East Harlem high school in New York City, he found that: (1) CVOE programs were instrumental in improving holding power, (2) cooperative students had better attendance records, and (3) the rate of graduation of cooperative students was six times higher than for regular vocational education students.

In a study which assessed agreement among North Carolina's industrial cooperative training coordinators regarding national guidelines, Smith (70), p. 114, found that coordinators ranked the following ten selection criteria as most important.

1. The coordinator determines the final selection of students who are considered for industrial cooperative education.
2. All interested student applicants are given a complete understanding of the program before they are enrolled.
3. The applicant meets the minimum age, grade, and other standards before selection.
4. The selection takes place in the Spring.
5. A student application form is used.
6. The student's school record is reviewed in the selection process.
7. The coordinator and counselors work closely in the selection of students.
8. A definite policy for student selection is followed.
9. The student's interests and qualifications fit some available job in the community.
10. The student's school record is reviewed in the selection process.

Pender (57) p. 7, listed the important considerations for selecting students for cooperative programs as: (1) age; (2) needs; (3) interests; (4) aptitudes; (5) abilities; (6) scholastic average; (7) attendance record; (8) appearance; and (9) interpersonal relations.

Both schools of thought on student selection present cogent arguments. Their basic differences probably result from diverse perceptions of CVOE. If a number of vocational/ occupational educational practitioners are asked to define CVOE, divergent responses are certain to result. As defined in this book, CVOE connotes many types of occupationally oriented experiential programs, which serve clientele with varying abilities and educational levels. CVOE is one of the vehicles which can be utilized to foster career development. For example, if mentally handicapped students need to develop manipulative skills and attitudes necessary to satisfactory performance of simple, repetitive operations which will permit them to become productive members of society, CVOE may be the best vehicle. Conversely, if academically talented students need to develop technical competencies necessary to successful performance of sophisticated manipulative and mental tasks which will assure that they become productive members of society, CVOE may be the best vehicle.

The overriding concern of professionals should be what CVOE programs can contribute to student's educational/occupational development rather than what students can contribute to an LEA, program, or coordinator. As was indicated in Chapter 5, after planners assess needs and aspirations of students to be served by CVOE, decisions can be made re types of programs and types of students which should be served by respective programs. Two basic questions must be considered:

1. What specific developmental outcomes are desirable for student clientele?
2. What types of CVOE programs will foster desired outcomes?

CVOE programs should be developed to meet the career development needs of the student clientele served by the LEA. "Student selection criteria" should take a subordinate role to "program development criteria." *Students should not be selected to ensure program success. Programs should be developed and implemented to ensure student success.* The primary objective of CVOE is not to develop successful programs; it is to develop students who can be successful in the world of work. Thus, it is conceivable that CVOE programs in a given LEA will be significantly different from those in other LEA's. CVOE programs should be developed in accord with local objectives which reflect real career development needs of student clientele. Futhermore, student clientele and employers should understand the objectives of CVOE programs in the LEA.

The results of the student and community surveys (See Chapter 4.) conducted by the LEA should provide adequate bases for decisions re occupations in the local community which may support implementation of CVOE and re populations which can benefit from CVOE. Characteristics of target populations should dicate program purposes. Some student purposes for which CVOE programs may be developed are:

1. develop entry level manipulative skills.
2. apply skills developed in laboratory classes.
3. explore several occupations or clusters.

4. develop attitudes and interpersonal skills necessary to job success.

5. remain in school.

Obviously, one type of CVOE program cannot effectively serve the diverse needs of "misfits" and "perfect fits." Generally, one program cannot serve several divergent groups. Since individuals are diverse, one type of CVOE program is no more educationally desirable than another. A CVOE program established to provide economically deprived students with resources necessary to attendance is neither more nor less desirable than is a CVOE program designed to develop midmanagement personnel.

Traditional student selection processes are no longer applicable to most programs in most LEA's. Whereas certain programs such as health occupations programs which lend to licensure may have to satisfy licensing agency stipulations concerning entrance criteria, in the main, cooperative education should be turned around. That is, programs such as distributive education or office occupations should exist to serve students with a wide range of characteristics rather than to serve narrow definitions of program purposes and only a few occupational titles. Furthermore, entrance requirements must be defensible in courts of law and are increasingly difficult to defend on mental measurements bases. In a great many LEA's with widely divergent clientele, the process for relating students and programs has changed from *selecting* to *matching*. Students' career development needs are matched with program purposes. Thus, judicious student ingression depends upon understandings of the purposes of specific CVOE programs, i.e., understandings of student clientele, counselors, teachers, coordinators, employers, and others.

## DETERMINING STUDENT PROFILES

Good matching of student needs and program purposes depends upon at least two types of information, i.e., information relative to purposes of CVOE programs and information relative to characteristics of individual prospective CVOE students. Matching of student needs and program purposes requires information in several categories.

### Career Awareness and Occupational Understanding

One basic principle of CVOE is that students will be placed in occupations which are consistent with their expressed vocational objectives. Expressed vocational objective should be the major factor in deciding which CVOE program is best suited for a given student. For example, if CVOE programs in an LEA serve particular occupational areas, students who express interests in respective occupational clusters should receive primary consideration. However, matching decisions cannot be made on bases of expressed occupational preference alone. Frequently, students do not have accurate perceptions of competency requirements and working conditions of particular occupations. The authors are reminded of a young man who indicated a desire to become a building construction technologist. When asked, "What does a building construction technologist do?" he responded, "I haven't the foggiest notion." In future, career education may increase knowledge of occupations, generally. However, some students and some occupations will always require special opportunities to develop understandings before deciding upon a CVOE program. Presently, it is obvious that many individuals gravitate toward occupations by chance rather than via informed choice. Therefore, LEA's must attempt to ascertain students':

1. knowledge of the world of work,
2. understanding of occupations,
3. perceived career goals and aspirations,
4. plans for furthering education, and
5. plans for place of residence.

If students are genuinely understanding of at least some occupations, matching of students and CVOE programs requires answers to questions such as:

1. What are my present abilities?
2. What are my capabilities over the long haul? Over the short haul?
3. What are my interests and motivations respective to work?
4. What are the requirements of the occupation I have chosen?
5. Are my occupational choice and my abilities and my capabilities compatible?

These questions seem simple enough. But, obtaining answers to such questions is extremely difficult. Many types of information from several sources must be assimilated before answers can be formulated. The admonishment "know thyself" is very difficult to heed, especially in the occupational domain.

### Aptitudes, Interests, and Abilities

Most LEA's accumulate information on students from the time they enter formal education. Cumulative records maintained by LEA's and transferred to other LEA's are an excellent source of information for use in matching students with programs. Typically, they provide:

1. intelligence test scores,

2. achievement test scores in areas such as reading, vocabulary, language usage, mathematics, science, and spatial relations,
3. aptitude test scores,
4. academic records,
5. records of behavioral problems,
6. attendance records,
7. health records, and
8. interest or preference scale scores.

These types of information should be used by professionals who guide student decisions re educational and occupational development. Such information should not be used to restrict student opportunities.[1] Because many students respond to environments in the world of work quite differently from the ways they have responded to educational environments, records should be utilized in student-centered guidance, i.e., to help students arrive at conclusions concerning abilities, aptitudes, occupational choice, etc. Information re scholastic performance, mechanical aptitude, manual dexterity, and supervisory potential, for example, may bear upon a variety of decisions.

Frequently, previous employment experience of a prospective CVOE student provides insights re abilities, aptitudes, and interests. Hobbies and leisure activities also provide information which standarized tests cannot provide.

### Physical Condition

Attention should also be given to matching physical requirements of jobs and abilities of students. In the main, this is not a crucial variable. But, in extreme cases it is paramount. Students with physical handicaps or restrictions may be well advised to consider some occupations and not to consider others. Such considerations should depend upon true physical demands of occupations, valid assessments of capabilities, and individual will. All students should understand physical requirements of jobs in occupational areas they are considering.

### Personality and Behavior

Many of the factors which are important to job success cannot be assessed by measures available to educators. How does one, for example, measure motivation, dependability, honesty, sense of humor, persis-

---

[1] Again, this is not to challenge defensible restrictions such as are still imposed by some licensing bodies on, say, convicted felons. Nevertheless, CVOE personnel are admonished to be alert to the liberalization of such restrictions.

tence, initiative, drive, desire, attitude toward others, attitude toward work, reliability, responsibility, and other factors which influence job success? Educators and employers tend to predict performance of prospective CVOE students on bases of behavior patterns developed during prior associations with the LEA. This is the natural procedure because, in most instances, the record of association with an LEA is the available source of information relevant to personality and behavior.

For at least two reasons, this procedure should be employed with extreme caution. First, attitudes and behavior patterns displayed by many students in their associations with an LEA are very dissimilar from patterns displayed outside the LEA. Many young students and some not-so-young students relate very differently to the real world and to the world of schooling. Witness that often when confronted with the concept that attitudes and behavior patterns displayed in an LEA will deter job success students display shock and indignation. Responses such as, "You don't think I would act that way on the job do you?" and "You don't think I would be late for work, do you?" are common. Granted, many authorities support the notion that behaviors exhibited in institutions are rather accurate predictors of behaviors which will be exhibited in the world of work. However, observed discrepancies challenge wholesale use of this assumption. The great bulk of responsible and intelligent people respond rather similarly no matter where they may be for what purpose. But, some who best satisfy institutional expectations may perform very differently on the job and, conversely, some who seem never to "get along" on the inside may perform marvelously well on the job. These realizations suggest (1) that ingression to cooperative education should not depend unduly upon prior behavior patterns and (2) that coordination and supervision on the job should be very well done, especially at the very beginning of a student's transition to a training station. This is an extremely important opportunity for good to go bad and bad to go good— so-to-speak.

Second, CVOE programs are developed to provide students opportunity to develop skills necessary to success in the world of work. But, skills are not limited to the obvious mental and manual tasks of an occupation. Witness the following typical statement of program outcomes.

The_____CVOE program provides opportunity for participants to develop:

1. positive attitudes toward work,
2. ability to work well with others,
3. responsibility,
4. citizenship, and
5. job knowledge and skills.

These outcomes imply that something is going to happen to the student. Behaviors are going to be changed. If only students who display attitudes and behaviors necessary to job success are enrolled in CVOE, development toward such outcomes should not be listed. Because CVOE has time and time again been shown to be an effective vehicle for shaping positive attitudes, it is ludicrous to lay claim to developing desirable attitudes and exclude students with undesirable behaviors from CVOE.

Admittedly, some students in nearly all LEA's do not display attitudes and behaviors necessary to placement in the world of work. If substantial numbers of such students are being served by an LEA, special classes should be developed and implemented to assist them to become employable. (A student must be placed at a training station in order to be enrolled in CVOE.) Meanwhile, potential employers should be apprised of program purposes, student characteristics, and the need to supervise students so that early experiences are successful and cumulative. Employers must understand the challenge of any CVOE program and participate (or not participate) with full understanding of responsibilities and rewards.

### Education and Employment History

Two additional features of profiles which are used to match student needs and interests with CVOE program types are prior educational and employment experiences. Performance in various courses and extracurricular activities provide additional information about interests and abilities. Employment history is certain to provide information useful to vocational choice and placement. For example, students should not be placed in jobs which provide little opportunity for new learning.

## MATCHING STUDENT PROFILES WITH PROGRAM PURPOSES

CVOE programs are developed and implemented to meet identified career development needs of student clientele. Program policies and procedures should be established with those needs uppermost in mind. Time invested in ascertaining needs, aspirations, abilities, and behavior characteristics of prospective CVOE students pays dividends only if results are used to assure that individuals are placed in the particular types of CVOE programs which best meet their occupational development needs. In sum, the intent is to match characteristics of student clientele, competency requirements and constraints of jobs, and CVOE program purposes. Individual participation in CVOE should be based on answers to questions such as:

(1) What are the needs and occupational aspirations of the student?

(2) What type of CVOE program would best meet those identified needs?

The Minnesota Guide for Cooperative Vocational Education (44), p. 23, lists concerns which bear on matching students, jobs, and programs.

### Expected Student Outcomes

1. In order to achieve unity of purpose among those concerned with a local cooperative vocational education program and to maintain harmonious operation, a carefully planned statement of expected student outcomes is necessary.
2. A viable statement of expected student outcomes is based on data, information, and reason rather than on the emotionally tinged opinions of individuals and groups. These outcomes become the basis of program evaluation.
3. Three primary factors in formulating a statement of expected student outcomes are the needs of the students to be served, the requirements of the occupations for which training is pursued, and the capabilities of a good citizen-worker.
4. Because of the constraints on the school and cooperating employers the vocational education needs of all students cannot be served by cooperative education alone; choices among student groups to be served must be made. The needs and characteristics of the selected group(s) should be identified and studied in order to arrive at a statement of expected student outcomes.
5. The expected student outcomes of a cooperative vocational section representing one occupational field should not be copied for a section representing another field because of the inherent differences in emphasis on areas of occupational competency among the fields.
6. Factors which influence the expected student outcomes are: characteristics of the students to be served, educational achievement level of the program, availability of related course offerings, and the characteristics of the local community and individual school. Schools in low-income areas probably would strive for different outcomes than those in wealthy communities.
7. When preparing expected student outcomes, program planners and implementors should consider the differences in occupational competency patterns within occupational fields.

### WORKING WITH OTHER PERSONNEL

An employer's decision to employ (or not to employ) a CVOE student ultimately determines acceptance into a CVOE program. Other events in the student ingression and orientation process must occur prior to the time of the employer's decision. Determinations regarding which students shall participate in which CVOE programs should be the shared responsibility of CVOE, other instructional, counseling, and administrative personnel. Of course, the weight of these types of professionals in such determinations varies from LEA to LEA. But, in a given LEA, at least several kinds of personnel can help to assure success by contributing to ingression and orientation of CVOE students.

For example, in most LEA's there will be several types of CVOE programs and many types of students. Some CVOE programs will be mandatory for students in certain programs, and some will be elective. Programs may also vary in duration from a few weeks to several years. Because of such variances, an intrastaff informational program must be maintained. Various LEA personnel must be cognizant of purposes and operational characteristics of the several CVOE programs, the better to contribute to students' decisions. For example, classroom/laboratory teachers in programs which lead to CVOE should familiarize students with CVOE purposes and procedures. (See Chapter 16 re Internal Public Relations.)

An LEA's student personnel or guidance unit should be central to the student/program matching process. Personnel in the student services department should be well qualified in career counseling and testing, cognizant of employment trends, and knowledgeable about students enrolled in the LEA. Especially in LEA's wherein registration and scheduling functions are centered in the student services unit, CVOE personnel must make every effort to assure that counselors and others are knowledgeable about and have empathy for the several kinds of ongoing and planned programs. Counselors are strategically situated to influence student/program match. For example, they are usually responsible for collection and maintenance of student records which are essential to matters discussed earlier in this chapter.

Many benefits accrue from involving faculty in the CVOE program ingression process. It is well to assure faculty input. One way to assure involvement is to require prospective CVOE students to obtain three or four written recommendations from teachers regarding suitability for a particular CVOE program. Teachers can offer judgments concerning characteristics such as ability to learn, capacity for work, judgment, initiative, appearance, leadership potential, response to supervision, and dependability. Such data could be used to complement information used to establish a student profile. But, its major use should be to guide students into CVOE programs which best serve individual career development needs. It should not be used to exclude students.

Because all personnel will not be supportive of CVOE, because new personnel will be joining an LEA, and because programs change, the internal public relations job is never done. Although CVOE personnel are ultimately responsible for the success of the student ingression process, they must collect and disseminate information continuously. All publics associated with the LEA should understand various CVOE programs. Information services are probably the most important aspect of the student ingression process. If an effective and multifaceted information system is developed, implemented, and maintained, many of the problems associated with the process of matching student needs and program purposes will be greatly eased. (See Chapter 16.)

## INTERVIEWING PROSPECTIVE STUDENT APPLICANTS

It is well to require applicants to CVOE programs to complete application forms similar in format to the one shown in Fig. 9-1. These forms should be available from vocational/occupational teachers, guidance and counseling staff, CVOE supervisor(s), and teacher-coordinators. It is relatively easy to design an application blank which may be utilized for all CVOE programs offered by an LEA. CVOE personnel should include items which ease locating applicants in attendance or not in attendance. Items which are readily available in students' records should not be incorporated. Information regarding current employment is useful in several ways.

Because much of the work of placing students occurs at training stations between terms, it is important that teacher-coordinators be able to contact applicants when the LEA is not in session. An application form should facilitate contact to arrange personal interviews with CVOE personnel and with potential employers.

### The Interview

In an initial interview, a teacher-coordinator and a student should exchange information and ideas. The teacher-coordinator should try to learn more about the prospective student and the student should attempt to learn more about the CVOE program(s). Some teacher-coordinators prefer to have the student fill out an extensive personal data sheet during the initial interview. Such sheets contain items relative to marital status, subjects required for program completion, educational and occupational plans, hobbies and special interests, reasons for leaving prior employment, and other matters deemed important by individual professionals. Personal data sheets may be used as interview guides. Together a data sheet and an interview can assure that relevant data are collected.

However, a less formalized process of information sharing is appro-

## Application Form for CVOE Program

Date _____

(stamp specific program name here)

Name _____Grade level_____

Street _____

City_____, State_____Zip code_____

Telephone Number _____

Occupational                                                    Social Security

Preference _____ Age_____Number_____

### Present Class Schedule

| Period | Class | Rm# | Period | Class | Rm# |
|--------|-------|-----|--------|-------|-----|
| 1 |  |  |  |  |  |
| 2 |  |  |  |  |  |
| 3 |  |  |  |  |  |

Are you working currently: Yes____ No____
If yes, Please indicate name of your place of employment.

Employer _____

Employer's

Address _____

Please return completed application to:

_____        _____
(Teacher-Coordinator)                                    (Room)

Fig. 9-1.  Sample application form for CVOE program.

priate in many situations. Because it is essential that both parties (coordinator and student) receive information, the teacher-coordinator should attempt to create a pleasant, relaxed situation which will foster a free flow of information—both ways. The interviewer/interviewee concept may inhibit the student's willingness to share important information, or to question the coordinator about the CVOE program(s). Attempts should be made to put the student at ease during the initial interview process. Some coordinators who use informal interviews maintain a list of items which should be covered sometime during the interview. The following are appropriate items.

1. Purpose of the CVOE program(s).
2. Special program policies and procedures.
3. Parental approval forms for younger students.

4. Discussion of student career plans.
5. Discussion of opportunities in and limitations of the chosen occupational cluster.
6. Social Security Cards and work permits.
7. Past work history.
8. Past and future educational experiences.

After the initial interview, the teacher-coordinator should start a file on the prospective student. This file may ultimately contain such items as:

1. completed application,
2. personal data sheet,
3. training agreement,
4. training plan,
5. wage and hour report,
6. job interview schedule,
7. scholastic records, and
8. work permit.

## ORIENTING PROSPECTIVE STUDENT APPLICATIONS

As was indicated earlier in this chapter, an employer makes the final decision relative to a student's admission to the CVOE program. Influence of CVOE personnel on this matter is extremely important. The success or failure of a student during an interview with an employer depends very much upon orientation provided by the coordinator. The process of preparing prospective CVOE students for initial contact at training stations is very critical to employment prospects.

In keeping with program policies, most coordinators attempt to place CVOE students at training stations prior to the beginning of regularly scheduled classes at the start of a term. (This target is sometimes advanced to a few days after classes begin.) Thus, most teacher-coordinators prepare students for job interviews before a term begins. All aspects, including the most elementary, of applying for a job should be thoroughly covered with prospective CVOE students. Students may be rejected for not approaching the interview properly. Common reasons for rejecting students are:

1. failure to complete a job application properly,
2. improper attire,
3. arriving for the interview late—or not at all,
4. bringing a companion to the interview,
5. being unable to communicate easily with the interviewer,
6. communicating too freely with the interiewer,

7. being ignorant of the employing enterprise, and
8. chewing gum or smoking.

Group and individual orientation sessions should be conducted prior to scheduling job interviews. The teacher-coordinator should orient all applicants to proper interview techniques. Students should learn (1) what should, and should not, be stressed during an interview, (2) how to present strengths and qualifications in positive ways, (3) how to respond to typical interview questions, (4) basic rules for filling out applications, (5) what to do at the end of the interview, and (6) how to follow up on an interview. Most students do not understand such matters.

When possible, more than one student should be interviewed for each prospective training station. (This will not be possible if only one student has applied for a particular occupation.) The practice is defensible from at least two standpoints. First, scheduling more than one student to be interviewed at a prospective training station is more in keeping with regular employment practices. Students will be involved in competitive hiring situations more like those in which the LEA is not involved. Second, scheduling more than one student diminishes the "student-which-you-sent-me" syndrome. Responsibility for selecting from among students gives employers opportunity to apply judgment re which students are best suited for respective training stations. Furthermore, it will be natural for employers to work a little harder to ensure successful experiences for students whom they have chosen as contrasted to students who were chosen for them.

Another activity appropriate to the orientation process is to prepare a schedule of classes (or program of studies) for each potential CVOE student. This activity should be completed in cooperation with whoever is responsible for scheduling and may be quite involved. To assure continuity of the student's educational experience no matter whether she/he is employed, two schedules should be developed. One should anticipate employment and the other should be a schedule of regular classes. If efforts to place a prospective student at a suitable training station are unsuccessful by a designated time, he/she should be directed to follow the regular schedule of classes. If a student is properly placed at a suitable training station, she/he should be directed to follow the CVOE schedule of classes and activities.

Some LEA's use the dual schedule procedure to ease orientation and placement of CVOE students after a term begins—say within the first two weeks of a new term. This procedure has advantages and disadvantages. It provides more time for the coordinator to place prospective CVOE students at suitable training stations. But, students should not be "shelved" while they are waiting to be interviewed for jobs. Rather, with the dual schedule procedure they should follow a schedule of regular classes. Then, coordinators can work during the first two weeks of a new term to place additional students. It is much less disruptive to withdraw from regular classes than to enroll students in regular classes long after they were begun. Faculty members are much more receptive to losing students than to enrolling them two weeks late.

### Summary

The process of enrolling students in CVOE programs has undergone significant changes. Emphasis has shifted from "selection" to "matching." Matching involves ascertaining the career-related needs, aspirations, interests, abilities, and capabilities of diverse student clientele. A simplified label for this nearly impossible task is *student career profiling*. When student career-profiles have been determined, decisions can be made re types of CVOE programs in which they should be placed. Student profile/CVOE program matching involves counselors, coordinators, other teachers, employers, parents, and (most importantly) the student. This process is much more difficult than the traditional CVOE student-selection process. With matching, emphasis shifts from *developing successful programs* to *developing successful students*. The process is in concert with the general shift in education from orientation to *teaching* to emphasis on *learning*.

### Activities

1. Develop a one-page paper on what should be included in an individual's career profile.
2. List ten behavior characteristics which significantly affect employment success. Defend each of the ten.
3. Develop a two-page paper on why low achievers should *not* participate in CVOE.
4. Develop a two-page typewritten paper on why low achievers should participate in CVOE.
5. Visit a local office of a state employment service, and determine what assistance it could give to CVOE student ingression.
6. List ten or more major objectives for CVOE programs.
7. Outline a 15-minute oral report on "CVOE Programs Should Serve Only Better and Best Students."
8. Develop a list of 10 or more items to cover during the initial coordinator/student interview.
9. Interview personnel of two CVOE programs regarding student-selection or ingression. Contrast processes used for the two programs.

10. Develop a plan for conducting a job interview orientation session for prospective CVOE students.
11. List 10 points which should be emphasized as prospective CVOE students are scheduled for job interviews.
12. Interview two employment directors to determine what they look for in prospective employees. Compare and contrast what they say in a short paper.

# Chapter 10

# Establishing Training Stations

The training station is a laboratory utilized to develop skills necessary to proficiency in an occupation or occupational cluster. Student-trainees make significant time commitments to learning under actual conditions in productive environments. Coakley (11), p. 22, defined the purpose of a training station:

> . . . only part of the student's education takes place in school. The experience on the job provides for the mental and emotional growth as well as the development of work habits and attitudes. For these reasons, the training station is a vital part in the education of student-trainees. It is important that the teacher-coordinator, student, employer, and parents understand that this is an educational program rather than a placement agency for students wanting part-time work. Placing the student on a job is one of the most important duties of a teacher-coordinator. The coordinator should make every effort to match the job for the student with his objective. To do this the coordinator must know both the student and the job.

Because the laboratory of cooperative education is the employment community, development of training stations is very essential to the conduct of cooperative vocational/occupational education (CVOE) programs. This chapter deals with considerations CVOE personnel should make in the establishment of training stations. Chapter 13 deals with continued development of established training stations.

CVOE professionals make two assumptions re training stations: (1) training stations should serve as educational vehicles rather than as devices for earning alone, and (2) experiences at training stations should contribute to the development of knowledge, skills, and attitudes which are essential to proficiency in an occupation or an occupational cluster directly related to individual student career objectives.

Some of the outcomes of reading this chapter are:

1. Understanding characteristics of desirable and undesirable training stations.

2. Understanding processes involved in contacting potential employers of CVOE students.
3. Understanding the importance of developing desirable training partnerships.
4. Ability to develop training agreements, plans, and memoranda.

### CHARACTERISTICS OF DESIRABLE TRAINING STATIONS

Training stations should provide appropriate career-oriented experiences for CVOE students. They should be developed by the local educational agency's (LEA's) official representative, i.e., a teacher-coordinator or a cooperative education supervisor. All too many CVOE students are permitted to or even made responsible for obtaining employment prior to being admitted to CVOE programs. Such practice significantly lightens the workload of CVOE personnel. But, it nearly always has more negative than positive effects. When CVOE personnel establish training stations, they are able to stress matters related to training, that is, they can foster positive attitudes toward training. The training function must be stressed from the time of initial contact. In most instances, employers hire people to maximize productivity. Without unduly sacrificing this principle over the short term and without any sacrifice over the long term, employers should hire CVOE students for the primary purpose of training. Establishing primacy of the training emphasis is a major concern. Put another way, teacher-coordinators establish *training stations;* they do not aquire *jobs* for CVOE students. The career development needs, as contrasted to financial needs, of individual students should be the major, guiding factor in the establishment of training stations.

#### Locating Training Stations

CVOE personnel should utilize a number of resources to identify potential places of employment. Surveys conducted during early planning stages are primary sources of information about employers. Properly done manpower surveys provide information re various types of establishments in the community. In addition to names and addresses of establishments, well-done surveys indicate the types of occupations in each establishment and present and projected needs. Followup surveys of graduates and early leavers and of their employers provide information. Furthermore, employers who consistently hire graduates are among the establishments which are most likely to provide training stations.

The commercial pages of telephone directories provide addresses and other information about establishments by categories. All or nearly all of the potential employers for many programs are listed in several categories. For narrowly defined programs—say for a licensure occupation—potential employers may be listed in one category, e.g., beauty shops.

The local office of the state employment service is a good source of information about employers who wish to hire people for specified jobs. One of the primary functions of the employment service is to assist people in acquiring jobs. Employment statistics, especially re specific manpower demand areas, can be very useful over the short term for establishing training stations; and manpower trend data, maintained by the employment service, can be very useful to long-term planning. Because positive working relationships with personnel of state employment offices can be beneficial to all parties, they are relatively easy to develop.

Various ones of a variety of associations can provide information about employment opportunities, and individual members of most of them can establish training stations and/or influence others in their places of employment to establish training stations. Chambers of commerce, economic development corporations, labor organizations, professional associations, specialized businessmen's associations, personnel directors' associations, office managers' associations, etc., can provide leads to job opportunities for CVOE students.

The help-wanted sections of the local newspapers should be read often by teacher-coordinators. Advertisements provide important leads to potential training stations. Regular review of help-wanted advertisements provides good clues to employment trends in some occupations in the community.

As was indicated in Chapter 8, advisory committee members who represent the constituents mentioned above should be primary and early contacts. One of the advisory committee functions which is best performed by community representatives is assisting coordinators with contacts which assure placement of student-learners.

### Training Station Criteria

Obviously, LEA's must attempt to form partnerships only with employers[1] who satisfy criteria which assure emphasis on training as defined above. The goal is to utilize training stations to provide opportunities for acquiring knowledge, skills, and attitudes which are congruent with student career objectives. Training stations consist of human and physical elements; that is, sponsors[2], equipment, and work places, and/or

---

[1] In the literature of cooperative education, "employer" means establishment which employs student-learners.

[2] "Sponsor" means a person in an establishment to whom a CVOE student(s) is responsible, i.e., supervisor.

customers, etc. Criteria for evaluating elements of potential training stations help CVOE personnel answer the following questions:

1. Will the potential employer be able and willing to provide adequate supervision?
2. Are equipment and facilities adequate from the standpoints of safety and other legal standards and from the standpoint of essential learnings?
3. Will the employer assure that sponsors rotate students through assignments according to plan to maximize learning?
4. Will the employer and sponsor(s) provide constructive evaluation of student progress?
5. Do the employer and sponsor(s) have integrity and the respect of their peers?

Programs have been terminated because coordinators have been too quick to form partnerships with employers who proved to be disreputable. Advisory committee and personal assessments of potential employers must be utilized to assure adherence to training station selection criteria.

The Tennessee handbook (73), p. 51, lists the following criteria for selecting suitable training stations:

1. Would the establishment provide a training station rather than a work station?
2. Is the employer sincerely interested in cooperative education *training*?
3. Do the employer and his employees have sincere interest in providing on-the-job laboratory experience for the trainees?
4. Are the objectives of the program understood and accepted by the employer?
5. Is the employer or sponsor able and willing to provide employment for the student during the *entire* school year?
6. Will standards supply a sufficient number of hours of profitable training?
7. Does the firm under consideration have equipment and the type of work adequate to provide good training?
8 Will the trainee be trained under desirable working conditions?
9. Are those to be assigned as sponsors enthusiastic about the program?
10. Will all of the trainee's on-the-job experiences be supervised by a competent person?
11. What is the reputation of the employer in the community?
12. Does the employer carefully select his employees?
13. Are wages comparable to wages paid for similar occupations in the community?
14. Does the employer or sponsor recognize the value of technical training in these occupations?

15. Is the firm conveniently located with respect to the student, the school, and the coordinator?

Because the quality of a CVOE program is in large part determined by the nature of the on-the-job experiences provided by the employer, CVOE personnel must adopt selection criteria prior to making initial contact with prospective employers. Another listing of such criteria follows:

1. Congruence of the position with student goals.
2. Safe working environment.
3. Broad rather than routine and repetitive experiences.
4. Adequate and enlightened supervision.
5. Location within easy commuting distance and time standards.
6. Wages and benefits equal to other beginners in the occupation.
7. Facilities and equipment which are safe, representative of those used in the occupation generally, and modern.
8. Sufficient number of working hours throughout the period of program.
9. Compliance with state and federal laws.
10. Integrity and respect of peers in similar establishments.

The importance of the on-the-job portion of CVOE experiences cannot be overemphasized. Application of learnings in real situations is the basic advantage of CVOE. Therefore, partnerships with employers must be established with great care and strengthened to assure maximum training benefit for student clientele.

## INITIATING TRAINING PARTNERSHIPS

Initial contact with potential employers should be for information sharing. The teacher-coordinator should explain the purpose and describe operational features of the CVOE program(s) to the employer and should learn as much as possible about work in the establishment. A good technique is to send a brochure to the potential employer prior to personal contact. Coordinators should learn as much as possible about the form and operation of an enterprise prior to meeting with people who are responsible for its personal functions. Products, services, recent developments, organization history, and projected activities are examples of what should be learned prior to an initial interview. Many coordinators maintain a card file of potential training stations. Cards are a ready reference for name of organization, types of jobs available, names of contacts, and records of CVOE participation. Cards may be categorized alphabetically by name of organization and according to types of jobs. Such cards are useful for reviewing facts immediately prior to contacting employers.

### Information Sharing

During contacts with employers, teacher-coordinators should share information with and learn things from employers. Primary attention should be given to developing empathy for the training function. As early as possible, the primary purpose(s) of the particular CVOE program should be explained. The issue of productivity arises during many interviews. Coordinators should stress the primacy of training over production, admit that student-learners may take some time to perform as well as experienced employees, and submit that student-learners "catch up" faster than do other new employees. That students in CVOE are expected to be productive and are helped to be so by supervisors *and* coordinators should be made clear. These and other features of CVOE can be underscored during explanations of the partnership of the employer and the LEA. What each of the partners must contribute to and benefits which are derived from CVOE as students develop competencies should be noted. (See Chapter 1.)

Potential employers of CVOE students will be most desirous of information regarding:

1. the relationship of the LEA's instructional emphasis to on-the-job experience,
2. the amount of time CVOE students are required to work,
3. the fact that wages must be commensurate with wages paid other workers of similar experience,
4. courses which are directly related to students' work,
5. coordinator visits to the job site,
6. employer responsibility for evaluation,
7. training agreements and plans,
8. special assistance from coordinators, and
9. students' career objectives and long-term benefits to relevant fields.

Some of the things which teacher-coordinators should assess during early contacts with establishments are:

1. willingness to participate in a CVOE program(s),
2. types of occupations in the establishment,
3. attitudes toward the training function,
4. working conditions in the establishment, and
5. satisfaction of criteria listed in the first section of this chapter.

### Approaches

The objective of an initial visit to an employer should influence approaches taken by the teacher-coordinator. If the coordinator is trying to place students who have applied to a CVOE program, the approach will be different from the one he would use to identify training stations for possible use in the future. Informing and selling are not identical processes, and coordinators do not stop short of selling. A coordinator is a salesperson. He/she attempts to convince employers that they will benefit from participation in a CVOE program(s). Prospective employers must be sold on student-learners, programs, the LEA, and CVOE personnel. If the coordinator is attempting to place students, his/her approach should be more student- than program-oriented. Information about the type of students who have applied should be emphasized and closure should entail scheduling an interview(s) for the CVOE student(s).

In all contacts with employers, CVOE personnel should remember loyalties. Personnel are official representatives of the LEA. The LEA is established to serve students. Thus personnel represent students, i.e., are student advocates. Care should be exercised to assure that needs of students are given primary consideration. Coordinators should not be motivated to help satisfy immediate manpower needs if learning is compromised and should not place students indiscriminately, i.e., each potential training station should be thoroughly evaluated and some should be rejected, even if time and number of students seem to suggest otherwise.

### Whom to Contact

Type, size, and operating procedures of establishments and kinds of occupations in which students are to be placed determine who should be contacted re potential training stations. First-line supervisors, personnel directors, top management, owners, and others are appropriate contacts in various establishments. Often, members of advisory committees can help teacher-coordinators to determine whom to contact. Many cooperative education authorities suggest that initial contacts be with top management. A carte blanche recommendation is not good. Establishment policies and practices vary a great deal. In some organizations all hiring and other personnel matters are managed by one office. In others, different kinds of personnel are hired by different officers. What is standard practice in a private enterprise may be different for similar kinds of employment in the public sector. Generally, initial contact should be with the individual or individuals who are responsible for hiring. But, especially when contacts are made tactfully and graciously, it may be best to contact an individual who will have empathy for CVOE and will influence others to support it. It is important to avoid contributing to differences in an establishment. For example, it may be necessary to make two or more contacts to avoid situations wherein top management or personnel people order supervisors to participate in CVOE, even though they may lack understandings which are necessary to voluntary participation and full contribution.

### Additional Considerations

Heeding the following suggestions helps to assure successful encounters:

1. Make an appointment with the "proper" representative of the prospective training establishment.
2. Find out as much as possible about the establishment prior to the appointment.
3. Outline points to be emphasized during the interview.
4. Be on time, proceed with good speed, and conclude the interview graciously.
5. Do not dominate the conversation.
6. Respond to objections pleasantly with informative rather than defensive arguments.
7. Be honest, sincere, and optimistic.
8. Show genuine interest in the needs and ideas of the employer.
9. Do not "oversell."

The Kansas manual (37), p. 9, lists the following considerations for initial contact with prospective employers:

1. Find out who top management is
   a. Through Advisory Committee, preferably
   b. Or, from secretary or receptionist of company
   c. Or, by telephone call

2. Make an appointment or call
   a. Through Advisory Committee member if possible
   b. By telephone if a very busy person
   c. Ask for best hours upon which to call personally

3. Explain the program
   a. If management does not understand it, tell a complete story
   b. Question for completeness of understanding, tactfully
   c. Quote experience of other business; name field and community if possible

4. Explain latest developments
   a. If trainees already placed with company
   b. Be brief but thorough

5. Mail selected information at    a. From statistics of program
    intervals, not "en masse"     b. From descriptive reports
                                   c. Try to relate to management's interests
                                      as discovered

Salient points of an interview should be recorded afterward. Names of other personnel who should be contacted, commitments of any kind, questions which must be answered later, and next steps should be written down so that memory need not be trusted. Such records make CVOE businessiike and help to provide continuity through personnel changes.

## DEVELOPING TRAINING MEMORANDA

Training agreements and training plans have been used as management tools by practitioners of CVOE for many years. Some states require that public LEA's file training agreements with the SEA for all CVOE students. All CVOE programs funded under the Vocational Education Amendments of 1968 (P.L. 90-579) Part G are required to have training agreements for all students. Training agreements and plans do much to assure the primacy of the training in CVOE. Training agreements should be developed for all students (or each employer) and training plans should be developed for each student in CVOE.

### Training Agreements

Training agreements delineate responsibilities of several parties, i.e., the student, the employer, and the LEA. The following types of information should be contained in the training agreement:

1. purpose of the CVOE program,
2. student career goals,
3. responsibilities of the student,
4. responsibilities of the employer,
5. responsibilities of the LEA,
6. schedule of wages,
7. length of training period and schedule of hours to be worked,
8. name and age of the student,
9. name of the employing agency,
10. name of the LEA, and
11. signatures of the principal parties—student, employer, and coordinator. (And parent where applicable.)

Sample Training Agreements 1 and 2 (Figs. 10-1 and 10-2) are illustrative of formats and statements which are recommended in the literature and by SEA's.

---

### Cooperative Education -
### Training Agreement

By this agreement the _____(training agency)_____will permit

_____(student)_____ to enter its establishment for

the purpose of securing training and knowledge in _____
(occupation)

All persons concerned jointly agree to the following conditions:

1. That the training will extend from _____ 19_____ to _____
   19_____ five days per week.
2. That the trainee and the training agency will have a probation period of
   _____ weeks. At the end of this period the trainee, training
   agency, or the coordinator may terminate this agreement.
3. The trainee will divide his time: in school _____.
   Laboratory period _____.
4. The trainee will be supervised by: in school _____.
   Laboratory period _____.
5. The school will make provision for the student to receive related and
   technical instruction in the above occupation.
6. The training during the laboratory period shall be progressive. It shall
   provide for the trainee's passing from one job to another in order that
   the trainee may become proficient in different phases of the
   occupation.
7. All complaints shall be made to and adjusted by the coordinator.
8. The coordinator shall have authority to transfer or withdraw the trainee
   at any time.
9. The trainee may work after 4:00 p.m. and/or on Saturdays as he may
   arrange with the training agency.
10. The student promises to abide by all implied and stated terms
    included in this memorandum. The student shall be bound during the
    laboratory period by the ordinary school regulations. The parent or
    guardian shall be responsible for the conduct of the student while in
    training.

SIGNED: _____

_____                    _____
(Employer)                              (Student)

_____                    _____
(Coordinator)                        (Parent or Guardian)

Fig. 10-1.   Sample Training Agreement 1.

**Training Agreement**

School _____City_____Date_____

The _____(training agency)_____ will permit _____(student)_____

to enter their establishment for the purpose of gaining knowledge and experience as (a) (an) _____(occupation)_____ _____(beginning wage)_____

The course of training is designed to operate for a_____month period with a minimum of fifteen hours per week. The training will be in accordance with the outline of training below, made and agreed upon by the employer and coordinator.

**Training Plan**
(FOR ALL OCCUPATIONS)

1. The school will make provision for the student to receive related instruction.
2. The status of the student while in training shall be that of student-learner.
3. The student while in training shall progress from job to job in order to gain experience in various operations.
4. The schedule of compensation shall be in accordance with existing local standards, labor laws, and policies.
5. The coordinator will assist with adjustment of any problems of the student.
6. The parent or guardian shall be responsible for the conduct of the student while in training.
7. The coordinator shall have authority to transfer or withdraw the student when he deems such action to be to the best interests of those concerned.
8. The student promises to abide by all implied and stated terms included in this training plan.
9. The student shall be subject to discharge at any time because of inefficiency or because of conditions within the industry or concern.
10. This training plan may be canceled at any time provided due notice is given to all parties concerned.

(FOR HAZARDOUS OCCUPATIONS ONLY)

A. The work of the student-learner in occupations declared hazardous shall be incidental to his training, shall be intermittent and for short periods of time, and shall be under the direct and close supervision of a qualified and experienced person.
B. Safety instruction shall be given by the school and correlated by the employer with on-the-job training.

_____
(Employer)                    (Title)              (Parent or guardian)

_____
(Coordinator)                               (Student)

Original to Training Agency, Duplicate to Parent, and Triplicate to Coordinator

Fig. 10-2.   Sample Training Agreement 2.

The United States Department of Health, Education, and Welfare (HEW) publication, *Zero In on Cooperative Vocational Education Training Agreements* (76), p. 1, lists four reasons why agreements are essential:

1. As a planning document, it serves as a vehicle for directing and evaluating learning experiences;
2. As an information document, it helps employers to appreciate their teaching role and to understand the purposes of cooperative vocational education;
3. As a permanent record, it is useful for subsequent placement services and followup studies;
4. As a career decision-making document, it builds student satisfaction in fulfilling a prevailing career interest.

Training agreements are indispensable management tools for assuring quality of cooperative experiences. They are among the more important features of high-quality CVOE programs. Teacher-coordinators should explain agreements and obtain signatures of all parties prior to placing students at training stations. Copies of the signed agreements should be maintained by the LEA, employers, and students. Training agreements are not legal documents. They may be terminated by any party upon due notice. Although agreements are not binding contracts, they do add formality and do foster understandings of the expectations of principal participants in CVOE programs.

### Training Plans

CVOE professionals and legislation require that on-the-job experiences of cooperative programs be (1) planned, (2) relevant to student's training objectives, (3) correlated with instruction provided by LEA's, and (4) adequately supervised. Training plans are management tools which insure that relevant sequences of on-the-job experiences are provided CVOE students. Via plans, teacher-coordinators correlate on-the-job experiences with related learnings in LEA's. Learning effectiveness is generally proportional to the degree of congruence between on-the-job experiences and instruction/ learning provided by LEA's. Training plans describe total CVOE experiences and show how major parts, i.e., related instruction and the on-the-job experiences, fit together in complete training experiences.

Training plans in common use range from a few simple statements relating to the type of work in which the student will be engaged, to comprehensive job analyses entailing several pages and much work. Most training plans describe the following elements:

1. A schedule of specific job tasks of an occupation,

2. Provisions for instruction in safety, and
3. Supporting classroom instructional components.

Plans should describe tasks which an individual must learn to perform in order to be proficient in an occupation or occupational cluster. They should provide:

1. Directions for students,
2. Guidelines for employers and supervisors who assign tasks to students,
3. Guidelines for employer evaluation of student progress, and
4. Guidelines for scheduling and presenting related experiences in an LEA.

Developing training plans is one of the major tasks of the teacher-coordinator role. Plans should be developed in consultation with employers, students, and members of advisory committees. Teacher-coordinators must provide initiative and assume responsibility for completing training plans. Development should begin with a clear definition of career objectives. It is often best to consult the *Dictionary of Occupational Titles (DOT)* to develop a concise job description. The *DOT* can also be used to make initial identification of functions which workers in an occupation must perform.

The major step in development of a training plan is task analysis. A task analysis is a listing of the tasks which must be performed by a practitioner of a certain occupation. Vocational/occupational educators have long since done job analyses and developed training plans for a great many occupations. It is well to use published analyses and training plans as guides for development of particular training plans.[3]

With assistance from training sponsors and other individuals knowledgeable of the occupation(s) to be analyzed, a teacher-coordinator should make a list of the general training areas of an occupation. For dental assistant, general training areas might be:

1. chairside assisting,
2. dental office management,
3. dental anatomy,
4. dental pathology,
5. sterilization,
6. anesthesia,

---

[3]Some sources of published analyses and/or training plans are
1. Division of Vocational Education State Department of Education, *Occupational Training Plans for Use in Cooperative Programs,* Columbus, Ohio.
2. Department of Industrial Education, The University of Missouri, Columbia, Missouri.
3. Division of Extension, Industrial Education Department, The University of Texas, Austin, Texas.
4. Ohio Trade and Industrial Education, Education Instructional Materials Laboratory, The Ohio State University, Columbus, Ohio.
5. Vocational and Industrial Education Department, University of Alabama, Alabama.
6. American Technical Society, 848 E. 58th Street, Chicago, Illinois.

  7. dental roentgenology,
  8. oral hygiene and pedodontia,
  9. diet and nutrition,
 10. orthodontia,
 11. pharmacology,
 12. emerging treatment,
 13. impression materials and models,
 14. base plates and bites, and
 15. inlays and crowns.

After broad areas of training have been listed, tasks which are performed in each area should be listed. The following tasks might be listed for training areas 1 and 2.

*Training Area 1* — Chairside Assisting

  1. Greet, seat, and prepare patient.
  2. Arrange instruments.
  3. Hold pumice and fill cup with water.
  4. Blow air on tooth.
  5. Hold suction near patient's mouth.

*Training Area 2* — Dental Office Management

  1. Maintain neat and clean office.
  2. Arrange appointments.
  3. Meet, greet, and seat patients.
  4. Answer telephone calls.
  5. Keep books.
  6. Etc., etc.

When one is preparing to teach a specific task to an employee, the process should be carried one step further. This step is often referred to as task-detailing. Task-detail lists provide tasks for instructional planning. Task-detailing consists of analyzing a particular task to outline step-by-step procedures which are performed in completing the task. The task-detailing process yields organized and logical plans for teaching skills. The process yields too much detail for training plans.

After the task-listing process has been completed, the teacher-coordinator should know what an individual has to learn in order to be proficient in an occupation. Then the teacher-coordinator should determine what an individual needs to *know* to be proficient in an occupation. The task list, consisting of the jobs an employee must be able to do, should be used to guide determination of what an employee has to *know*. The following illustrates how "do" and "know" should be correlated.

*Training Area 1* — Chairside Assisting

Tasks a dental assistant must be able
to *"do."*

1. Greet, seat, and prepare patients.
2. Arrange instruments.
3. Mold pumice and fill cup with water.
4. Blow air on tooth.
5. Hold suction near patient's mouth.

Related information a dental assistant must *"know"*
1. Human relations and communications.
2. Names and use of instruments.
3. Dental prophylaxis.
4. Cavity preparation.
5. Abrasive techniques.

When the teacher-coordinator has developed lists of tasks and related information, decisions can be made regarding training and instruction which the employer can provide and training and instruction which the LEA can provide.

Many formats may be utilized for training plan development. The sample training plan (Fig. 10-3) illustrates a format which has been used by a great many teacher-coordinators. A plan should not be developed without input from a training sponsor or supervisor and the respective student. But teacher-coordinators must realize that development of training plans involves major time commitments which training sponsors are not able to make. It is well for the teacher-coordinator to develop a candidate plan and then get additional input from a training sponsor(s). Such meetings provide opportunity to decide which learnings will be provided in the LEA and which will be provided on the job, how long the student should work in each training area, and what sequence of experiences will be best for the student. They also provide opportunities for stressing the salutary efforts of early successes on the job.

After a training plan has been refined and agreed upon by all parties concerned, i.e., the training sponsor, student, and teacher-coordinator, copies should be used regularly by each. The training plan should be the guide for or the key to the total training experience for an individual. It should be utilized to direct a student's on-the-job and LEA learning experiences. Furthermore, a training plan should guide assessments of progress toward training goals.

**Training Plan**

_____     _____
            (Occupation)                              (OE Code#)


Training Sponsor _____Telephone_____
Trainee _____Telephone_____
Job Description  _____
               _____
               _____
               _____

| Training Areas and Tasks | Time Required | Responsible OJT    LEA | Date Mastered | Initial | Related Information |
|---|---|---|---|---|---|
| I.  (Training Area)<br>A.<br>B. (Tasks)<br>C.<br>D.<br><br>II. (Training Area)<br>A.<br>B. (Tasks)<br>C.<br>D. | | | | | 1<br>2<br>3<br>4<br>5<br>6<br>7<br>8<br>9<br>10<br>11 |

Fig. 10-3.  Sample training plan.

**Training Memoranda**

Training memoranda consist of completed training agreements and training plans. That is, a training memorandum consists of (1) a training agreement which describes responsibilities of the three parties to the agreement and (2) a training plan which delineates learning experiences. To assure proper quality and quantity of experiences, a training memorandum should be developed for each CVOE student. However, many CVOE practitioners discover that development of comprehensive training plans involves more time than they can allot to this part of the teacher-coordinator role. The sample training memorandum (Fig. 10-4) is a combination training agreement and training plan. Whereas the authors advocate development of more comprehensive training plans, they also recognize that some teacher-coordinators work under serious time limitations. Some minimal attention to the primacy of the training function is better than no attention at all.

## Training Memorandum

_____PROGRAM

This training memorandum is for the purpose of (1) establishing the general conditions of the student-learner's employment and (2) indicating the on-the-job areas of experience in which the student-learner will be working. This memorandum is not to be considered as a legal document by either agency.

1. AGREEMENT: The employer, _____, agrees to
(Company Name)

employ _____who is enrolled in cooperative
(Student-Learner)

education at_____ for the purpose of receiving

training and experience in _____. The employ-
(Occupation)

ment period will begin on _____, and extend through
(Date)

_____, and will be for ____hours per week. There will be an
(Date)

orientation period ____days during which an employment termination or continuation decision will be made on the appropriateness of the job in meeting the student's occupational objective, and the student's ability to function adequately on the job. The beginning wage will be____per hour with future consideration of increases directly proportional to the increased productivity of the student.

a. The **EMPLOYER** agrees to:
   (1) Supervise the student trainee on-the-job;
   (2) Rotate the student through the various areas of the job in accordance with the jointly developed training plan;
   (3) Consult with the teacher-coordinator on student performance, evaluations, and any other areas of concerns which arise concerning the performance or conduct of the student-learner; and

Fig. 10-4. Sample training memorandum. (Cont'd on next page.)

(4) Adhere to all state and federal regulations relative to safety, wages, and laobr laws.

b. The COORDINATOR agrees to:
(1) Provide and/or coordinate instruction directly related to occupation;
(2) Visit the training station periodically to assess the progress and needs of the student-learner;
(3) Review training plan with student and employer to ascertain its adequacy and implementation;
(4) Assist the company in the training function; and
(5) Represent the LEA in all matters resulting from the employment of the student-learner.

c. The **STUDENT** agrees to:
(1) Be punctual and dependable in working the hours designated;
(2) Inform the employer if he has to miss work;
(3) Conform to all the rules and regulations of the training station;
(4) Exhibit a cooperative attitude, proper dress, and proper work habits; and
(5) Consult with the teacher-coordinator on any difficulties arising on the training station.

2. TRAINING PLAN: JOB TITLE: _____
   OE CODE:_____. Name and address of employing firm:
   _____

   Name of Supervisor_____

| Experience to be Provided | Approximate Work-time per Experience | Evaluation Of Experiences | Study Areas Provided by LEA |
|---|---|---|---|
| (attach other pages as needed) | | | |

**APPROVALS**

_____ _____  _____ _____
(Employer)        (Date)  (Student)          (Date)

_____ _____  _____ _____
(Coordinator)     (Date)  (Other)            (Date)

**Fig. 10-4.  Sample training memorandum.**

**Summary**

Development of training stations which provide opportunities to develop knowledges, skills, and attitudes necessary to success in chosen occupational clusters is one of the most important functions of CVOE personnel. To assure that on-the-job experiences are of high quality, considerable attention must be given to the selection of training stations. Selection and development of training stations must assure primacy of the training function in the total CVOE experience. It is important to enlist participation of employers who can and will provide learning experiences which are relevant to the career objectives of individual CVOE students.

On-the-job experiences are often said to be the arena in which products of formal learning are applied. In CVOE, on-the-job experiences not only provide for application but also provide formal learning experiences. Partnerships which are formed by the LEA and employers in the community must be nurtured for purposes of expanding and improving training opportunities for CVOE student clientele.

Maintenance of training emphases in CVOE experiences can be made easier by development and use of proper training agreements and training plans (training memoranda). Training memoranda delineate responsibilities over simple work experiences through careful sequencing and correlation of student experiences on the job and in the LEA. Planning, sequencing, and correlating depend upon development of comprehensive training plans in accord with training needs of individual students.

**Activities**

1. Make a list of the civic and social organizations which may provide assistance in establishing training stations.
2. Visit an establishment to ascertain
   a. types of occupations,
   b. projected manpower needs, and
   c. willingness or unwillingness to participate in CVOE.
3. Use a help-wanted section of a newspaper to identify ten or more occupations which might be served by CVOE programs.
4. Develop a list of ten or more criteria for selecting training stations. Organize the list in order of importance. Defend the order in two pages or less.
5. Develop a list of five or more characteristics of undesirable training stations.
6. Interview a personnel director to determine characteristics he/she seeks in various kinds of personnel.
7. Develop half-page or shorter descriptions for two occupations.

8. Develop a one-page training agreement which contains the essential elements described in this chapter.
9. Develop a schematic model of steps for developing a complete training memorandum.

Section **Four**

# Conduct and Operation of Cooperative Vocational/Occupational Education (CVOE) Programs

# Chapter 11

# Planning Instruction

Most successful cooperative vocational/occupational education (CVOE) programs require that student-trainees participate in related classes or seminars during the term(s) in which they are enrolled in the experiential portion of the program. Related classes meet from one to five hours per week, depending on type and level of program. Most secondary LEA's require that cooperative students participate in a related class which meets one period each day. Many post-secondary LEA's require that CVOE students enroll in a one-hour seminar during the term in which they are enrolled. Several factors influence form and function of related classes. For example, in strategic programs, LEA's provide significant amounts of occupationally related instruction; but in tactical programs instruction may be provided in completely different ways.

Because certain types of information are essential to job success in all manner of occupations and because some specialized information is necessary to success in nearly all occupations, teacher-coordinators must plan, develop, deliver, and evaluate related instruction and learnings. Teacher-coordinators must be especially careful to assure appropriate and relevant learnings in related classes or seminars.

Some of the outcomes of reading this chapter are:

1. Understanding the role and function of the teacher-coordinator in CVOE instructional planning.
2. Understanding major types of instruction topics provided via related classes.
3. Understanding procedures for instructional planning.
4. Appreciation of selected principles of learning, such as immediacy of application.

## DETERMINING WHAT TO TEACH

Instructional content of CVOE related classes should vary considerably from program to program. But several categories of instruction should be included on all related classes. The two types of content most often included are called (1) *General* related instruction and (2) specific related instruction. General related instruction includes topics which are important for all workers, and specific related instruction includes topics which make an individual more proficient in an occupation or occupational cluster.

Mason and Haines (41), p.191, identified three types of occupational competencies: (1) *general* occupational competencies, (2) *specific occupational* competencies, and (3) *specific job* competencies. General occupational competencies include topics such as employer-employee relations, job safety, grooming, and labor-management relations. Specific occupational competencies include skills which are needed by workers in an occupational cluster. For example, basic welding operations may be essential to workers in many metalworking occupations. Basic typing skills are essential to many kinds of office jobs. Specific job competencies include skills which are essential to proficiency in a particular job.

Meyer, Crawford, and Klaurens (43), p.214, classified vocational competencies needed by young workers into three distinct areas: "(1) technical competencies — skills and knowledges, (2) occupational adjustment competencies — those needed by all workers regardless of occupation; and (3) career development competencies — those relating to self-understanding and occupational awareness."

To progress toward career goals, CVOE students must be successful in several areas of learning. These entail not only occupationally related skills but also personal, social, and civic skills, which are necessary to rewarding participation in the larger society. Therefore, in this book, content of CVOE related classes is described in two broad categories: (1) *occupational related instruction* and (2) *general related instruction*.

Instruction in related classes should satisfy two conditions. First, it should be *individualized*. In many CVOE programs students work in several different occupations or jobs. In all programs, students are at different career, personal, and social development levels at a given time. Therefore, instruction should relate to needs of individual student-learners. Second, instruction should be *correlated with on-the-job experiences*. Learnings in related classes should be applicable to job tasks.

CVOE personnel should begin instructional planning by referring to training plans. (See Chapter 10.) A well-developed training plan contains a comprehensive occupational analysis. An analysis is a list of what a worker must know and do to perform satisfactorily. A well-developed training plan also delineates instructional responsibilities of the training sponsor and the LEA. Some types of learning can best be accomplished on the job and some are best accomplished in an organized classroom situation.

**Occupational Related Instruction**

Occupational related instruction topics for related classes are identified as a training sponsor and a coordinator develop a training plan. Some tactical CVOE programs do not require major involvement of the teacher-coordinator in development and delivery of instruction which is directly related to a particular occupation. But, most programs require that teacher-coordinators devote a major portion of their time to these tasks. Fortunately, for CVOE personnel (and students) there are a number of sources of good- and high-quality curriculum guides for various occupations. Demands on their time require that CVOE personnel acquire large amounts of curriculum materials from commercial publishers, corporations, universities, and other agencies of government. If they make good use of published materials, teacher-coordinators have to develop only very specialized materials. State curriculum materials centers are good places to begin searches for instructional materials for related classes. For example, the Illinois Division of Vocational and Technical Education publication *An Annotated Bibliography of Instructional Materials in Cooperative Occupational Education* (27) was developed to assist CVOE personnel in selecting materials. This publication describes over five hundred individual curriculum materials which are supplied by hundreds of publishers. Most occupational study guides for CVOE contain teachers' guides, programmed or individualized student learning booklets, reference books, tests, and answer keys. Some best known and most respected sources of CVOE instructional materials are in the Appendix.

Teacher-coordinators must plan learning experiences for individuals. Having begun instructional planning with an occupational or job analysis from a training plan, CVOE personnel should continue instructional planning by determining relevant abilities and accomplishments of the student. Together, these determinations guide decisions regarding such matters as what needs to be accomplished in the related class and how rapidly it can be accomplished.

**General Related Instruction**

Many essential instructional topics do not relate directly to student jobs. Such topics are referred to as *general related instruction*. Several state vocational education agencies, e.g., Arizona, Florida, Louisiana, Missouri, Michigan, North Carolina, Ohio, and universities, e.g., University of Texas and University of Minnesota, have developed general related study guides for CVOE. CVOE personnel should build libraries of such materials. General related instruction topics may be classified in the categories: (1) career related, (2) personal and social, and (3) consumer economics.

Some career related topics are:

1. Orientation to CVOE records and reports,
2. Applying for a job,
3. Preparing for an interview,
4. Employer and employee responsibilities and expectations,
5. Legal aspects of youth employment,
6. Labor/management relations,
7. Job safety,
8. Agencies affecting employment,
9. Working with others,
10. Career patterns — choosing and planning a career,
11. Learning on the job,
12. How to keep a job, and
13. Changing jobs.

Some personal and social topics are:

1. Human relations,
2. Communications,
3. Personal hygiene, grooming and appearance,
4. Personality development, and
5. Drug abuse.

Some consumer education topics are:

1. Banking,
2. Savings,
3. Investments,
4. Interest,
5. Checking accounts,
6. Money management,
7. Budgeting,
8. Income tax,
9. Insurance,
10. Installment buying, and
11. Social security.

Even though many general related topics, suggested by publisher curriculum guides and commonly treated in related courses, are treated in required courses at one or more levels, most teacher-coordinators include them on the principles of repetition and use. Because CVOE is for many students the first opportunity to be wage-earning, review of personal, social, and economic matters is entirely appropriate prior to and during the time when principles of good behavior are applied in the real world of work and personal affairs.

As has been indicated in earlier chapters, many CVOE programs are conducted for students who have identified learning disabilities. The content of related classes for such programs may vary significantly from that of more traditional programs. It is not uncommon to find programmed instruction/learning for basic skills (reading, math, etc.) development in related classes. Furthermore, in CVOE programs conducted to serve the educational/occupational needs of early school leavers, basic education courses are often contained in related classes so that participants may be helped in every possible way to pass General Education Development (GED) tests and receive high school diplomas. Teacher-coordinators must determine content for CVOE related classes on the basis of identified needs of individual students. Each student has unique educational needs. Satisfaction of these needs will increase short-term employability and career development options. Type, quality, and quantity of both general related and occupational related learnings should depend upon students served.

## ORGANIZING INSTRUCTION

When appropriate related-class content has been determined, the teacher-coordinator can turn to the task of organizing content for presentation. Obviously, several units regarding program characteristics are an appropriate beginning. Most coordinators devote the first several related-class sessions to an orientation to the CVOE program. Policies and regulations, student and employer expectations, and forms and reports should be treated in such sessions. Early meetings are also the time to use techniques which assure that students get acquainted with one another, to explain the values of membership in the student organization, and to begin to develop esprit de corps.

Organizing instruction involves sequencing of topics for related classes. It also involves closely related decisions regarding how much time to devote to each topic. Normally, teacher-coordinators intersperse a number of general related topics with occupational related instruction. It is common practice to present most general related topics via group instruction processes and most occupational related topics via individualized methods. The major consideration in organizing occupational related class topics is what the student needs for job success at a given time. This consideration cannot be carefully done unless the teacher-coordinator, training sponsor, and student are in accord on matters such as a training plan and their respective responsibilities. Much of the coordinator role consists (1) of tactful reminders to sponsor and student of training and learning responsibilities and (2) of fitting related class learnings to what is expected on the job. Immediacy of application at training stations should govern order of learning in related classes. Job knowledges and skills should be learned as they are needed. To satisfy this condition and because students' knowledge and skill development needs vary from training station to training station, occupational related learning should be facilitated by individualized methods insofar as possible.

Considerations for organizing general related topics are not so simple. Teacher-coordinators should attempt to sequence learnings in accord with student needs and interests. For example, such topics as income tax and social security should be introduced before students receive their first pay checks. Similarly, savings, investments, and interest should be treated early so that new wage earners may design individual investment plans and see actual results during the term.

A strategy which may be utilized for sequencing topics for related classes is diagrammed in Fig. 11-1. At the beginning of the term, a major portion of related class time is utilized for career-related topics, i.e., topics which are important to job success. As the term progresses (and hopefully as student-trainees progress), more related class time is devoted to their occupations. Put another way, as the term progresses, students move to individualized learning modes for occupational related knowledges and skills. It is well to present general related topics throughout the term. This practice combines group instruction for topics of common concern with individualized instruction for topics of individual concern. Thus, the learning environment is varied and motivating.

## Strategy for Sequencing Topics for Related Classes

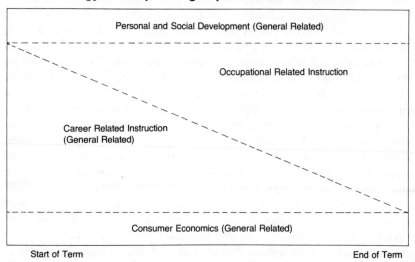

Fig. 11-1. Strategy for sequencing topics for related classes.

One sequencing strategy is not applicable to all types of CVOE. Some require only general related instruction. Some require only occupational related instruction. But, most programs incorporate some of each. Characteristics of student clientele and training plans should dictate what is taught, when it is taught, and how it is taught.

### CORRELATING RELATED CLASS AND ON-THE-JOB EXPERIENCES

The two conditions of related instruction stated early in this chapter were that it be (1) individualized, and (2) correlated with on-the-job experiences. Instruction provided in the LEA should be closely correlated with instruction provided at the training station. Because of work flow and other demands of training stations, a logical progression of learnings which might be appropriate in a laboratory class cannot be followed. Because changing conditions at training stations may necessitate deviation from sequences outlined in training plans, teacher-coordinators must continuously monitor training station and related class experiences, the better to match related-class experiences with those at training stations. Periodic visits to training stations are inadequate to this task.

One method for assessing the need to adjust in-school experiences is the weekly activity report (Fig. 11-2). Activity reports should be done carefully by individual students and collected each week by the teacher-coordinator. After students become acclimated to their use, activity reports show clearly whether learning activities at training stations and in related classes are correlated. An activity report provides information which is useful in three ways. First, as indicated, it can be used to determine appropriateness of learnings in a related class. Second, it can be used together with other information to plan coordination visits. When used together with reports of regular coordination visits, activity reports do much to assure satisfaction of conditions of the partnership, established for cooperative education students.

Quality of CVOE programs depends in large measure upon correlation of contributions of training stations and the LEA. Benefits are maximized when instructional contributions of the LEA are correlated with and supportive of learnings in the employment community.

### Summary

The related class is an important component of a CVOE program. Some knowledges and skills are best learned via classroom delivery. The types of instruction provided in related classes may be divided into two

## Weekly Activity Report

Student Name: _____ Date: From: _____ To: _____

| Day | On-The-Job Learning Activities | Related Class Learning Activities |
|---|---|---|
| Mon. | | |
| Tues. | | |
| Wed. | | |
| Thurs. | | |
| Fri. | | |
| Sat. | | |
| Sun. | | |

Student Remarks: (Please report any unusual or important developments below or on the back of form) _____

**Fig. 11-2. Sample weekly activity report.**

categories. One category includes competencies which are needed by all
productive members of society, and the other includes knowledges and
skills which are needed by individuals in a particular occupation or job.
The first category is *general related instruction* and the second is *occupational related instruction*. One type of related instruction is not more
important than the other. Both types of learnings are important to CVOE
students.

Related instruction should satisfy two conditions. (1) It should be developed to meet individual needs. (2) It should be closely correlated with instruction provided at the training station. Congruence of learning opportunities provided by the LEA and by participating employers determines, in large measure, the effectiveness of the CVOE program.

Instructional planning for related classes should begin with analyses of training plans developed for student-trainees and of student characteristics. Occupational related instruction should result from analyses of student personnel, social, employment, and consumer maturation. The principle of immediacy of application should govern sequencing of topics for related classes. Learning is enhanced when students relate immediate needs to classroom experiences.

### Activities

1. Develop a unit of instruction with objectives, learning activities, and evaluation components, for a career-related topic, a consumer economics topic, and a personal or social topic.
2. Develop a one-page argument that general related instruction should *not* be an integral part of CVOE.
3. Develop an outline of general related instruction topics which would be appropriate for the CVOE program with which you are or are likely to be most closely associated.
4. Prepare a topical outline for the first two weeks of related instruction for that program.
5. Develop a list of twenty or more competencies which you feel are needed for job success, regardless of occupational specialty.
6. Secure related-class curriculum guides for two occupations. List their strengths and weaknesses.
7. Visit a state curriculum materials laboratory. List available CVOE instructional resources.

# Chapter 12

# Executing Instruction

In Chapter 11 the factors which affect decisions re teaching and learning in cooperative vocational/occupational education (CVOE) related classes were dealt with. This chapter deals with methods, techniques, and facilities which are associated with high-quality instruction/learning programs. The chapter is focused on how teacher-coordinators may foster atmospheres which are conducive to learning.

The problems associated with instruction in CVOE are quite different from such problems in traditional subjects. The content of related classes affects, and is affected by, students' on-the job experiences. In traditional subjects, there is usually a rather definitive course outline for a term or several terms. In most local education agencies (LEA's), vocational instruction is delivered in traditional classrooms and laboratories for utilization some time in the future. That is, students are prepared for jobs they hope to hold after completion of the program. Contrastingly, CVOE entails immediate application. In CVOE, it is important that student-trainees learn knowledges, skills, and attitudes which are applicable to current job needs. This feature of cooperative education adds a special dimension to teaching/learning processes.

If all students worked at identical jobs and if all students had an identical capacity for learning, a teacher-coordinator's role in conducting a related class would be greatly simplified. But it is highly improbable that even two students will be at the same level of development on job-related learnings at any given time. In the main, CVOE must be individualized.

One of the more frequent criticisms of education is that, although it is given that individuals learn differently, LEA's make only token efforts to provide individualized content and to provide for a variety of learning modes.

This chapter cannot entail basic analysis of teaching/learning processes. Readers who have not previously studied learning theories, instructional planning, and teaching strategies and who are or will be responsible for planning, development, implementation, and evaluation of CVOE programs should study such matters—preferably via university courses. The purpose of this chapter is to present suggestions which may be used to establish conditions which maximize learnings of individual student/trainees.

Some of the outcomes of reading this chapter are:

1. Understanding purposes of related instruction.
2. Ability to plan a CVOE facility.
3. Understanding four-step teaching.
4. Understanding instructional methods which are appropriate to CVOE.
5. Understanding the purpose of evaluation of student progress.
6. Understanding the teacher-coordinator's role in teaching/learning.

## INSTRUCTIONAL RATIONALE

An ethos for instructional delivery in CVOE related classes is suggested by Glaser (18), p.5. "We must design the effective conditions under which individuals are provided with the opportunities and rewards to perform at their best and in their own way." In an article in *Educational Researcher*, Glaser identified and characterized selective and adaptive learning modes. The selective mode provides limited flexibility for meeting individual learning variations. The adaptive mode provides maximum flexibility for meeting unique learning needs of individuals. The selective educational delivery is concerned with separating grain from chaff. People who do not fit the traditional academic learning pattern are eliminated at certain checkpoints. Glaser's adaptive mode assumes that learning is influenced by environment. Put another way, various methods, techniques, and instructional practices, applied in accord with unique learning characteristics of individuals, will result in desired learning outcomes.

Some CVOE personnel utilize both selective and adaptive learning modes. Quite properly, adaptive learning patterns are nearly always fostered at training stations. But, all too often, selective learning patterns are employed in related classes. Teacher-coordinators should strive to develop competency-based instructional systems in related classes as well as at training stations. In well-coordinated CVOE, training station and much of related class learnings are adaptive, i.e., are suited to timely, individual needs.

The concept of competency-based instruction for CVOE related classes which is being developed here may be significantly different from that associated with traditional vocational education. In traditional vocational education, competency-based instruction begins with identification of competencies which an individual must possess to be proficient in a particular occupational specialty and proceeds with development of performance objectives, based on a list of competencies. Instructors determine which processes should be used to bring learners to previously defined performance standards. Through evaluation processes, the instructor can determine when each student achieves specified objectives. A great variety of instructional techniques can be utilized until desired learning outcomes occur. Casual observation suggests that this would be a rather simple and effective delivery system for CVOE related classes. However, adoption of traditional vocational education systems is complicated by at least three factors. First, all student-learners in a related class may not be preparing for the same occupation. This is the typical condition. Competencies required for proficiency in one occupation may be significantly different from those required in another. Second, one may be reasonably certain that individuals enrolled in CVOE programs will, at given moments, be at different levels of career, educational, psychomotor, and other aspects of development. Third, each student has unique learning modes. Each learns various things best by peculiar combinations of reading, listening, observing, and doing.

Obviously, teacher-coordinators can deal with such variables only by employing many methods and techniques. One of these, but not a panacea, is individualized instruction. Individualized instruction strategies have great utility in CVOE. However, individualized instruction may be ineffective for many students. For example, for some, individualized instruction may be too lonely and lead to inactivity rather than effective learning. Many individuals learn more effectively through personal interaction with human beings. The effects of peer and instructor interaction upon learning processes have been assessed scientifically. Peers and instructors can have synergistic effects upon learning. That is, interaction among students and between students and teachers has significant bearing upon learning outcomes. Involving students in learning processes increases knowledge and skill development. Put another way, the affective domain affects all learning of concern to vocational/ occupational education.

Various methods and techniques must be employed in related classes. All major methods and techniques ranging from programmed instruction to "group gropes" are employed by conscientious teacher-coordinators. Major instructional methods and some techniques which have special significance in CVOE are introduced later in this chapter. Teacher-coordinators should select from among these and other techniques in accord with criteria such as:

1. Student learning objectives.

2. Student characteristics and attitudes, especially those related to learning modes.
3. Institutional milieu, expectations, and climate.
4. Teacher familiarity and facility with methods and techniques.
5. Cost.
6. Time.
7. Physical facilities.

## THE RELATED CLASS

### Organization

Law (36), p. 33, identified two types of related classroom organization, i.e., unit and diversified. Under the unit type of related classroom organization, all student-learners work to achieve similar occupational objectives. Related classes for office occupations, nursing, distributive education, and many other CVOE programs in which all students need to develop similar job competencies may be organized according to the unit format. Diversified related classroom organization is utilized when students are preparing for several different occupations.

In the main, CVOE related classes are organized to facilitate learning of general related and occupational related information. Manipulative[1] occupational related competencies should be developed at training stations or in laboratories in the LEA. In certain instances, the teacher-coordinator may need to arrange for provision of facilities and/or equipment with which students may develop specific manipulative competencies. However, the teacher-coordinator should make every possible effort to utilize laboratories in the LEA and training stations before attempting to acquire expensive equipment for the related class.

### Facilities

A particular CVOE program may utilize a related class facility for a limited number of hours each week. Utilization depends upon type and level of program and varies from one to ten (and, in rare instances, more) class periods per week. The facility described in Fig. 12-1 is a minimum, recommended learning center for all types of CVOE programs. Several related classes in various CVOE programs may use the facility, and other groups and individuals may use the study area by special arrangement. Related classes may be scheduled throughout the school day. If several classes use the facility, cabinets and storage space must be provided accordingly.

---

[1]Manipulation may be mental and/or manual.

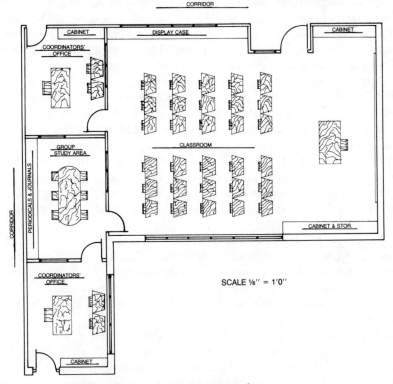

**Fig. 12-1.    Suggested CVOE related subjects classroom layout.**

Even though some CVOE programs have traditionally used simulated displays, special equipment, or peculiar paraphernalia, a facility like the one shown in the illustration can satisfy nearly all needs. Many related class learning activities which involve specialized equipment would better be left to the downtown teaching team. When an LEA uses specialized job-related equipment in related classes, it assumes that job competencies cannot be learned well on the job. The last three or four thousand years of human development seem to dispel the myth. Granted, some training stations do not have adequate facilities for learning all aspects of an occupation. In such cases, the teacher-coordinator should arrange for special experiences at other training stations or in the related class, according to student needs as contrasted to teacher whims or fancies.

Several "ity" words are important to the design of all learning laboratories and especially important to the design of CVOE facilities. *Flexibility, adaptability, versatility* are paramount to development of environments which are conducive to desired learnings. Provision must be made for large-group, small-group, and individual learning situations. This is best done with trapezoid tables, which may be easily maneuvered into various configurations. The long side of a trapezoid table accommodates two student-learners comfortably. The short side of a trapezoid table accommodates one student and necessary learning materials.

Cabinets in a related classroom should have bins or cubbyholes for each student's study materials, projects, etc. Reference books, study guides, instructional materials, audiovisual equipment, etc. should be kept in cabinets. It is well to use open shelves and inclined surfaces for reference books and materials in current use and locked storage for materials not in current use. A rack for trade and professional journals and other periodicals is a definite asset. Some CVOE students are required to subscribe to professional or trade journals. These and selected periodicals received by CVOE personnel and the LEA should be displayed and used in the related classroom.

An area for private group work and office space adequate to accommodate all CVOE personnel should be adjacent to the classroom. Telephones and secretarial services are necessary to the functioning and effectiveness of CVOE programs. Coordinator's offices should be adjacent to the related class with access doors to the related classroom and to the corridor.

CVOE facilities should be close to a building entrance. This location eases access for students, resource persons, and coordinators who come and go at various times throughout the day. Some coordinators advocate locating CVOE facilities close to guidance or student service offices and some advocate locating them close to occupational education facilities. Proximity to both is desirable. Local circumstances may suggest other locations and there will nearly always be compromises.

Equipment for the related class should satisfy local needs. The following are suggested minimums:

1. Trapezoid tables
2. Student chairs
3. Conference table
4. Instructor desks and chairs
5. Storage cabinets
6. Bookcases
7. Magazine racks
8. Secretarial desks and chairs
9. Typewriter
10. Audiovisual equipment
11. Telephone
12. Bulletin and chalkboards

13. Office visitor chairs
14. Filing cabinets
15. Display cases

Materials, office supplies, and postage should be adequate for duplicating instructional materials, record keeping, corresponding with advisors and employers, etc.

To enhance learning, CVOE facilities should be well designed and well appointed. Since CVOE personnel must perform in the varied roles of teacher, coordinator, and administrator, adequacy of offices and other facilities have a marked effect on the success of cooperative programs. Since the related class is the pivotal point of the cooperative experience, i.e., since related-class experiences integrate all school and work activities for individual students, the related classroom and auxiliary areas must be functional in every respect.

## Scheduling

Problems associated with scheduling related classes and on-the-job training vary from LEA to LEA and from program to program. Nearly all secondary and some post-secondary LEA's require that student-learners attend a related class for one hour each school day. In the typical pattern, students are scheduled for on-the-job learning experiences during the morning or afternoon and classes in the LEA when they are not working. In some programs, some students are scheduled for morning work/afternoon classes (Fig. 12-2) and some are scheduled for afternoon work/morning classes (Fig. 12-3).

Scheduling work in both mornings and afternoons has the advantage of increasing the number of training stations. It also satisfies establishments which require early morning or late afternoon part-time help. Teacher-coordinators should make efforts to assure that two CVOE students are not employed to displace a full-time employee. Placing one student in a position in the morning and another in the afternoon can make for bad public relations, especially if a union representative determines that a regular employee is thereby denied a job.

Many scheduling patterns are used in CVOE. Program level, program type, geography, and other factors determine what arrangement will be most conducive to learning efficiency. Some of the more common patterns are:

1. Students on the job in the morning and in classes in the afternoon. (See Fig. 12-2.)
2. Students in class in the morning and on the job in the afternoon. (See Fig. 12-3.)

## Schedule for Morning Work/Afternoon Classes

| Time | Subject |
|------|---------|
| 8:05—9:00 | on-the-job |
| 9:05—10:00 | on-the-job |
| 10:05—11:00 | on-the-job |
| 11:05—12:00 | on-the-job |
| 12:05—1:00 | CVOE Related Class |
| 1:05 —2:00 | History |
| 2:05—3:00 | English |
| 3:05—4:00 | Physical Education |

Fig. 12-2.   Sample morning work/afternoon classes schedule.

## Schedule for Afternoon Work/Morning Classes

| Time | Subject |
|------|---------|
| 8:05—9:00 | Physical Education |
| 9:05—10:00 | English |
| 10:05—11:00 | History |
| 11:05—12:00 | CVOE Related Class |
| 12:05—1:00 | on-the-job |
| 1:05—2:00 | on-the-job |
| 2:05—3:00 | on-the-job |
| 3:05—4:00 | on-the-job |

Fig. 12-3.   Sample afternoon work/morning classes schedule.

3. Students in class for one term and on the job for one term.
4. Some students on the job in the morning and some on the job in the afternoon.
5. Some students in school and some on the job on alternate days.
6. Some students on the job for two or three weeks and alternating with a like group of students.
7. Students on the job during summer months and/or other vacation periods.

Each scheduling pattern has advantages and disadvantages. For example, agricultural employment may be more readily available during spring, summer, and fall. Many distributive education training stations may be available only during late afternoon and early evening.

Many CVOE practitioners submit that students should spend a minimum number of hours on the job. Minimums range from fifteen to twenty-five hours per week. Such minimums have applied primarily to high school programs which require that students attend classes in the LEA for one half-day. Many LEA's also require that a major portion of time on the job be outside the normal school day. State guidelines and policies rescheduling of on-the-job training vary a great deal. Teacher-coordinators are advised to study state guidelines and local constraints prior to establishing a scheduling pattern(s).

It is widely maintained that student-trainees need to avail themselves of services provided by effective teacher-coordinators and other profession-als, such as counselors. Students need to identify with an official rep-resentative of the LEA, especially when problems arise on the job. The related class (along with club coordination activities) is the major vehicle for maintaining professional relationships with students. Nevertheless, some LEA's do not require a related class and provide little coordination. Such practices are not based on sound educational principles. Students, employers, and LEA's stand to lose from casual arrangements. CVOE is not work release. It is a highly effective educational plan for preparing students for the world of work—if conducted according to proven princi-ples

## FOUR-STEP TEACHING

Four-step teaching is a very simple and very accurate analysis of the teaching act. It is a very tried and very true analysis of all good teaching. It is a model of teaching for kindergarten, university, or CVOE. This section deals with a model for all kinds of teaching, using the demonstration method for purposes of illustration.[2]

The four steps of the teaching process are: *Preparation, Presentation, Application,* and *Testing.* This four-step outline of the teaching process was originated in Germany by the psychologist Herbart in the early 1800's. He used a five-step analysis, but in the 1860's this was shortened to four steps by a group of leaders in American teacher education.

Over the years, the idea that teaching is essentially Preparation, Presen-tation, Application, and Testing has been alternately praised and buried. The United States Army and a majority of schools of all kinds in the United Kingdom have not departed significantly from the kind of instruc-tion which is based on this analysis. Today, many prominent, young educational psychologists are again emphasizing the validity of this de-scription of the teaching act. Although it has suffered some severe criticisms, this four-step analysis is once again accepted in wide circles. It may appear as five or even six steps, and the steps may have different names, but the words don't change the music.

---

[2]Much of the material in this section is appropriate for teaching four-step teaching to training sponsors, who use the demonstration method more than any other in teaching student-learners.

**Preparation**

Preparation is, of course, the most important step in the teaching process. This step determines what will happen in all others. How well a teacher-coordinator does with this step determines in large measure how well learners will respond in succeeding steps.

There are two rather distinct elements in the preparation step. The preparation step is really a double-barreled step. Both barrels are important. The instructor must be sure to:

(1) prepare the lesson and

(2) prepare the learner(s) to receive what he/she plans to present.

For demonstrations the instructor knows well, preparing the lesson will not be very time consuming. Much of the time, planning will not be done on paper. The instructor should, however, have well in mind how he is going to (1) prepare the learner to receive skill instruction, (2) present the new skills, (3) permit the learner to apply what he has learned, and (4) test performance to decide whether production standards and other factors such as safety suggest more instruction.

It is well for people who have done little instruction or who have been dissatisfied with student performance to make some formal lesson plans. Demonstrations a teacher-coordinator must give repeatedly or ones which are most difficult to give should be planned on paper. It is also well to plan lessons on paper if other teacher-coordinators or students can use the plans to present the same lessons.

Lesson planning of the type good teacher-coordinators practice includes the following steps:

1. *Formulate Measurable Objectives*. Objectives should be referred to frequently as lesson planning continues. Objectives should be stated in terms of the behavior the learner should display after instruction. Doing this helps the instructor prepare appropriate presentations. Objectives are the guideposts for what follows in good teaching.

2. *Motivation*. The teacher-coordinator should consider ways of arousing desire to learn and should choose an approach, that is, should decide what to say to the student to motivate him—*more on this later*.

3. *List Instructional Materials*. The teacher-coordinator should prepare a list of all tools, equipment, written materials, teaching aids if any— everything he needs. This list will help him to assemble the proper materials before the lesson begins. Unless these are neatly assembled before instruction begins, the teacher-coordinator may have to interrupt the presentation to obtain a tool or some other item. Many lessons fail because of interruptions. People who receive instruction

need every advantage in learning. Interruptions to presentations also cost time.

4. *List Teaching Points*. If the demonstration involves teaching a procedure, such as assembling, teaching points will be the manipulative steps involved. These are the major points to be demonstrated. The person learning a new skill—whether it be manual or mental—needs steps in greater detail than does the person who is very familiar with the operation. Therefore, teacher-coordinators should incorporate more steps in lessons than accomplished workers think they use to perform the task. The student needs more detail than the experienced person is aware he uses.

5. *Determine Teaching Methods*. Teaching methods should vary a great deal. Teacher-coordinators seldom use lecture. Primarily, they use discussion and live demonstrations and methods described in the next section.

6. *Plan Application*. Decide what study or work to assign to the student to provide opportunity to apply what he/she has learned. In fifth grade arithmetic, this involves sample problems. Select tasks similar to the ones being taught.

7. *List Tools and Aids Student Will Need*. These are in addition to the ones used in the demonstration. For many applications, students will use the same things the teacher-coordinator uses. But, the teacher-coordinator must plan to have sufficient quantities, etc.

8. *Outline Performance Tests*.

   A. Decide upon a standard of performance.
   B. Remember that it is most important to tell people what is expected of them. Acquiring new knowledges and skills is often easier than learning what one is expected to master.
   C. The standard of performance should be made known as early as possible in the lesson. Students should know the "tolerances" so they may come up to expectations. People are made to feel important if their performance is checked regularly.

9. *List Instruments, Tools, Gauges, etc. Needed for Testing*. There will be none of these for many presentations. Checks and procedures should be the same during presentations as they are in job situations.

10. *Rearrange Lesson Notes*. Before a lesson is actually given, notes should be organized into readily accessible form. This form should be used when the materials are gathered for the actual lesson. For example, items 3, 7, and 9 are a list of things needed to complete a lesson.

    The lesson plan should be referred to during the actual lesson to assure that salient points are covered. Space does not permit a description of lesson plan formats, but many forms are acceptable, and the best one for a given instructor is the one which works for him.

In capsule form, the above are the things one must do to prepare good lessons. They are the "A" part of the preparation step.

The "B" part of the preparation step has to do with motivating the learner. Good motivation depends upon the assumption that all people operate under the belief that they can get along in the world. Ask any bum if he knows what's going on in the world and how to live in it, and he will think the question is silly, because it is obvious to him that he knows the score. Any student will give the same response. Human beings feel adequate to the world they confront—or they have serious personality problems.

In vocational/occupational classroom and laboratory situations, students want to feel adequate in the sense that they will be able to do what the occupations they hope to enter will demand of them. Students should simply be made to understand that the task or content being presented is important to successful performance of duties in whatever occupations they hope to enter. They should be made aware of the fact that good people in those job classifications are able to do what is to be learned. Insofar as instruction is correlated with experiences at training stations, students will understand that adequacy is jeopardized until they learn new skills and knowledges.

Teacher-coordinators should not pussyfoot about motivation. Rather, they should point out that tasks and content they plan to teach are important to acceptable performance and to success in productive organizations. They should make clear that certain standards of performance are expected and that instruction will make it possible for them to attain those standards. How this idea is put to individual student groups should vary somewhat, but the idea should not.

### Presentation

For illustration, the following remarks are limited to the demonstration method of teaching. The bread and butter of on-the-job and much related classroom instruction is the live demonstration. The following suggestions for using the demonstration method have implications for using other methods and special techniques.

1. Make sure that all the materials needed are at hand.
2. Make sure that students can see and hear. Be inventive. Think about using various audiovisual techniques. Think about using closed-circuit TV. Sometimes a filmed or taped TV demonstration is better than a live

demonstration. Sometimes mirrors are helpful in instruction. Consider the large overhead mirror in chemistry or physics—the experiment is viewed from above by the seated student just as it is viewed from above the instructor. Remember that the more real your instruction can be, the better. For example, students should follow the same procedure in instruction that they will be expected to follow on the job. Remember also that instruction must be safe to the student, the equipment, and the product or client.

3. Do whatever possible to avoid distractions. Certain times may be better than others for instructional purposes. Remember that people learn better when they are physically at their best—after breakfast or a restful coffee break, but not after a hasty lunch or a long work period. Assure that others stay out of the area. Prevent office girls, out-of-town visitors, or others from strolling through the area. Try to foresee and avoid distractions and interruptions.

4. Begin demonstrations by carefully explaining purposes and connecting what you plan to teach with what students already know. Put another way, before you begin, you should "tell 'em what you're gonna tell 'em." Then continue to "tell 'em" and, finally, "tell 'em what you told 'em."

5. Go slowly—students take from two to ten times longer to do a job than is required by experienced persons. Speed can increase only if steps in a task are learned thoroughly and in proper sequence. All operations should be performed with a high degree of skill; then the student learns what is expected at each step.

6. Pause at intervals and ask questions to determine whether students understand and are following the demonstration. In programmed instruction the advantage of frequent checks on learning is maximized. You can get some of the same advantages if you ask people questions periodically during presentations.

7. At the end of the demonstration, run over key points. ("Tell 'em what you told 'em.") Use questions. Be sure to review. *Always recapitulate.*

### Application

Application provides the best opportunity for learning by doing. Practice of a new task should begin as soon as possible after instruction. (On an assembly line, application comes immediately after instruction.) Delays between instruction and application are bad. Some suggestions for overcoming delays are: (1) Let the learner do as much of the work while you are demonstrating as possible—that is, combine the presentation and application steps. (2) Have the learner do a dry run after you have demonstrated the procedure—or you may do the dry run and have the learner do the actual job. (3) Do the job an extra time the same day or the next day. (4) Assist the student the first several times the job comes up again to assure that he'll make no costly mistakes. Think about the way you would gradually withdraw from the learning situation if you were teaching a youngster to ride a bicycle. Use judgment to balance good teaching with time and other limitations. Be inventive and do everything possible to assure that students' first attempts are successful.

### Testing and Evaluation

Insofar as teacher-coordinators are responsible for student performance, they should check to see that students comprehend presentations. Teachers should be sure to check on students the first few times they attempt new tasks. Sometimes, inspection is a more appropriate word than testing. The important thing to remember is that people need to know whether or not they have lived up to expectations. Mistakes corrected the first time a student performs a new task or solves a new problem would be much harder to correct if he/she were permitted to practice them for several days or weeks. Eventually, of course, the student should come to the point where he/she can test results and is ready to advance to new learnings.

The purpose of testing student performance is to inform the learner whether he/she has done things properly or has to relearn some part of the task. The sooner the student knows whether he/she is meeting expectations, the sooner he/she can make changes in procedures and move on to other learning tasks. Evaluation is often viewed as a terminal activity— something the teacher does after an instructional unit has been presented. When testing or evaluation is mentioned, tests, examinations, and quizzes come to mind. To most educators, evaluation is a process for arranging people neatly under the so-called normal curve. Evaluation is a security blanket for assigning letter grades and demonstrating academic rigor. Natural laws of probability and chance which yield the normal curve (and others) have dominated testing and evaluation in education for the past several decades. Benjamin S. Bloom (6) pointed out the folly of basing assessment of learning on chance events. Normal distributions are certain to result when students are tested on learning which has little, immediate application. This is one of the inadequacies of formal education which CVOE attempts to alleviate.

Because it is job-related, instruction in CVOE purports to move each and every student to mastery of specified competencies. The success of instruction/learning may be measured against prestated objectives. Instruction is evaluated; students are not in the traditional sense. Granted, instruction is assessed via measures of student performance; but, the primary purpose of evaluation is to assure proper selection and use of content and instructional methods and techniques to foster desired learning outcomes.

Consider some of student outcomes of related class instruction/ learning:

1. Ability to work harmoniously with other individuals.
2. Facility to respond to supervision.
3. Desirable personal and leadership characteristics.
4. Ability to secure a job and progress in an occupation.
5. Ability to develop job knowledges, skills, and attitudes on one's own.

The sum of CVOE teaching/learning should develop productive, successful, and happy individuals, i.e., integrated personalities. Presentation, application, and testing should be continuous and circular. Decisions regarding appropriateness of objectives and teaching/learning/working should depend upon observed results.

CVOE teaching/learning is more compatible with the pass/fail or better the complete/incomplete reporting system than with the letter grade system. Application of things learned should lead to success in the world-of-work. If student-learners are not developing knowledges, skills, and attitudes necessary to employment success, the instructional system is failing. CVOE should be without student failure.

## INSTRUCTIONAL METHODS AND TECHNIQUES

Given adequate facilities and manageable schedules, execution of instruction depends in major measure upon judicious use of a variety of methods and techniques. As stated in the first section of this chapter, methods and techniques employed by the teacher-coordinator in the classroom should be selected according to criteria. The most important of such criteria are objectives of learning outcomes and characteristics of student clientele. It is difficult to ascertain appropriate learning outcomes for each member of a related class. The information categories which were identified in Chapter 11 may be used to make broad definitions of both content and presentation/learning processes. However, students should have input to decisions regarding specific content and methodology. Some competencies are needed by all members of society and many are needed only by individuals in particular occupations. These are general related and occupational related competencies.

Because each CVOE program is different insofar as it serves a special clientele, has locally derived objectives, and functions under local constraints and with local resources, this section can deal only in general ways with presentation methods which have been variously effective. CVOE personnel must choose from among these methods and a great many techniques those which are best suited to unique circumstances.

Four oft-stated, general objectives of related classes are:

1. To learn technically related information associated with a particular occupation.
2. To develop interpersonal skills necessary to job success and to civic responsibility and community membership.
3. To develop leadership abilities.
4. To further career development.

Because a teacher-coordinator cannot have extensive, current experience in all of the occupations or with all of the content and methods which should be utilized in a related class, to achieve those student objectives (and objectives at subsequent levels of detail) he/she must assume the role of facilitator (or manager) of the learning environment. The following methods are inclusive of most presentation modes used by successful teacher-coordinators.

### Individual Study

Individual study has long been used in CVOE to provide each student the opportunity to learn things which are directly related to his/her occupational specialty. Even in unit-type CVOE classes, i.e., where all students are working in the same occupation, very much of job-related instruction/learning should be individualized because training stations for the same occupation vary significantly in such matters as sequence and frequency of tasks. In well-executed related classes, things learned have immediate application on the job. For example, take the cases of two auto mechanics/students in a CVOE program. One training station may assign a student-learner to tuneups and the other may assign a student-learner to front-end alignments. The student doing tuneups should study information units such as automotive electrical systems and the student doing alignments should study information units such as suspension systems.

Even for students who have very similar job-related information needs, learning should be individualized because people learn at different rates. Individualization allows each student to progress at speeds appropriate to his/her capabilities. Chapter 11 provided a list of sources of individualized study guides and references for CVOE related classes. Published materials should be used insofar as they satisfy student needs. When published study guides are not appropriate, other avenues must be pursued. One approach is to work with an expert, usually a training sponsor, to establish a sequence of job-related information units. Another approach is to work with advisors and/or vocational/occupational teachers and/or other resource persons to identify materials which can be procured and adapted to students' needs.

Individualized study is not the only method for presenting job-related technical information. It should be one of the primary methods. It should be combined with several group-study methods. Groups consisting of students working in very similar occupations should share on-the-job and related-class learning experiences, meet with resource people, go on field trips, etc. For example, auto mechanics students might meet with a regional service representative to discuss maintenance procedures and repair problems. Small groups might also be organized according to technical information needs which cut across occupations, e.g., handling money, OSHA compliance, and supervision.

A word of caution is in order re the use of published and teacher-prepared individual study guides. Often, study guides require texts and reference books. This should be taken into consideration when budgets are prepared and when purchase requisitions are prepared for study guides and other materials. Many texts and reference books will have utility for several years, but many should he purchased each term or each year so that the criteria of relevance to students' occupations and currency are satisfied.

### Discussion and Conference Groups

Cooperative education students should discuss a great many related-information topics, student organization activities, and other matters of common concern. Groups of various sizes should deal with various kinds of information topics. Groups should define topics, research topics on the job and elsewhere, make various kinds of presentations, conduct various kinds of discussions, and synthesize results in various ways. Some of the kinds of discussion and conference groups which are appropriate for related class learnings are: panel discussions, round tables, sixty-six groups, advocate conferences, and buzz sessions. Group discussions pool knowledge and adjust language and illustration to group needs. Some advantages of discussions and conferences are: they can assure high individual participation; they foster critical analysis of and reflection on many alternatives; they involve teamwork and cooperative efforts, making for additive inputs; they increase morale. Some disadvantages of discussions and conferences are: group leaders lack skills necessary to maximize inputs; participants lack listening skills; participants lack reserve and dominate time and/or attempt to force ideas on others; and they can mean excessive time expenditure.

Recommendations for using discussion and conference groups in CVOE related classes are:

1. Assure that students have or can quickly acquire knowledge pertinent to topics.
2. Assure that information rather than ignorance is pooled.
3. Use groups smaller than eleven.
4. Define topics or problems very clearly.
5. List and consider solutions and justifications on their merits.
6. Assure that stereotyping, bandwagon techniques, power plays, and other tactics of authoritarian participants fail.
7. Use questions to encourage participation of reticent members.
8. Consider benefits of learning outcomes over time inputs.
9. Create a relaxed, cooperative, and helpful climate.
10. Establish unwritten ground rules which assure fair hearings of all ideas and friendly disagreement and evaluation of ideas.

### Role Playing and Simulation

CVOE related classes are probably the single most appropriate classes in LEA's for use of role playing. Role playing is a participation or experiential method, which is especially appropriate for human relations learnings re such matters as interviewing, telephoning, and responding to supervision. Some authors define role playing as a special kind of discussion. It is most frequently used in related classes to set the stage for discussions. Role playing does not solve problems or transmit large quantities of information. Rather, it helps the actors, i.e., those who dramatize an event, to understand the feelings of others. Some advantages of role playing are: it increases appreciation of various viewpoints, positions, responsibilities, concerns, or relationships; it increases empathy for the other fellow; it enhances participation in discussions; it illustrates human relationships via people as contrasted to mere words; it heightens interest and understanding on the part of observers; and it develops appreciation of one's potential for various roles. Some disadvantages of role playing are: teacher-coordinators and students are unfamiliar with its varied uses; many are not used to acting and seldom prepare for roles; some actors grandstand; and many issues cannot be depicted via this method.

Recommendations for using role playing in CVOE related classes are:

1. Brief students re the roles they are to play and techniques for playing them.
2. Provide observers with a list of things for which they should watch.

3. Use several small groups so that all observers may be able to discuss issues.
4. Role-play several events in a chain, such as the steps in a grievance procedure or the steps in being interviewed in a personnel department and by a supervisor in the work area.
5. Have actors trade roles to learn opposing viewpoints.
6. Use stop action. That is, have observers discuss a scene already presented and then proceed with another scene.
7. Use role playing to emphasize human relations principles and to illustrate good worker-worker and worker-client or worker-customer communications.

**Demonstration**

This method is used in three primary ways in related classes. (1) Teacher-coordinators should, if possible and necessary, arrange to teach principles of four-step teaching and how to give live demonstrations to sponsors. (See the previous section of this chapter.) (2) Teacher-coordinators use the demonstration method, especially with small groups to present technical-related information. (3) They teach the demonstration method to students who then demonstrate an operation or process from their occupation to the class. This technique uses the demonstration method to present occupational information, refine skills, and develop poise, confidence, and public speaking skills. Some advantages of demonstration are: it appeals to several or all of the senses; it shows what an expert can do and how he/she does it; it can be followed by supervised application and thus corrections and reinforcements; and it can foster clear understanding of the relationships of what, how, and why. Some disadvantages of demonstration are: it depends upon equipment and facilities very much like the world of work; it is largely limited to technical as contrasted to human relations skills or concept development and it tends to cause students to mirror teachers and sponsors.

Recommendations for using demonstrations in CVOE related instruction are:

1. See previous section on four-step teaching.
2. Have experts do demonstrations.
3. Have students do return demonstrations.
4. Always explain why.
5. Proceed slowly, repeat, and limit length of demonstration.
6. Supervise applications by students making corrections and reemphasizing procedures in an easy and patient manner.
7. Provide time for questions and elicit questions.

**Case Study**

Teacher-coordinators often deal with human relations and leadership characteristics via the case-study method. Most case studies involve (1) presentation of a critical incident via film written or oral narrative, tape, or role playing, (2) open discussion or prestructured discussion, and (3) some kind of group or individual decision on the case. Teacher-coordinators often use studies which can be presented in several typed paragraphs. Many include questions which foster discussion and ultimately under- standing of principles which cases are designed to illustrate. Some advan- tages of case study are: it is realistic, especially if real cases are used; cases can parallel work experiences; it forces participation; it expands and extends earlier viewpoints and specialties; it illustrates the need for judg- ment and the fact that there is seldom a single solution to problems concerning people. Some disadvantages of case study are: writing cases is difficult; major concepts require long case studies and short cases tend to oversimplify; if the teacher-coordinator does not know the case, it is likely that not all relevant facts will be known; students waste a lot of time on irrelevancies; students lack much of the experience necessary to solve complex human problems; good discussion of cases requires a master discussion leader.

Recommendations for using case study in CVOE related classes are:

1. Use cases from actual experiences of past students, changing names and places.
2. Use a variety of cases to demonstrate the benefits of punctuality, attendance, honesty, integrity, loyalty, and other characteristics of good employees.
3. Use some cases from actual experiences of enrolled students and have the student concerned answer questions before others prepare solutions.
4. Use groups of four to six.
5. Have several groups discuss the same case, air solutions later, have group leaders argue for their decisions, and have the total group vote on decisions.
6. Use videotape or other audiovisual techniques to present cases.
7. Draw conclusions from each case. These may be principles, guidelines, do's and don't's, etc.

**Lecture**

Teacher-coordinators are well advised to use the lecture method spar- ingly. In pure form, this method is formal, unilateral oral communication. Because the lecturer is in complete control, there is little active participation and little opportunity for students to guide presentations to meet their needs. This method is best used to present important information which is needed by an entire class. Properly prepared and presented lectures can be as effective as other instructional techniques. Disrespect for the lecture method has resulted from improper and too-frequent use. Lectures must be well planned and should be augmented via audiovisual and other techniques. Teacher-coordinators should show enthusiasm for topics presented and should combine lecture with other methods such that, at various points, students can be involved in the learning process. Good lecturers are continually cognizant of students. They watch for nonverbal cues and employ teaching techniques, such as questioning, which bring students into the presentation. Some advantages of lecture are: it brings expertise to bear on the learning situation; it saves time if ideas and concepts are well organized and illustrated; it demonstrates the interrelatedness of a set of ideas; it permits careful and detailed planning; and it can assure that only precise imformation or informed opinions are presented. Some disadvantages of lecture are: it is easier to abuse than are most other methods; it works well only if students are skilled listeners; it appeals to only two senses; it requires an extremely good presenter; it assumes that listeners will remain motivated and can wait to apply what is being learned; and it is usually too structured to serve wide ability and experience ranges.

Recommendations for using lecture in CVOE related classes are:

1. Use lecture very sparingly during the first few weeks of a term and sparingly thereafter.
2. Combine lecture with discussion, incident processes, and other methods and techniques—give only short lectures.
3. Use lecture to introduce new units and for summarizing what has been learned from lessons presented via other techniques.
4. Use assignments, described beforehand, to motivate students to listen for information they will use later to answer questions, participate in discussions, or pursue other tasks.
5. Always outline key points at the start and review key points at the end.
6. Change pace by using humor, human interest stories, visuals, or other techniques.

### Resource Persons

Chapter 8 dealt with identification of resource persons for various purposes. Resource persons are very important to related-class experiences. They may be utilized for presentations in occupational and general related units. For example, a banker or insurance agent or an accountant might present information re financial topics. A union officer or business agent might deal with the role of unions in the economy. An Internal Revenue Service representative might discuss exemptions, deductions, etc. Some advantages of resource persons are: they relate real-life experiences; they take away good impressions and thus aid public relations; and they fill information voids which teachers and printed materials cannot satisfy. Some disadvantages of resource persons are: many have difficulty relating to students; having one segment of the community represented obligates the LEA to invite other segments; and some people may be persuasive rather than factual.

Recommendations for using resource persons in CVOE related classes are:

1. Use the following criteria to select resource persons.
   a. Adequate experience in relevant employment.
   b. Concern for students and young workers.
   c. Stage presence and other characteristics which are necessary to good presentations.
   d. Ability to follow presentation plan.
2. Make requests according to the resource person's wishes. Some organizations prefer that such requests be presented to management in writing. Be guided by the individual and by experience with the respective enterprise.
3. Plan ahead. Many people have complicated calendars and can meet obligations if they are contacted several weeks in advance and are given alternate dates.
4. Be prepared to greet resource persons fifteen minutes or more before presentation time to orient them to the task, i.e., to the topic, to the students and their needs, and to the space.
5. Provide for questions and discussion.
6. Introduce resource persons with accurate information, which helps students understand qualifications and career pattern development principles.
7. Express appreciation orally and in writing as soon as possible, emphasizing positive reactions of students.
8. Have advisors, employers, and students make suggestions re resource persons for selected topics.

### Techniques

The literature of educational methodology is far from definitive regarding what is a method and what is a technique. Suffice it to say (1) that the foregoing methods, i.e., individualized study, discussion and conference groups, role playing and simulation, demonstration, case study, lecture, and resource persons, are the methods which teacher-coordinators use most and (2) that the following are some of the techniques which they find helpful to support CVOE instruction/learning.

1. *Team Teaching.* Teacher-coordinators should work in various ways with counselors and other teachers. Recruiting, dealing with individual learning problems, meeting with parents, making various public appearances, and other tasks are sometimes best done by several professionals. Furthermore, coordinators may work as teams to assure that expertise is brought to bear, e.g., one teaches units on finance and another teaches units on leadership. Teacher-coordinators should also team with vocational/occupational laboratory teachers at times.

2. *Brainstorming.* This technique should be used to record ideas generated by students. A brainstorming session should be brief and duly motivated. Students should know that no contributions will be rejected, that they are obligated to speak as ideas are formed, and that there is no penalty for straying from the question or problem which is being brainstormed. The matter to be brainstormed should be clearly depicted by words and/or pictures. Brainstorming can be followed by various kinds of discussions or individual analysis in writing.

3. *Debate.* This technique is useful for introducing controversial issues for discussion. Two students or two teams of students research and present opposing viewpoints and rebut them. Then the entire class or small groups discuss these and perhaps additional viewpoints.

4. *Field Trips.* Chapter 8 described procedures for using field trips to benefit from external resources. Teacher-coordinators should make rather frequent use of trips to employment and community service agencies. Furthermore, groups of potential students and other people from the community who wish to tour CVOE and related facilities should be welcomed and informed via oral, printed, and pictorial media.

5. *Other Techniques.* CVOE personnel can make good use of the full array of audiovisual techniques and special techniques such as contests, civic projects, and games. Because research has not shown superiority of one method or technique over another for a given teaching/learning situation and because it has been demonstrated that learners respond to attention and novelty, techniques should be as varied as possible. Teacher-coordinators should become skilled re production and use of audiovisual techniques. They should work with para professionals and use commercial materials; but, they should also take pictures, narrate tapes, and in other ways generate local materials.

## Summary

Instruction/learning in CVOE related classes can be very exciting because it relates to on-the-job experiences. Desired learning outcomes may be achieved if (1) classes are well organized and conducted in adequate facilities and (2) presentations are designed in keeping with principles of four-step teaching and made via changing combinations of methods and techniques which are suited to objectives and student needs. Testing and evaluation should provide students and CVOE personnel with indices of progress and suggestions for improvement. Related-class experiences should be additive for students, staff, and visitors. They can and are nearly always illustrative of the accentuate-the-positive principle.

### Activities

1. Define "adaptive" and "selective" instructional modes.
2. Develop a list of twenty topics which may be presented in CVOE related classes by resource persons. Indicate what kind of person should present each topic.
3. List equipment which would be needed in a CVOE facility which houses different CVOE programs. Assume that classes will not exceed thirty-two.
4. Write a one-page case study which deals with a student-learner's relationship to a training sponsor. To a peer at work. To a peer in class.

Chapter *13*

# The Training Station

The training station is the major vehicle for developing desirable skills and attitudes in students served by cooperative vocational/occupational education (CVOE). In Chapter 10, factors to be considered in establishing training stations were described. This chapter deals with continued development of established training stations. Because the training station is one of the essential elements in the CVOE method of delivery, teacher-coordinators must be familiar with practices which maximize on-the-job experiences of cooperative education, i.e., with matters which affect the quality of on-the-job training and instruction.

Some of the outcomes of reading this chapter are understanding of the:

1. Purposes and importance of visits to training stations.
2. Procedures for planning, scheduling, and conducting visits to training stations.
3. Importance of maintaining records of visits to training stations.
4. Procedures for selection, orientation, and development of training sponsors.
5. Appropriate methods of training sponsor evaluation of student progress.

## VISITING TRAINING STATIONS

Congruence of training objectives of the local educational agency (LEA) and the training station significantly affect the quality of learning experiences. Individuals who conduct CVOE programs are called coordinators because they *coordinate* LEA and job-related experiences for benefit of student-trainees.One of the primary tools for assuring proper match and mix, i.e., for coordinating, is the training station visit.

### Purposes of Visits to Training Stations

Visits to training stations should be made for specific purposes. Some purposes for visits are:

1. Correlate on-the-job and LEA training efforts.
2. Become familiar with duties and responsibilities assigned to the CVOE student.
3. Become better acquainted with the training sponsor.
4. Assess student progress.
5. Determine whether training emphasis is being maintained.
6. Determine training sponsor's assessment of student competencies.
7. Assess adherence to the training agreement and plan.
8. Evaluate the training station.
9. Resolve problems.
10. Improve working relationships between the LEA and the training sponsor.
11. Obtain related instructional materials.
12. Encourage job rotation.
13. Examine the working environment.
14. Discuss instructional materials utilized in the LEA.
15. Cement the training partnership.
16. Seek assistance with related instruction.
17. Discuss hours of work.
18. Review state and federal laws and regulations relating to employment.
19. Assist the training sponsor with the training function.
20. Observe student performance.

Coordinators are much better received and much more effective when they go to training stations with specific purposes.

### Principles for Visiting Training Stations

Several principles should guide training station visitation. First, CVOE personnel should strive to conduct visits at times which are convenient to training sponsors and, preferably, when student-learners are working. Obviously, such times may be other than when an LEA is in session.

Second, CVOE personnel should make appointments for the first few visits to a given training station and should strive to develop a relationship which will make appointments unnecessary. As contrasted to making appointments for all visits, this approach makes for more efficient allocation and utilization of coordination time. When a coordinator is visiting a number of training stations in turn, it is very diffcult to estimate arrival times for each visit. Thus, it is desirable to strive for an open-door policy relative to visiting the *training station*.

Third, training stations should be visited at least once a month. Most CVOE practitioners advocate and some states mandate this practice.

Because a sequence of visits is necessary to (1) developing effective working relationships with employing agencies, and (2) assuring primacy of the training function, monthly visits are essential for nearly all training stations. Conditions at some excellent training stations are such that they need not be visited even as infrequently as once a month. Some of the factors which should be considered in determining frequency of visitation are:

1. Level of CVOE program.
2. Type of CVOE program.
3. Adequacy of supervision provided by the training sponsor.
4. Age and other characteristics of students.
5. Type of occupation being learned.

Frequency of visits should, in the main, be resolved on an individual student basis rather than on a program basis.

Fourth, when decisions are made for each student, a schedule of visits should be developed. The sample visitation schedule helps to assure that each student is visited each month (Fig. 13-1). In addition to monthly schedules, teacher-coordinators should schedule daily coordination time. Benefits accrue from providing tentative daily schedules to the coordinator's superior prior to leaving the LEA. This practice not only makes it possible to contact coordinators, if need be, but also fosters understanding of functioning CVOE programs. To conserve time and energy, the coordinator should attempt to group visits according to location.

Fifth, visits should be planned. Because purposes of visits vary, it is important that coordinators take necessary materials and prepare in other ways for visits. It may be necessary to take evaluation forms for one student, special instructional materials for another, and other documents for other students and sponsors. Training plans and records of student progress should be used for planning what is to be accomplished during visits.

Sixth, upon arriving at the training station, the teacher-coordinator should promptly state the purpose(s) of the visit. A professional, businesslike manner can do much to help personnel at training stations establish positive training attitudes

Seventh, efforts should be made to foster the "downtown teacher" concept. This concept is more easily developed by coordinators who view training sponsors as essential members of the LEA's instructional staff—which they are.

Eighth, during the visit, the coordinator should minimize interference with the normal duties of the student. There will have to be some interruptions for planning and evaluation. But careful preparation and in-school counseling can do much to reduce them.

## Schedule of Training Station Visits

| Student<br>Name | JAN | FEB | MAR | APR | MAY | JUN | JUL | AUG | SEP | OCT | NOV | DEC |
|---|---|---|---|---|---|---|---|---|---|---|---|---|
| | | | | | | | | | | | | |
| | | | | | | | | | | | | |
| | | | | | | | | | | | | |
| | | | | | | | | | | | | |
| | | | | | | | | | | | | |
| | | | | | | | | | | | | |
| | | | | | | | | | | | | |
| | | | | | | | | | | | | |
| | | | | | | | | | | | | |
| | | | | | | | | | | | | |
| | | | | | | | | | | | | |
| | | | | | | | | | | | | |
| | | | | | | | | | | | | |
| | | | | | | | | | | | | |
| | | | | | | | | | | | | |
| | | | | | | | | | | | | |
| | | | | | | | | | | | | |
| | | | | | | | | | | | | |
| | | | | | | | | | | | | |
| | | | | | | | | | | | | |
| | | | | | | | | | | | | |
| | | | | | | | | | | | | |

**Fig. 13-1.  Sample form for schedule of training station visits.**

Ninth, teacher-coordinators should avoid incurring personal obligations. The primary goal of the coordinating function is to assure quality
training experiences. But, it is not difficult to incur personal obligations to

the employer. Frequently, employers offer preferential service, such as free dental service, free automotive repair, or reduced prices for goods. Because such arrangements can lead to conflicts of interest which endanger the professional posture of the CVOE program, they should be declined graciously.

Tenth, written records should be made of all coordination activities. The sample monthly report is an example of management forms which are useful for this purpose (Fig. 13-2).

## Monthly Report of Cooperative Coordinator's Activities

(Program)

Name of LEA_____Month_____19_____
Date

| Code | | Student Name and Occupation | Comments Describing Activities and Accomplishments |
|---|---|---|---|
| | | | |
| | | | |
| | | | |
| | | | |
| | | | |
| | | | |
| | | | |

Coordinator's Signature  _____

CODE:

| | | |
|---|---|---|
| 1. Coordination | 5. Public relations | 9. Labor-management |
| 2. Instructional materials | 6. Administrative conducts | 10. Home visitations |
| 3. Promotional | 7. Club activities | 11. Other |
| 4. Guidance | 8. Advisory | |

Fig. 13-2.  Sample monthly report form of cooperative coordinator's activities.

This form serves three important functions:

1. It accounts for coordination time. The coordinator is not restricted. He comes and goes at various times during the day; he is likely to be almost anywhere in the community at almost any time. The Monthly Report of Coordinator's Activities protects the coordinator from accusations made by other teachers and people in the community who do not understand reasons for his/her being at various places at different times.
2. The form serves as a log to which the coordinator can refer for planning, scheduling, and other tasks. It is impossible to recall specific results of each of the many coordination, promotional, and public relations meetings which the coordinator makes in even one week.
3. The form is an excellent vehicle for communicating with superiors. Copies of the form should be sent to selected people each month to assure that they are aware of development of the CVOE program.

It is important to make entries accurately. Date, person contacted, and what transpired must be correct. However, the coordinator should not fill out the report in the presence of the person contacted. Record keeping should be done after meetings. Entries on this form should not be restricted to activities performed outside the LEA. Anything which is important and takes a significant time should be recorded—see codes at the bottom of the form.

### Coordinator Conduct

Many state manuals for cooperative education contain "do's" and "don'ts" for visiting training stations. Following is a potpourri of such suggestions.

**DO**

1. Be alert. Observe practices and procedures without appearing to snoop.
2. Be friendly without appearing to fraternize.
3. Show active interest in the work being performed.
4. Maintain records of what transpired during the visit.
5. Be sensitive to nonverbal clues which signal that a training sponsor desires to terminate a conference.
6. Maintain a professional and businesslike manner.
7. Meet with the student-trainee at the training station.
8. Show appreciation for the training efforts of the sponsor.
9. Explain the purpose of the visit.
10. Refer frequently to the training plan.

**DON'T**

1. Call errors, bad practices, or unsafe conditions to the attention of the trainee—these should be discussed tactfully with the training sponsor.
2. Attempt to demonstrate a procedure for the student or pose as an expert or authority on the activity being performed at the training station.
3. Make excessive demands on the training sponsor's time.
4. Interrupt the student-trainee's assigned duties.
5. Waste the trainee's time on unimportant issues.

Visits to training stations are necessary to correlating training for the benefit of student clientele. The major purpose of visits is to develop and maintain good, working relationships among the LEA, the employer, and the student, the better to assure primacy of the training function.

## ASSISTING TRAINING SPONSORS

*Training sponsor* is a title for individuals who have responsibility for on-the-job training of CVOE students. Training sponsors are important members of the CVOE instructional team. They may be chosen from any level of cooperating enterprises. In small establishments, training sponsors may be owners or top-level managers. In large establishments, they may appropriately be chosen from the ranks of experienced employees. Teacher-coordinators should work with employers to select training sponsors who will have responsible attitudes toward CVOE and students.

### Characteristics

Training sponsors should have the following qualities:

1. Mastery of technical skills of the occupation(s) to be learned.
2. Behavior which can serve as a role model.
3. Ability to communicate with student, coordinator, and fellow workers.
4. Interest in and aptitude for working with young people.
5. Interest in the training process.

### The Training Function

It is not uncommon for an individual to be a master of his/her occupation and not be able to facilitate learning of that occupation by another. Many people are reluctant to be involved in the teaching/learning process.

Often, master workmen say, "I told him how to do it, and he just doesn't seem to be able to catch on." Coordinators must help training sponsors improve training efficiency. Knowingly or unknowingly all enterprises are at least minimally involved in training new employees and retraining (or upgrading) experienced employees. Teacher-coordinators help cooperating employers with the training function, the better to improve on-the-job learning experiences.

One technique for fostering positive training emphases is to schedule a meal function for training sponsors early in a term. It is sometimes well to have one function for new training sponsors and employers and one for training sponsors who have been cooperating with the CVOE program for a considerable time. During the function, presentations may be made to define the roles which must be assumed by the LEA and by employing agencies to assure desired training results. Some points which should be emphasized are:

1. Importance of training sponsors in the CVOE process.
2. Overall operation of the CVOE program.
3. Importance of on-the-job instruction.
4. Features of other programs offered by the LEA, which may be helpful to employers.
5. Importance of training plans.

An evening meal function is a good opportunity for a teacher-coordinator or a resource person to demonstrate the four-step teaching method. Understanding and use of preparation, presentation, application, and evaluation can improve training on the job. Many coordinators place students on the job, talk about training, and offer little positive assistance to training sponsors. Training of CVOE students may be significantly different from previous experiences of training sponsors. Coordinators should not portray "know-it-all" attitudes. But, they should work with training sponsors on common problems, e.g, how to present and assure mastery of various job tasks.

Primacy of the training function may be assured by reemphasizing values which can be derived from following a training plan at the beginning of each term. Training sponsors need to be reminded about training plans. So do LEA personnel. All too often, training plans are developed and made part of students' personal data files instead of being used as action plans for training. Some of the important contributions of training plans which teacher-coordinators should emphasize are:

1. They help to assure quality and comprehensiveness of training experiences.
2. They guide assignment and rotation of the CVOE student.

3. They provide bases for realistic evaluation of student progress.

4. They provide bases for systematic training.

A training plan should provide student, training sponsor, and teacher-coordinator clear understanding of things to be accomplished as the student progresses toward career goals.

Teacher-coordinators can assist training sponsors with the conduct of the CVOE program in many ways. Some of these are:

1. Informing sponsors of in-service training opportunities provided by the LEA.

2. Keeping sponsors informed of student progress in the LEA portion of the program.

3. Conducting in-service training sessions for sponsors.

4. Suggesting on-the-job experiences for students.

5. Assisting with student evaluation processes.

6. Seeking input for related classes.

7. Inviting sponsors to special functions presented by the LEA.

8. Explaining the importance of CVOE management forms.

9. Keeping paperwork to a minimum.

Because training sponsors perform many of the functions performed by LEA laboratory instructors, it is imperative that teacher-coordinators provide training sponsors assistance in developing training, evaluating, and counseling skills. Some important principles of the on-the-job instructional phase of CVOE are:

1. Training sponsors are responsible for on-the-job instruction.

2. Teacher-coordinators should assist training sponsors with the training function.

3. Continuous evaluation of student progress should be conducted by the training sponsor and by the teacher-coordinator.

4. Instruction should be directly related to student career objectives.

5. Records of student progress should be maintained.

### ASSESSING STUDENT PROGRESS ON THE JOB

Evaluation of CVOE student progress should be systematic and continuous. Because training sponsors share responsibility for helping students develop mental, manipulative, and interpersonal skills necessary to job success, they should also share responsibility for on-the-job evaluation. Evaluation should determine whether performance objectives have been met and whether proper performance objectives have been formulated. Instructional resources should be directed to achievement of job-related performance objectives. And performance should be assessed regularly.

Criteria by which students are evaluated on the job may be significantly different from criteria utilized in the LEA. The authors are reminded of an episode which occurred in an associate degree automotive technology program and which illustrates this fact. Students enrolled in the program were required to participate in a CVOE experience near the end of the two-year program. The student who had earned the highest grade point average was placed in a large automotive dealership. Near midterm, the teacher-coordinator visited the training station to assess the student's progress. The first few statements made by the service manager seemed to support the coordinator's expectations. It was revealed that the student had passed a state-sponsored automotive competency examination and was the only employee who successfully completed all five parts of the test. But the training sponsor went on to say that he believed the student would never develop into a productive auto mechanic. Knowledge and skill are one thing. Success on the job is something more.

Performance-based evaluation depends upon at least three factors, i.e., the process to be learned, an acceptable standard of performance, and the time element. The automotive student in the previous example knew how to perform tasks required of an auto mechanic within acceptable standards of performance. But his speed did not improve through repetition. Productivity rates are important in the world of work. Students who do not develop acceptable rates will likely fail. Too many LEA's place disproportionate emphasis upon job content over job performance, i.e., upon *why* and *how* as contrasted to *do*.

Most LEA's do not evalute how students get along with fellow workers. Yet, human relations at work are very critical to job success. Those who have studied factors related to job failure report that the majority of people who are dismissed from jobs are dismissed because they are unable to "get along" with peers and/or supervisors. Related-class experiences and early evaluative sessions at training stations should make clear to student-learners how they may achieve rapport and productive relationships at work.

In most jobs the following are as important to employability as are job skills:

1. Initiative
2. Dependability
3. Appearance
4. Cooperativeness
5. Interest in work
6. Communication skills
7. Tact
8. Personal hygiene
9. Ability to follow directions
10. Ability to take criticism
11. Interpersonal relations

Periodic on-the-job evaluations by employers are made to discover student strengths and weaknesses. Employer's Student Worker Evaluation Form 1 (Fig. 13-3) serves this purpose. One advantage of this

## Employer's Student Worker Evaluation Form 1

_____ (Program) _____

| LEA | Location | Phone |

| Student | Training Agency | Phone |

RATING CODE: 1. Very Poor, 2. Poor, 3. Average, 4. Good, 5. Very Good.

| CHARACTERISTICS | GRADING PERIODS | | | | | |
|---|---|---|---|---|---|---|
| | FIRST | SECOND | THIRD | FOURTH | FIFTH | SIXTH |
| 1. QUALITY OF WORK: Compare with others of equal age and experience. | | | | | | |
| 2. QUANTITY OF WORK: Compare with others of equal age and experience. | | | | | | |
| 3. DEPENDABILITY: Able to follow instructions. | | | | | | |
| 4. INITIATIVE: Does things without being told. | | | | | | |
| 5. ATTITUDES TOWARD SUPERVISION: With regard to accepting criticism. | | | | | | |
| 6. SAFETY PRACTICES: How well does the student-learner observe safety rules? | | | | | | |
| 7. GENERAL ATTITUDE: Consider attitude toward job, superiors, & other employees. | | | | | | |
| 8. ATTENDANCE: Compare actual attendance with hours assigned. | | | | | | |
| 9. PUNCTUALITY: Consider times late. Do not consider reasons. | | | | | | |
| 10. APPEARANCE: Compare with standards set with other employees in the occupation. | | | | | | |

Evaluation Period 1___ Date_____ Signed _____
Evaluation Period 2___ Date_____ Signed _____
Evaluation Period 3___ Date_____ Signed _____
Evaluation Period 4___ Date_____ Signed _____
Evaluation Period 5___ Date_____ Signed _____
Evaluation Period 6___ Date_____ Signed _____

## (PLEASE MAKE COMMENTS ON BACK)

Fig. 13-3. Sample employer's student worker evaluation form (Form 1). (Cont'd on next page.)

## Employer's Student Worker Evaluation Form 1 (Con'td)

### COMMENTS

First Grading Period _____

_____

_____

_____

_____

Second Grading Period _____

_____

_____

_____

_____

Third Grading Period _____

_____

_____

_____

_____

Fourth Grading Period _____

_____

_____

_____

_____

Fifth Grading Period _____

_____

_____

_____

_____

Sixth Grading Period _____

_____

_____

_____

_____

Fig. 13-3. Sample employer's student worker evaluation form (Form 1).

form is that several evaluations may be made on a single sheet. Thus, it is easier to detect student growth on the ten factors over an extended period of time. Improvement or regression from one grading period to the next may be observed for each factor. However, this format tends to influence training sponsors to base current evaluations upon scores which they gave during previous evaluation periods.

Training sponsors should be encouraged to consult with students during evaluation and to point up strengths and weaknesses. Often, training sponsors fail to follow this procedure and teacher-coordinators counsel students regarding employer evaluations by default. Naturally, students do not always agree with training sponsor evaluations. In such instances, teacher-coordinators are placed in difficult positions. They have to justify evaluations with less than adequate information. Therefore, coordinators should encourage training sponsors to complete evaluations and go over results with students.

The type of evaluation instrument used for on-the-job evaluation of trainee performance should depend in large measure upon types of CVOE program, and desired student outcomes. Sample Employer's Student Worker Evaluation Forms 2 and 3 illustrate two other evaluation instruments which serve this purpose (Figs. 13-4 and 13-5).

Although many LEA's assign grades for the experiential portion of CVOE programs, the authors advocate the pass/fail marking system for on-the-job experience. In most institutions which are committed to the assignment of letter grades, it is relatively easy to obtain a variance for on-the-job experiences because letter grades present a potentially difficult situation. Because a CVOE program will likely be in partnership with several employers with students in different occupations, it is unreasonable to assume that grading policies will be consistent across establishments. Some sponsors may think that only the best students deserve a grade above "C." Others may think that all students are above average. For this and other reasons, teacher-coordinators should reserve final authority for awarding letter grades for on-the-job experiences — if letter grades must be given. Thus, it is mandatory that teacher-coordinators visit training stations frequently enough to become familiar with each student's performance.

Several techniques are utilized by teacher-coordinators to provide training sponsors with evaluation forms. Some coordinators mail instruments to employers several weeks before the end of an evaluation period. Some have students hand-carry the forms; and some deliver the instruments during regular coordination visits. The authors advocate the last procedure. This provides opportunity to instruct training sponsors

## Employer's Student Worker Evaluation Form 2

Name of Student_____ Date of Evaluation_____
Employer_____ Period of Evaluation_____ to_____
Directions:

  Please evaluate the CVOE student on the following factors by checking the appropriate blank following each of the 20 statements. Your evaluation should be based on a comparison of the student with workers of similar age and training.

| | HIGHEST 5 | 4 | 3 | 2 | LOWEST 1 |
|---|---|---|---|---|---|
| **PERSONAL QUALIFICATION** | | | | | |
| 1. How dependable and punctual is the student? | | | | | |
| 2. Does the student work well with others? | | | | | |
| 3. Is the student's appearance and dress suitable? | | | | | |
| 4. Is the student physically suited to the work? | | | | | |
| **CAPACITY** | | | | | |
| 5. Does the student learn rapidly when shown how to do a job? | | | | | |
| 6. Does the student display initiative and independent thinking? | | | | | |
| **ATTITUDE TOWARD JOB** | | | | | |
| 7. Is the student interested in the work? | | | | | |
| 8. Does the student perform work willingly? | | | | | |
| 9. Does the student accept responsibility? | | | | | |
| **JOB PERFORMANCE** | | | | | |
| 10. Is the student's knowledge of the work adequate at the present stage? | | | | | |
| 11. Is the student safety minded? | | | | | |
| 12. Is the student conscientious in the use of equipment? | | | | | |
| 13. Rate quality of work. | | | | | |
| 14. Rate accuracy of work. | | | | | |
| **TRAINING PLAN** | | | | | |
| 15. Do you periodically review the training plan yourself to determine the student's actual vs. planned exposure to various work experiences? | | | | | |
| 16. Is the student progressing through the various training plan at an acceptable rate? | | | | | |
| 17. Have you occasionally discussed the student's progress with the student? | | | | | |
| **EMPLOYER ATTITUDE** | | | | | |
| 18. Has participating in the Occupational Internship Program been a successful and profitable venture for you? | | | | | |
| 19. Would you participate in the program again? | | | | | |

20. Additional Comments:

21. _____     _____
      (Signature of Training Sponsor)                      (Date)

**Fig. 13-4. Sample employer's student worker evaluation form (Form 2).**

## Employer's Student Worker Evaluation Form 3

Note:   (To be completed by LEA)

SECTION I

Name _____
(Last)                          (First)                          (Initial)

Academic Major _____

Employing Firm: Name _____

Address _____

Date term started _____Will complete_____

Department _____Job title_____

Supervisor's name _____Title_____

Brief Job Description: _____

_____

Comments: _____

_____

Date turned in to Supervisor _____

SECTION II

| | Excellent | Superior | Average | Below Average | Unacceptable | Comments |
|---|---|---|---|---|---|---|
| 1. Relationship with others | | | | | | |
| 2. Judgment | | | | | | |
| 3. Ability to learn | | | | | | |
| 4. Attitude toward work | | | | | | |
| 5. Dependability | | | | | | |
| 6. Quality of work | | | | | | |
| 7. Communication skill: Oral | | | | | | |
| 8. Communication skill: Written | | | | | | |

| | Outstanding | Good | +Average− | Marginal | Unsatisfactory |
|---|---|---|---|---|---|
| Overall Performance | | | | | |

Comments: _____

_____

Have you discussed this evaluation with the co-op ☐Yes ☐No

Signature of Supervisor _____Date_____

Fig. 13-5.  Sample employer's student worker evaluation form (Form 3).

regarding the evaluation process and to answer questions about standards, etc.

Some of the principles which employers and coordinators should consider as they evaluate student progress are:

1. The coordinator should assist the training sponsor in evaluating student performance.
2. The training sponsor should counsel the student regarding the evaluation.
3. The teacher-coordinator should review the evaluation with the student.
4. The evaluation form (and process) should be explained to the training sponsor prior to the evaluation.
5. The teacher-coordinator should reserve final judgment on grades.
6. Pass/fail options are better than letter grades.
7. Evaluation forms should be filed in student folders.

### Summary

Continued development of established training stations is one of the most important functions of the teacher-coordinator. Training station visits are necessary (1) to develop effective working relationships between employing enterprises and the LEA and (2) to assure primacy of the training function. Efforts expended by the teacher-coordinator in development of training sponsors (and stations) return dividends in improved training for CVOE students.

The training sponsor is an important member of the LEA's instructional staff. Therefore, the teacher-coordinator is obligated to help sponsors acquire skills of a professional trainer. The teacher-coordinator should provide sponsors assistance in developing training, evaluating, and counseling skills.

The degree of congruence between things taught at the LEA and at training stations determines the effectiveness of CVOE programs. Coordinators must correlate the efforts of both agencies.

### Activities

1. Develop a calendar of events for the in-service development of participating training sponsors.
2. Develop five performance objectives which describe: (a) behavior to be exhibited, (b) a performance standard(s), and (c) a criterion or criteria.
3. Develop a form which may be utilized by a teacher-coordinator to prepare a daily itinerary of coordination activity.

4. Develop a form which may be utilized to record results of a coordination visit.
5. Prepare an agenda for an orientation meeting for training sponsors.
6. Develop an evaluation instrument which may be utilized by training sponsors of a:
   a. career exploration program,
   b. high school office occupations program, and
   c. post-secondary middle-management program.

# Chapter 14

# Program Management

Teacher-coordinators have many functions, e.g., planning, conducting programs, counseling, public relations, and administration. The various functions of cooperative vocational/occupational education (CVOE) must be managed efficiently and simultaneously. The teacher-coordinator may be likened to a juggler who must keep as many as six balls in the air at one time. If the juggler doesn't apply the right force in the right direction on each ball at the right time, his act comes to an embarrassing end. CVOE personnel manage many more than six things. Witness some essential subsystems of a functioning CVOE program:

1. advisory committee
2. student ingression and orientation
3. related instruction
4. public relations
5. training station identification and development
6. student organization
7. training station evaluation of student progress
8. instructional materials acquisition and maintenance
9. safety compliance and instruction
10. report and record maintenance
11. training-sponsor development
12. program evaluation and renewal

Teacher-coordinator functions are complicated by various publics. Local educational agency (LEA) expectations are normally easy to understand. The expectations of enterprises which employ students, state and federal agencies, community service groups, students, and parents are sometimes difficult to understand. More so than other LEA functions, these publics place great demands upon the management of CVOE programs.

Other chapters of this book contain many suggestions for accomplishing various tasks associated with the teacher-coordinator's job. They include many management forms. This chapter contains sample forms for management functions which are not treated in other chapters. Forms included in this chapter are in common use. Forms found in other chapters are not duplicated here. But, in several cases, variations are duplicated. Management forms help CVOE personnel assure proper functioning of subsystems. Proper functioning of subsystems is essential to the quality, efficiency, and effectiveness of programs. Management forms serve accountabily requirements, improve services to students, and make the teacher-coordinator's job easier. They replace guesswork and memory with good plans and records.

Some of the outcomes of reading this chapter are understanding:

1. Several subsystems of CVOE programs.
2. Needs for and uses of various management forms.
3. Management aspects of the teacher-coordinator's role.

### STUDENT INGRESSION AND ORIENTATION

Several forms are used by teacher-coordinators to support student ingression and orientation functions. This section includes six forms. Teacher-coordinators should consider several factors before adopting or adapting these forms. Principal among these is age of students. Generally, the younger the students the more forms are necessary. For example, parents of students who are younger than eighteen are usually asked to complete one or more approval forms. Program objectives also influence type and format of management forms. For example, if the program is one in which a major portion of manipulative skills is to be developed at training stations, that goal should be reflected in management forms.

A sample student application form is shown in Fig. 14-1. Teacher-coordinators must have basic information re students who wish to participate in CVOE. Many prospective students obtain these forms from counselors. Many students also approach teacher-coordinators to talk about programs and request application forms. In LEA's which conduct several CVOE programs, an application form should be designed so that it serves all programs. Counselors and CVOE personnel can readily determine which teacher-coordinator should receive a given application. A student application form should assure that teacher-coordinators can locate and contact applicants.

Some teacher-coordinators collect information on applicants prior to scheduling individual interviews. Several forms in common use are specifically designed for that purpose. An attendance, discipline, and health form is shown in Fig. 14-2. Coordinators should be aware of such matters, because they may influence job placement. As was emphasized in Chapter 9, attendance and discipline patterns established in the LEA may not

## Student Application for Cooperative Education Program

Type of Program Desired \_\_\_\_\_AO, \_\_\_\_\_DE, \_\_\_\_\_HERO, \_\_\_\_\_HO,\_\_\_\_ ICE, \_\_\_\_\_OO.

(Check one if known)

Name _____

(Last)                         (First)                    (Initial)

Date of Birth_____Date of Application_____

Address _____Social Security Number_____

Parent or Guardian _____Telephone_____

Homeroom Teacher_____Year in School_____

Now Attending_____High School_____Counselor

### Current Schedule of Classes

| Time' | Course | Location | Time | Course | Location |
|---|---|---|---|---|---|
| 1. | | | 4. | | |
| 2. | | | 5. | | |
| 3 | | | 6. | | |

Plans After Graduation _____

Do you have a driver's license?_____

Will you be able to provide transportation to a job if you are enrolled in cooperative Education?_____

_____

(parent's signature)

_____

(student's signature)

**Fig. 14-1.   Sample student application form for cooperative education program.**

be accurate indicators of how students will respond in the world of work. However, teacher-coordinators should discuss such matters with applicants during initial interviews. The Attendance, Discipline, and Health Record form (see Fig. 14-2) should be sent to the students counselor, attendance officer, and school nurse (or equivalents) for completion.

A teacher evaluation form for CVOE applicants can be found in Fig. 14-3. A student's former and present teachers can provide information

## Attendance, Discipline, and Health Record

Student's Name _____Date_____

                    (Last)    (First)    (Initial)

|  | Freshman Year | Sophomore Year | Junior Year | Senior Year |
|---|---|---|---|---|
| Absences | _____ | _____ | _____ | _____ |
| Tardinesses | _____ | _____ | _____ | _____ |
| Detentions | _____ | _____ | _____ | _____ |

Comments regarding student's behavior.

_____

_____

_____

_____

Date _____        Dean_____

**Health Record:**
Is the above student in good health? _____
List physical defects or limitations which might affect job performance in cooperative education.

_____

_____

_____

Date _____        _____
                                             (school nurse)

Return this form to: _____
                                       (coordinator)

**Fig. 14-2.**   Sample attendance, discipline, and health record.

which helps CVOE personnel counsel applicants. Involving teachers in student ingression procedures helps them understand CVOE.

Additional data on prospective students may be obtained by meeting with counselors to review student files. Records of courses taken, aptitude test results, intelligence test scores, interest inventory reports, anecdotal reports, and other types of information enhance understanding of individuals.

## Teacher Evaluation Form for CVOE Applicant

Dear Fellow Teacher:

_____has applied for admission to the Cooperative Vocational/Occupational Education Program. Many factors influence success on-the-job. Your perceptions of this applicant will assist me counsel the applicant regarding appropriateness of the program. Information will be confidential. Thank you for valued assistance.

---

For each characteristic listed, circle the word which best describes the applicant.

 1. Ability to learn......................................................Quick  Fair  Slow
 2. Capacity for work................Unusual  Industrious  Average  Poor
 3. Judgment...................................Uncanny  Sound  Average  Poor
 4. Initiative.........................................Exceptional  High  Fair  None
 5. Appearance ..........................Very neat  Neat  Careless  Slovenly
 6. Leadership quality....................Pronounced  High  Average  Low
 7. Desire to make good ...............Pronounced  High  Average  Low
 8. Ability to take orders................Outstanding  High  Average  Low
 9. Reliable.................................................Very  Ordinary  Unreliable
10. Perseverance......................Unlimited  Ample  Monderate  Weak
11. General conduct...........................Courteous  Discourteous  Rude
12. Accepts criticism ........................Readily  Indifferently  Reluctantly
13. Ability to mix...................................Natural  Fairly good  Doubtful
14. Would you employ this person?......_____Yes  _____No
Remarks: _____

---

Return to: _____

(teacher-coordinator)

Signed  _____

(teacher)

**Fig. 14-3.  Sample teacher evaluation form for CVOE applicant.**

 

    Some coordinators use a student interview form which guides the initial interview (Fig. 14-4). It is especially helpful for ascertaining appropriateness of the occupational area chosen by an applicant. Policies re CVOE programs should be discussed with applicants during initial interviews. There is no better time to begin to develop understandings of goals and expectations of CVOE personnel, employers, etc.

## Student Interview Form for Cooperative Vocational Education

Name _____

| | Help or Information Needed | | |
|---|---|---|---|
| | Much | Some | Little or None |
| 1. Do you know definitely the fields of work in which you are most interested? | | | |
| 2. Have you analyzed carefully your skills and abilities? | | | |
| 3. Have you determined the type of work for which your particular personality is best suited? | | | |
| 4. Have you considered carefully the employment outlook in your chosen field? | | | |
| 5. Do you know the general requirements of this occupation(s)? | | | |
| 6. Do you know how to find reliable information about your chosen occupation? | | | |
| 7. Do you know the most important factors to keep in mind when you are interviewed by an employer? | | | |
| 8. Do you know what factors your employer is likely to consider when you are ready for a raise or a promotion? | | | |
| 9. Do you know how to decide whether or not a job is one with a future? | | | |
| 10. Have you a clear idea of what you consider essential to success in life? | | | |

Corrdinator's Comments:

**Fig. 14-4.   Sample student interview form for CVOE program.**

Many LEA's require that CVOE students sign a student agreement form which defines certain policies and sets forth program rules and regulations (Fig. 14-5). Level of program (secondary or post-secondary),

## Student Agreement for CVOE Program

The _____Cooperative Vocational Education program provides classroom and work experiences. To achieve career goals, a student must accept certain responsibilities.

As a condition of admittance to the CVOE program, agrees:

That placement on-the-job is the responsibility of the teacher-coordinator.

To be in regular attendance at school and on the job, including days when school is not in session and when my employer expects me.

To be on time at school and on the job.

To notify my training sponsor as soon as I know I will be absent from work for good cause.

To notify my coordinator and my training sponsor as early in the day as possible on days that I am absent from school.

That if I am absent from school I must also be absent from work on that day.

To conduct myself on the job in a manner which reflects positively upon me and the CVOE program.

To perform all of my duties in a commendable manner and to complete study assigments thoroughly and on time.

To conduct myself in a satisfactory manner on-the-job and in the classroom least my training be discontinued and I be removed from the program.

To attend functions the Cooperative Education class sponsors.

To pay normal fees and special (and reasonable) charges for class activities, e.g., banquet, conferences, field trips.

To work toward group and individual goals.

That the teacher-coordinator has the same authority over me on-the-job as in the classroom.

That the Coordinator is the recognized authority for making adjustments to my training on-the-job.

To obey all traffic laws while commuting to and from my training station.

To remain at the training-station assigned by my teacher-coordinator.

Fig. 14-5. Sample student agreement form for CVOE program. (Cont'd on next page.)

To dress in a manner acceptable to employer and LEA standards.

That if I am required to leave school for disciplinary reasons, I cannot report to my training station because it is the same as other subjects.

That if I am required to leave school for disciplinary reasons, I cannot report to my training station because it is the same as other subjects.

To resign or change jobs only after discussing my situation with my parents and coordinator.

To work 15-20 hours each week to be eligible for credit.

I fully understand the above statements, and agree to cooperate in carrying them out to the fullest of my ability.

Student's Signature _____ Date _____

Parent's Signature _____ Date _____

Fig. 14-5.    Sample student agreement form for CVOE program.

student characteristics, philosophy of the LEA and SEA, and other factors must be considered in developing policy and forms.

Teacher-coordinators who serve students under eighteen should use some technique for informing parents of prospective participants about the CVOE program. Parental encouragement and assistance are important for success in CVOE. A typical parental approval form used at the secondary level is shown in Fig. 14-6.

## THE COORDINATING FUNCTION

By definition, one of a teacher-coordinator's primary responsibilities is correlating the LEA's and the training station's instructional responsibilities. Agreements and plans developed as employers and students join the program (see Chapter 10) provide bases for correlation activities. Practicing teacher-coordinators use various systems and forms.

A Student Location Card (Fig. 14-7) permits ready location of students and eases the planning of training station visits and provision of various services in the LEA. Student location cards should be printed on a 3'' x 5'' or 5'' x 7'' format. A card should be established for each student and should be updated as changes occur.

Many CVOE personnel issue CVOE student identification and introduction cards. Formats for these cards can be seen in Fig. 14-8. An identification card should be carried by students for use if they are asked

**Parental Approval Form for CVOE Program**

TO:

_____has indicated a desire to enroll in the
_____ program. Success in cooperative education
depends in major part upon support which parents provide.

To assure that you are well acquainted with the Program, we ask that
you make note of the following. ("Student-learner" refers to your son or
daughter.)
1. The student-learner will take two regular high school subjects, phys-
   cial education and the cooperative education programs.
2. One period of the day will be spent in the Cooperative education
   Related Class.
3. A minimum of fifteen hours per week will be spent on-the-job.
4. There will be a try-out period to see whether the student-learner is
   suited for the job. If needs be, job change or enrollment in other
   school subjects will be arranged.
5. Successful completion of cooperative education results in two credits
   which apply to graduation.
Be assured that I will advise and counsel your child regarding good
conduct in school and on-the-job.

Coordinator's Signature_____Date_____
I understand purposes of the Cooperative Education Program and
approve of my child's participation for the_____term.
Parent's Signature _____Date_____

Fig. 14-6.  Sample parental approval form for CVOE program.

why they are away from the LEA. The introduction card should be used
for each employment interview and may remain with the potential
employer. It is especially useful with employers who hire only CVOE
students.

A Monthly Coordinator's Report form (Fig. 14-9) serves three important
functions. (1) As indicated in Chapter 13, there is sometimes a need to
account for a coordinator's time and whereabouts. Colleagues and
superiors can discover from the form that a coordinator accomplishes
many things in many places. (2) Since a coordinator cannot recall specifics
of each promotion, coordination, or public relations contact, this form
serves as a log of activities and is referred to as schedules, evaluations,

## Student Location Card

(Front)

Name _____
Occupation _____
Home Address _____
Home Phone _____
Date Enrolled _____
Employer _____
Employer's Address _____
Training Sponsor _____
Business Phone _____
Student Classification ____Fr, ____Soph, ____Jr, ____Sr.
Notes _____

(Back)

| Work Schedule | | | Class Schedule | | |
|---|---|---|---|---|---|
| Day | From | To | Period | Subject | Room |
| Mon. | _____ | _____ | 1 | _____ | ____ |
| Tues. | _____ | _____ | 2 | _____ | ____ |
| Wed. | _____ | _____ | 3 | _____ | ____ |
| Thurs. | _____ | _____ | 4 | _____ | ____ |
| Fri. | _____ | _____ | 5 | _____ | ____ |
| Sat. | _____ | _____ | 6 | _____ | ____ |
| Sun. | _____ | _____ | 7 | _____ | ____ |

Fig. 14-7.   Sample form for locating a student in CVOE program.

etc. are planned. (3) This form is excellent for communicating with superiors and other LEA personnel. A copy should be submitted to the coordinator's supervisor. Entries on the form should be accurate in every respect and thorough even though they must be abbreviated. The coordinator should not fill out the report in the presence of the person contacted. He/she should make entries immediately after each meeting. Entries should not be restricted to activities conducted outside of the LEA. Rather, anything which is important and/or which takes significant coordinator time should be recorded.

A Weekly Activity Report form for recording daily on-the-job and related-class activities of a student-learner is shown in Fig. 14-10. This

## Student Identification and Introduction Cards for CVOE

```
                              CVOE
                        Identification Card

This certifies that _____
is a member of the  _____
CVOE Program at _____ and
is employed by _____.
Permission is granted for absence from school after_____ p.m. on
Monday, Tuesday, Wednesday, Thursday, Friday.
        Principal  _____
Date_____Teacher-Coordinator  _____
```

```
          Cooperative Education Student Introduction Card

M  _____
Date _____
Company  _____
Appointment_____o'clock.
        This will introduce  _____
who has applied for the  _____
CVOE Program at _____
        This applicant will be available for employment every school day
at _____p.m. and all day on Saturday.
Applicant's age  _____
Social Security No.  _____
Teacher-Coordinator  _____
```

Fig. 14-8.  Sample identification card (top) and introduction card (bottom) for CVOE students.

form is important, since it forces the coordinator to note what a student is doing at the training station and in the related class. This form may be used to check progress on items in a training plan. Each student should update his form at the beginning of each related-class period and give the form to the coordinator on Monday of each week. The coordinator should analyze each form to determine quality and appropriateness of on-the-job activities and to make adjustments in the sequence of related class activities. Effectiveness of a CVOE program can be greatly improved by close coordination of job and classroom experiences made possible by careful use of this form.

## Monthly Coordinator's Report

CVOE Program _____Month_____Year_____

| Date | Code | Miles Traveled | Student's Name and Occupation | Comments Describing Activities |
|------|------|----------------|-------------------------------|-------------------------------|
|      |      |                |                               |                               |
|      |      |                |                               |                               |
|      |      |                |                               |                               |
|      |      |                |                               |                               |
|      |      |                |                               |                               |
|      |      |                |                               |                               |

Coordinator _____Mileage for Month_____

Code:

| | | |
|---|---|---|
| 1. Coordination | 5. Guidance | 9. Labor-management |
| 2. Instruction materials | 6. Administrative contacts | 10. Home visitation |
| 3. Promotional | 7. Advisory committee activities | 11. Other |
| 4. Public relations | 8. Club | |

Fig. 14-9.   Sample coordinator's monthly report form.

In most LEA's it is well to monitor progress of CVOE students in other courses. Normally, performance in other courses is improved when students participate in CVOE programs. But, sometimes performance in other courses suffers as a result of participation. A Grade Report form (Fig. 14-11) may be used to monitor student progress in all courses. The form may be used to structure counseling sessions and to support decisions re working hours, study habits, etc. Forms should be completed by each student at the beginning of each term and updated at the end of each grading period.

For various reasons, nearly all LEA's must maintain accurate daily wage and hour records (Fig. 14-12). Most coordinators require that students maintain forms and turn them in at the end of each month. Forms

## Student's Weekly Activity Report

Student's Name _____ Date: From_____ to_____

| Day | On-the-job Activities | Classroom Activities |
|-----|----------------------|---------------------|
| Mon. | | |
| Tues. | | |
| Wed. | | |
| Thurs. | | |
| Fri. | | |
| Sat. | | |
| Sun. | | |

Student Remarks (important developments) _____

_____

New Job Experiences _____

_____

_____

**Fig. 14-10.    Sample student's weekly activity report form.**

should be filed in student folders each month after data is transferred to a yearly report form.

Some LEA's provide vehicles for coordination activities. The common practice is to reimburse CVOE personnel for mileage traveled in their own automobiles. An Expense Record form which may be used for preparing travel vouchers is shown in Fig. 14-13.

### OTHER FORMS

Various forms which are useful for CVOE program management appear elsewhere in this book. Forms for ascertaining student and commun-

## Grade Report Form

Student's Name _____School Term_____
Counselor's Name _____

| Period | Subject | Grade | | | | | |
|--------|---------|-----|-----|-----|-----|-----|-----|
|        |         | 1st | 2nd | 3rd | 4th | 5th | 6th |
| 1      |         |     |     |     |     |     |     |
| 2      |         |     |     |     |     |     |     |
| 3      |         |     |     |     |     |     |     |
| 4      |         |     |     |     |     |     |     |
| 5      |         |     |     |     |     |     |     |
| 6      |         |     |     |     |     |     |     |
| 7      |         |     |     |     |     |     |     |
| 8      |         |     |     |     |     |     |     |
| Average by Grading Period | | | | | | | |

**Student Comments:**

First Grading Period _____

Second _____

Third _____

Fourth _____

Fifth _____

Sixth _____

**Fig. 14-11.   Sample grade report form.**

ity needs are in Chapter 4. Forms and letters useful for organizing and utilizing steering and advisory committees can be found in Chapters 6 and 8. Forms and permits relevant to labor laws are in Chapter 9. Chapters 11 and 12 contain many forms which support management of related classes.

## Daily Wage-Hour Report

| Day of Week | Day of Month | Hours Worked School Days | Hours Worked Other Days | $ Rec'd School Days | $ Rec'd Other Days |
|---|---|---|---|---|---|
| | 1 | | | | |
| | 2 | | | | |
| | 3 | | | | |
| | 4 | | | | |
| | 5 | | | | |
| | 6 | | | | |
| | 7 | | | | |
| | 8 | | | | |
| | 9 | | | | |
| | 10 | | | | |
| | 11 | | | | |
| | 12 | | | | |
| | 13 | | | | |
| | 14 | | | | |
| | 15 | | | | |
| | 16 | | | | |
| | 17 | | | | |
| | 18 | | | | |
| | 19 | | | | |
| | 20 | | | | |
| | 21 | | | | |
| | 22 | | | | |
| | 23 | | | | |
| | 24 | | | | |
| | 25 | | | | |
| | 26 | | | | |
| | 27 | | | | |
| | 28 | | | | |
| | 29 | | | | |
| | 30 | | | | |
| | 31 | | | | |
| TOTALS | | | | | |

Total hours worked in this month _____    Total hours worked to date _____

Total wages earned in this month _____    Total wages earned to date _____

**Fig. 14-12.  Sample daily wage-hour report form.**

Chapter 17 contains several forms which may be used to support various evaluation activities. Forms and other illustrations may be readily located by consulting the List of Illustrations at the front of the book.

As indicated repeatedly in this book, CVOE personnel should consult with state education agency (SEA) people re many things. In many states, manuals and other materials re CVOE contain management forms. Needless to say, required report forms deserve special attention.

## Coordinator's Expense Record

Coordinator's Name _____Program_____
For First_____, Second_____, Third_____, Fourth_____Quarter.
Date Submitted _____

| Date | Activity Performed | Miles Traveled | Other Expenses (Please Specify) |
|---|---|---|---|
| | | | |
| | | | |
| | | | |
| | | | |
| | | | |
| | | | |
| | | | |
| | | | |
| | | | |
| | | | |
| | | | |
| | | | |
| | | | |
| | | | |
| | | | |
| | | | |
| | | | |
| | | | |
| TOTALS | | | |

Signatures:

_____          _____miles @  _____
(Teacher-Coordinator)                      $ _____
                                           Other Expenses
_____          $ _____
(Director)                                 Total $ _____

**Fig. 14-13.  Sample form for coordinator's expense record.**

## Summary

Several CVOE subsystems must be managed effectively. In addition to the traditional teaching function, teacher-coordinators must maintain an advisory committee, a student ingression and orientation subsystem, manpower and student need data bases, a training station acquisition and development subsystem, a public relations program, a student organization, equipment and supply inventories, an evaluation subsystem, instructional correlation and control subsystems, and other subsystems. To assure proper functioning of subsystems, and other subsystems. To assure proper functioning of subsystems which are essential to program effectiveness, CVOE personnel must make good use of management forms.

## Activities

Consider the CVOE program for which you are responsible or may soon be responsible.

1. Modify forms in Figs. 14-1 through 14-6 accordingly.
2. Modify forms in Figs. 14-7 through 14-13 accordingly.
3. List five advantages and five disadvantages of obtaining teacher evaluations of prospective CVOE students.
4. Draft a letter which explains the purpose and operation of a CVOE program to:

   a. prospective training sponsors,
   b. prospective students,
   c. parents of prospective CVOE students,
   d. fellow teachers.

Chapter *15*

# Vocational/Occupational
# Student Organizations

Leaders in various segments of vocational/occupational education are supportive of the concept that student organizations should be integral with instruction and learning. Vocational/occupational student organizations are fostered by agencies of government at federal and state levels and by professional associations. Means of support vary from state to state and from LEA to LEA. At minimum, state vocational education agencies encourage student organizations and provide guidance to teachers who wish to form new groups. At maximum, SEA's require that LEA's have active student organizations. For example, in many states, agriculture occupations programs entail Future Farmers of America chapters without exception, and agriculture teachers, supervisors in the SEA, and teacher educators assume that program planning, conduct, and evaluation include consideration of FFA as a program component, integral with and equivalent to other components.

Some of the outcomes of reading this chapter are:

1. Understanding characteristics of the various types of student organizations.
2. Understanding local, regional, state, and national structures of the several established organizations.
3. Understanding advisor responsibilities and liabilities.
4. Appreciating the need to balance several kinds of student organization activities.
5. Understanding hints for assisting student organizations.

## COMMON CHARACTERISTICS OF ORGANIZATIONS

As one would expect of organizations with very similar purposes, organizations in respective occupational areas have several things in common. Among these are:

1. Formal organization as private not-for-profit corporations.
2. Well-defined structures for national, state (and in some states regional), and local programs and activities.
3. Provision for secondary, post-secondary, and their collegiate affiliates.
4. Foundation in local vocational/occupational programs.
5. Vocational/occupational education advisors at local and state levels.
6. Executive directors or secretaries and national headquarters staffs.
7. Periodicals, handbooks, manuals, and other publications which guide and support local activities.
8. Supply services for various printed materials such as leadership handbooks, jewelry, clothing, insignia, trophies and other awards, and items such as candy for sales campaigns.
9. A system of membership dues and solicitation of contributions to support national, state, and local activities.
10. Local activities which are balanced for purposes of leadership development, fund raising, citizenship development, service, socialization, and contact and conference participation.

## NATIONAL ORGANIZATIONS

### Distributive Education Clubs of America (DECA)

National *Distributive Education Clubs of America (DECA)* began in 1947 with seventeen charter states. It was officially chartered under the laws of Virginia in 1950. It fosters cocurricular programs for students who are preparing for employment in marketing and distribution. There are secondary and post-secondary chapters in all states and territories. DECA includes five kinds of members: high school, community or junior college, college or university, alumni, and professional, i.e., university, state agency, and other distributive education professionals. Participation in club activities develops economic responsibility, literacy, vocational competency, leadership characteristics, social intelligence, and civic consciousness. National programs include the DECA Program of Youth Activity, National Leadership Conference, and a quarterly magazine DECA distributor. Requests for information re available materials and services should be addressed to:

Executive Director
Distributive Education Clubs of America
200 Park Avenue
Falls Church, VA 22046

**Future Business Leaders of America (FBLA)**

National *Future Business Leaders of America (FBLA)* began in 1946 under sponsorship of what is now the *National Business Association*, an affiliate of the National Education Association. FBLA functions at the secondary level and at the post-secondary level as Phi Beta Lambda (PBL established in 1958). The two kinds of local chapters serve students in business education courses with career objectives in business, marketing, and management. Chapters may be formed for students in specialties such as data processing, or office occupations or for all manner of business education students. Participation in club activities develops competencies for the understanding of and development in business occupations, aggressive business leadership, improvements in home and community, citizenship, and organized recreation. National programs include a magazine, *Tomorrow's Business Leader,* and a leadership conference, following state and local conferences. Projects, achievement degrees, and elective offices at the three levels provide incentives for members. Requests for information re available materials and services should be addressed to:

Executive Director
Future Business Leaders of America
1201 Sixteenth Street, N.W.
Washington, D.C. 20036

**Future Farmers of America (FFA)**

National *Future Farmers of America (FFA)* began in 1928. State and local chapters were begun as early as 1917. FFA was granted a charter by the Congress in 1950. Membership is open to students in public secondary school programs, funded under vocational education legislation. Membership was opened to girls in 1969. The three levels of the organization are governed according to fundamentals of true democracy. Each member has a voice re programs, policies, rules, and regulations and commensurate responsibilities as an individual and cooperating organization member. Each chapter plans activities and a specified number of orderly meetings. Public speaking and parliamentary procedures are among the more essential activities of FFA contest and award systems. National programs include awards programs for individuals and state and local chapters; a very rigorous and achievement-based degree system: Greenhand, Chapter Farmer, State Farmer, and American Farmer; a bimonthly magazine, *The National Future Farmer;* and incentive awards via *The Future Farmers of America Foundation, Inc.,* which are financed by donations from corporations, associations, and individuals. Requests for information re available materials and services should be addressed to:

Executive Secretary
Future Farmers of America
The National FFA Center
P.O. Box 15160
Alexandria, VA 22309

### Future Homemakers of America (FHA) and Home Economics Related Occupations (HERO)

National *Future Homemakers of America (FHA)* began in 1945. It fosters programs for public and private junior and senior high school students enrolled in home economics and home economics occupations courses such as food services, clothing services, and child care. (Post-secondary students may belong to affiliates of the *American Home Economics Association.)* There are three kinds of FHA chapters: (1) FHA chapters for home economics and family living, (2) HERO-FHA chapters for students preparing for careers in *Home Economics Related Occupations* (HERO), and (3) FHA-HERO combination chapters. FHA is sponsored by the United States Office of Education and the *American Home Economics Association.* It cooperates with the Home Economics Division of the American Vocational Association and the Home Economics Education Association of the National Education Association on various professional programs and projects. Increasingly, HERO-FHA chapters engage in activities similar to those of DECA, FBLA, FFA, OEA, and VICA. Activities include formal meetings, social events, displays, and contests. The principal national programs are the National Program of Work which every four years results in a guidebook for classroom-related activities and a magazine, *Teen Times,* which is published five times a year. Requests regarding available materials and services should be addressed to:

National Advisor
Future Homemakers of America
2010 Massachusetts Avenue, N.W.
Washington, D.C. 20036

### Office Education Association (OEA)

National *Office Education Association (OEA)* began in 1966. OEA has secondary and post-secondary divisions and is open to vocational office education students. Its purposes are to promote and stimulate ideals, skills, and aptitudes which are important and necessary to future office workers. Activities foster development of individual leadership, responsibility, and understandings of group effort. Activities include educational, social, and service events. National programs include competitive events involving vocational skills and personal development and leadership contests. Requests for information regarding available materials and services should be addressed to:

Executive Director
Office Education Association
20 Leland Avenue
Columbus, Ohio 43214

### Vocational Industrial Clubs of America (VICA)

National *Vocational Industrial Clubs of America (VICA)* began in 1965. VICA has secondary and post-secondary divisions. It serves students enrolled in trade, technical, industrial and health occupations programs. Among VICA goals are appreciation of the dignity of work and of standards of trade ethics, workmanship, scholarship, and safety. Parliamentary procedures, democratic decision making, public speaking, skill contests, essays, job interviews, and other projects are conducted at local, state, and national levels. VICA is associated with the National Association of State Supervisors of Trade and Industrial Education, United States Office of Education, United States Chamber of Commerce, and AFL-CIO. National programs include competitive and individual achievement awards programs and a quarterly magazine, *VICA*. Requests for information regarding available materials and services should be addressed to:

Executive Director
Vocational Industrial Clubs of America
105 N. Virginia Avenue
Falls Church, VA 22046

### OTHER ORGANIZATIONS

Whenever possible, student organizations should be affiliated with state and national organizations — the better to benefit from contests and conferences. However, some cooperative vocational/occupational education (CVOE) programs prepare people for occupations which are obviously not of concern to one of the established national organizations. (Like trade and industrial education, VICA serves a wide range of students. Cosmetology, welding, health occupations, and many other specialty groups benefit greatly from VICA.) Highly specialized post-secondary (or secondary) programs, especially those aimed at licensure in health and personal service occupations, might better entail student organizations which ex<sup>i</sup>st as separate entities and/or are affiliated with respective regional or state professional associations. Such organizations would do well to emulate the programs and activities of the established vocational/occupational organizations.

All vocational/occupational student organizations would do well to consider association with other local and/or state groups. Obviously, local chapters should be associated in various ways with local advisory committees. In many LEA's, the number and structure of student organizations and advisory committees are exactly parallel. Decisions regarding the number and relationships of CVOE programs, organizations, and committees depend upon very similar data. They might also benefit in various ways via relationships with local employer and employee groups, trade and professional associations, economic development groups, personnel associations, and civic groups. Fund-raising, civic, and social activities may be enhanced by association and cooperation with such groups.

## ADVISOR RESPONSIBILITIES

In nearly all instances, the advisor of a local student organization is the teacher-coordinator of the respective cooperative program. (Some student organizations function in programs which do not entail cooperative experiences.) Gooch (19), p. 7, classified coordinator responsibilities re student organizations into eight categories: (1) organizing, (2) promoting, (3) operating the club, (4) assisting student leaders, (5) providing advice and direction, (6) supervising all activities, (7) affiliating with state and national organizations, and (8) correlating activities with the cooperative program. Coordinators who sponsor student organizations are certain to have some involvement in each of these categories. Specific responsibilities in each category will be affected by the type of CVOE program, requirements of national and state affiliates, student abilities and interests, and conditions in the LEA.

## SAMPLE ACTIVITIES

A student organization should engage in a variety of activities. During a school year or term, activities should focus variously upon educational, fund raising, civic, service, social-recreational, competitive, and leadership purposes. Some activities satisfy one or more of these purposes with little contribution to the others. All activities have at least some social reward; but, some do not develop leadership characteristics or civic responsibility—and some deplete rather than add to the treasury. It is important for educational and other reasons such as motivation that activities be varied in form and purpose.

The following are ideas which might stimulate thought re planning of activities.

| | |
|---|---|
| Field Trip | Radio Program |
| Resource Person | Television Program |
| Organizational Meeting | Assembly Program |
| Election of Officers | News Release |
| Get-Out-the-Vote | Alumni Night |
| Town Clean-Up | Game Night |
| Leadership Conference | Dance |
| Regional Contests | Contest Night |
| State Contests | Magazine Sales |
| Employer Breakfast | Recruitment Presentations |
| Employer Banquet | Magazine Articles |
| Homecoming Float | Storefront Display |
| Faculty Appreciation | Freshman Orientation |
| Halloween Party | Followup Studies |
| Laboratory Safety Inspection | Candy Sales |
| Robert's Rules of Order | Community Survey |
| Bulletin Board | School/College Display Case |
| Big Brother/Sister Project | Auction |
| Repair Services | Flower Fund |
| Carnival Booth | Design Contest |
| Skill Contest | Monitor City Council |
| Liaison with State Vocational | Monitor Legislature |
| Association | Student Council Representation |

National organization magazines, guidebooks, and the professional literature of vocational/occupational and cooperative education also provide ideas for activities. But, in the main, ideas and plans for activities should be generated locally. Students should use brainstorming and other techniques to fit activities to local needs and conditions—while preparing for participation in regional, state, and hopefully national conferences and contests. Activities should be planned early in the year and facilities and the like should be scheduled well in advance. It is well to publish a calendar of major events so that members and others, such as media people, can protect their calendars and attend. A calling-card-size calendar is effective.

## HINTS FOR ADVISORS

National student organizations provide advisor handbooks which deal with organizing clubs, electing officers, conducting meetings, recruiting members, fund raising, and many more tasks which the teacher-coordinator-sponsor must understand, assist, and supervise. The following are hints re some of these tasks. Especially for information regarding activities which are peculiar to a given student organization, sponsors should consult published manuals and guidebooks.

1. Schedule time and place of meetings in accord with student schedules and local custom.
2. Observe institutional policies, apprise appropriate persons of organization activities, and secure necessary approvals.
3. Use related class time for some meetings.
4. Plan agenda well in advance with officers and/or standing and ad hoc committee chairmen.
5. Correlate some activities with related class units, e.g., career information, money management, civic responsibility.
6. Help students to plan finance activities in several ways.
7. Adjust dues according to ability to pay and show clearly what dues buy.
8. Have executive committee prepare dues proposal for approval at a regular meeting.
9. Require two-thirds majority approval of all matters relating to individuals' money.
10. Discuss merits of short-term fund-raising activities over continuing activities, such as regular sales or services. Study national publications and talk to counterparts in similar LEA's to get ideas.
11. Discuss merits of fund raising via the savings plan, e.g., students save a portion of training station earnings to fund a major trip.
12. Avoid solicitation of contributions. It is better to ask community members and groups to contribute to the ongoing program so that successive students will be benefited. (See Chapter 8.)
13. Benefit from past experiences and arrangements. But, for most activities let students "do their thing" as contrasted to copying what has been done during previous years.
14. Establish some traditions, e.g., a spring employer appreciation banquet, regular participation in state conferences and contests.
15. Have delegates to state meetings pay a fraction—say a third—of their expenses.
16. Treat teacher liability re organization activities the same as re regular teacher-coordinator responsibilities. Pay special attention to safety

for organization activities, supervise thoroughly, and teach safety as at any other time.

17. Apprise superiors, students, and parents re time, place, and purpose of all activities.
18. Assure that LEA and personal liability insurance applies to organization activities and that activities comply with LEA policies and regulations.
19. Evaluate student organizations together with other CVOE program components. (See Chapter 17.) Use student evaluation.
20. Realize the public relations potential of activities. (See Chapter 16.)
21. Attempt to assure that each student has prime responsibility for at least one facet of one activity each term. Also engage each student in successful experiences. All cannot be officers, delegates, or chairmen, but each student can complete some project successfully.
22. Cooperate with other groups on some activities, e.g., publicity, sales campaigns, banquets, dances, trips.
23. Assure that activities are student- and learning-centered.
24. Have each student make several presentations before at least a small group each term.
25. Assure that officers and committee chairman use conference leadership techniques to enlist all to participate in discussions, voice opinions, and commit themselves to planned activities.

### Summary

Some CVOE students and personnel submit that student organizations are as important as related classes and training stations. From the standpoint of fully participating students, legs of the CVOE triangle—study, work, socialize—are understood as distinguishable but closely correlated experiences which depend upon and support each other. Student organizations are truly the icing on the CVOE cake. Without student organization activities, CVOE can be vapid. Functioning, assertive student organizations add to the benefits which students, employers, LEA's, parents, and communities enjoy from CVOE. Student organizations put back many more opportunities for socialization with peers than is taken away by absence during work periods. The several organizations which have sound national, state, regional, and local structures have many things in common; yet, they have peculiarities because activities are correlated with related-class and occupational specialties. Advisors should be as sincere and responsible re student organizations as they are regarding other CVOE components. Activities should be varied and balanced across major purposes: educational, fund raising, civic, service, social-recreational, competitive, and leadership.

## Activities

1. Examine a state CVOE manual to discover what it says about student organizations. List major items of information which it contains and which are not contained in this chapter, e.g., regulations, schedule of state conferences and contests, state officer elections.
2. Obtain the current advisor's manual and promotional literature of the student organization you advise or are likely to advise in an LEA. Discover (a) the number of state and local chapters, (b) number of members, (c) procedures for establishing a chapter, and (d) schedule of national conferences and contests.
3. Interview a coordinator and/or student organization officer. Determine what activities are planned for the next several months and how they relate to classroom experiences. Categorize the activities as educational, fund raising, etc. Discover what steps are taken to assure that each member (a) has prime responsibility for some facet of a group activity and (b) succeeds at some activity.

# Chapter 16

# Public Relations

Public or community relations programs should be conducted according to well-laid plans. "The purposes, objectives, policies, procedures, and other information about cooperative vocational education should be communicated to a variety of specific audiences through various media." [Minnesota (44), p. 83.] Public relations programs must be continuous for many reasons, chief among them the fact that new people are continually joining various publics. The major function of public relations programs is to develop good will. In short, this is done by using internal and external resources to publicize learning successes, quality programs, and efficient management practices to various publics via various media.

CVOE personnel and their superiors who are responsible for a total LEA public relations program should observe the following principles, which were espoused by the *American Association of School Administrators* (1).

Public relations:

1. Must be positive in nature.
2. Must be a continuous program.
3. Must be honest in both intent and execution.
4. Should be comprehensive in character.
5. Must be simple in meaning and conception.
6. Should be sensitive to the attitude and level of understanding of the public.

These principles require no explanation. But, item three deserves emphasis. Public relations should depict CVOE honestly, i.e., should engage in activities which inform accurately and should not use tactics which sell shoddy products or even good products to the wrong people.

Some of the outcomes of reading this chapter are *understanding:*

1. The information needs of various CVOE publics.
2. Public relations vehicles and techniques for using them.

3. The function of a public relations calendar.
4. The importance of approvals for public relations policy.

## TYPES OF PUBLICS AND HOW TO REACH THEM

The real and expressed needs and concerns of specific audiences should determine the nature of information programs. Content and method should depend upon receivers. The following are CVOE's major publics.

### Potential Students, Enrolled Students, and Graduates

Public relations for educational enterprises must begin with students. Maintaining an effective learning program is *the* one best approach to good relationships with clientele and the many kinds of people with which they are associated. CVOE experiences should be so meaningful to students that they exude enthusiasm and knowledge in their contacts in school, home, and community.

Some of the techniques which are effective with potential students attending the LEA and "feeder" institutions are:

1. Maintaining relevant and effective learning experiences.
2. Working with librarians and counselors to assure ample career information and intelligent career planning.
3. Maintaining attractive classrooms, laboratories, auxiliary areas, and bulletin boards and displays.
4. Recognizing outstanding achievement in school and communities, newspapers and broadcast media, honors convocations, graduations, and other special events.
5. Reporting special interest features of classroom, laboratory, and work-site activities via the same media.
6. Sponsoring assembly programs, career-day activities, and special events for internal and external students who are potential enrollees.
7. Arranging field trips to student-learner work sites for potential students.
8. Sponsoring CVOE and other student organizations.
9. Involving enrolled students and/or alumni in as many of the above as possible.

Early leavers require special public relations efforts. Two kinds of leavers require somewhat different approaches. The first kind is withdrawals or students who "clear the base" properly, i.e., leave officially. These people and, in most instances, a relative should be interviewed by a counselor for many reasons, among them to determine what, if any, CVOE program might serve the leaver in the future. The second kind is dropouts or students who leave without notice. Secondary school CVOE personnel should obtain lists of names and addresses of dropouts for use in future surveys and recruitment activities. CVOE personnel in post-secondary institutions should do likewise for leavers. If a post-secondary institution offers a program(s) for high school leavers, names and addresses should be sought from feeder schools.

Several approaches may be used to reach the leaver audience:

1. Direct mailings to leavers.
2. Direct mailings to relatives of leavers.
3. Direct mailings to known employers of leavers.
4. CVOE personnel and alumni face-to-face contacts with leavers.
5. Radio and television spots featuring CVOE and academic programs for leavers.

In addition to involvement in the above, enrolled students can assist public relations efforts via the following:

1. Membership and leadership roles in other than CVOE student groups, including student government, honor societies, athletics, and other extracurricular activities.
2. Membership on standing and ad hoc committees and the governing board in LEA's which involve students in governance.
3. Involvement in similar organizations in the community and in special community events and observations, e.g., fairs, carnivals, fund drives, blood donation drives.

In addition to aiding in the above, alumni can abet public relations efforts via the following:

1. Providing pictures and success stories for use in various aspects of the public relations program.
2. Conducting tours for potential students, LEA personnel, advisors, evaluators, and others.
3. Contributing to funds for scholarships and other awards for needy and advanced students.

Especially in post-secondary institutions such public relations efforts might be undertaken via formal CVOE alumni groups.

### Parents, Guardians, and Spouses

Parents, guardians, and spouses are nearly as important as students to public relations. Close relatives greatly affect student attitudes. Most families want to be assured that programs lead to wholesome, rewarding, and progressive employment. Many also want to be assured that further education, including university study, is not jeopardized by the CVOE alternative. Relatives also want to be assured that social status in the LEA is not impaired by participation in a career-oriented program.

Public relations vehicles which are effective for informing relatives are:

1. Presentations and conversations at meetings of parent-teacher groups.
2. Special meetings with CVOE parents, guardians, and spouses.
3. Direct mail brochures, articles concerning accomplishments, and announcements regarding special events.
4. Items released to local media.
5. Personal contacts with CVOE personnel in the community and in homes.
6. Telephone calls.
7. Student-parent or spouse banquets or field trips.

Whenever possible, CVOE personnel should talk to parents or spouses of individuals to indicate that a student has a career plan and is pursuing it and that some *one* person in the LEA is responsible for assuring that he is served as an individual. Relatives should also be informed of progress and how they may assist it.

### Other Student-Contact Personnel

Teachers, librarians, counselors, coaches, and other LEA personnel, in their various student-contact roles, are essential audiences. They have ample opportunities to influence student attitudes toward and knowledge of CVOE and career pattern development. Professionals evaluate programs, courses, and learning experiences via observable behavioral changes and conversations with students. Students' maturation, including improved social and academic performance does much to promote understanding and appreciation of CVOE. Associations with CVOE personnel also affect the thinking of other professionals. One of the functions of public relations programs should be to illustrate that the contributions of CVOE and other personnel are complementary in the total development of students.

Some of the vehicles for informing other student-contact personnel are:

1. Participating in faculty meetings, committee work, etc.
2. Exchanging ideas and sharing professional literature, instructional materials, etc.
3. Distributing brochures and announcements.
4. Involving other staff members in special events as speakers, greeters, guides, etc.

5. Doing likewise for special events relevant to other curricular areas.
6. Working with guidance personnel on testing, student surveys, student and employer followup, and student recruitment missions.
7. Working with guidance personnel on financial aids and placement for part-time, summer, and permanent work.
8. Distributing information re placement and findings of followup studies.

### Administrators

Administrators have concerns similar to those of student-contact personnel and are also interested in all matters concerning allocation of resources and/or interfaces with the community. Chief administrative officers, their assistants, heads of service units such as guidance and records, and selected leaders of academic units which serve CVOE students should receive copies of all public relations items. Indeed, in situations where one or more administrators are responsible for aspects of the total public relations program, CVOE personnel will have to get approvals for plans and for many or all items and events.

Some of the vehicles which are especially useful for keeping administrators informed are:

1. Detailed annual reports. These should contain information which is required by funding and licensing agencies and at least the following items:

    a. Enrollment by age, sex, occupational specialty, etc., to show trends over several years.
    b. A description of related instruction units and special experiences such as those afforded by field trips and resource persons.
    c. Hours worked and wages earned by each student.
    d. A description of work stations by employer, occupation, and location.
    e. Number of visits to establish work stations, number of visits to student-learners, and number of visits to community agencies, parents, etc.
    f. A description of cooperative efforts with guidance personnel, especially such matters as student and employer followup, permanent job placement, and placement for advanced study.
    g. Description of advisory committee efforts—probably via copies of minutes.
    h. Description of CVOE club accomplishments—probably via meeting minutes and news releases.
    i. A listing of public relations efforts, e.g., number and title of inter-

nal and external special presentations, trips, etc.; number of news releases.

j.  Description of in-service professional development activities.

2. Quarterly reports which reflect similar information, perhaps in less detail.
3. Weekly wages and hours reports.
4. Inviting administrators to visit classes and training stations.
5. Inviting administrators to accompany students on field trips.
6. Inviting administrators to hear resource persons and have lunch or refreshments with special presenters.
7. Involving administrators in the work of advisory committees and/or student clubs, especially year-end activities.
8. Supporting institution-wide efforts in public relations, safety, extracurricular activities—whatever as full partners—both staff and students.
9. Executing all internal communications tasks in businesslike manner.

### Employees and Employers

In nearly all instances, it is well to conduct public relations efforts aimed at employees and employers simultaneously. (See Chapter 6, Steering Committees, and Chapter 8, Utilizing External Resources, especially sections on advisory committees.) Respected individuals such as officers of unions and trade and professional associations need to know program purposes, objectives, policies, procedures, accomplishments, etc. Furthermore, the contributions of employees and employers to learning experiences should be emphasized in various public relations efforts. In general, publicity efforts directed toward employees and employers should emphasize benefits of participation in a cooperative program. (See lists of benefits to employees and employers in Chapter 1.)

The major vehicles for informing employers and employees are, of course, advisory committee contacts and associations with student-learners and CVOE personnel at work sites. They are also informed by:

1. Printed materials of various kinds.
2. Annual reports.
3. Meetings of service clubs, and trade and professional associations.
4. Surveys to establish work stations.
5. Employer followup studies.
6. Community and adult education programs.
7. CVOE personnel who work part-time and/or summers and/or during sabbaticals.

8. News releases acknowledging contributions of equipment, material, supplies, etc.
9. News releases concerning field trips and presentations by resource persons.
10. Participation in awards and recognition assemblies or banquets.
11. Participation in program evaluation.

### Community Groups

In addition to employee and employer associations, other community groups are important audiences of CVOE public relations programs. Such groups include individuals with wide influence in the community.

Some of the types of groups are service clubs; social action groups, such as *Urban League* and *American Civil Liberties Union;* welfare agencies; and religious groups, such as a local group or council of religious leaders.

Some of the special ways to inform such groups are:

1. CVOE personnel and/or students making presentations at meetings.
2. Placing CVOE students at work stations in the offices of groups which support a permanent, salaried staff.
3. Contracting to do meaningful, paid work for special events, e.g., CVOE students man booths at fairs and trade shows, CVOE students construct floats or other decorations, CVOE students manage and conduct various surveys, fund drives, or campaigns. (Such projects should match learning objectives of particular CVOE student programs.)
4. CVOE and other LEA personnel join and participate in community groups, according to personal needs and convictions.

### Funding and Regulating Agencies

It is well to provide more than required information to agencies which fund and/or control such matters as licensing of graduates. Selected people in state education agencies and federal, state, and county or city regulatory agencies should be on mailing lists for brochures and special releases.

Some examples of informing agency personnel re CVOE activities are:

1. Sending annual reports to CVOE consultants in the SEA.
2. Inviting licensing agency officials to graduation ceremonies or awards and recognition banquets — sometimes as speakers.
3. Sending news releases regarding new equipment acquisitions and regular safety inspections to respective regulatory agency.

4. Sending findings of self-motivated evaluations to counterparts in SEA and licensing agencies.
5. Sending news releases regarding student placement to scholarship contributors.

## VEHICLES FOR PUBLIC RELATIONS

It would be well at this point to review the major vehicles for conducting public relations programs.

1. Informal personal contact is far and away the number one vehicle. CVOE personnel and students, more than any other vehicle, satisfy the continuity principle of public relations.
2. Special presentations, such as speeches by CVOE personnel other than LEA personnel and students, are similarly important. Insofar as possible, special presentations should be illustrated with pictures, slides, slide-tapes, etc.
3. Newspaper articles are usually the most important of public media.
4. Radio and television have potential for being as important as newspapers.
5. Printed materials such as brochures and posters are essential vehicles, especially for reaching potential students and other educators. Among the most useful vehicles are brochures which double as mailing pieces.
6. LEA catalogs, bulletins, student newspapers, house organs, and yearbooks are essential to publicizing CVOE programs and emphasizing special events and accomplishments.
7. Letters, LEA reports, meeting minutes, evaluation reports, etc. are essential for informing many internal and selected external publics.
8. Special LEA and community events add frosting to the public relations cake. Participation in parades, fairs, trade shows, open house, American Education Week, and other events which attract people from diverse community segments demonstrates that CVOE is a full, participating citizen and partner in the larger community.
9. Complimentary items such as pencils, key chains, tumblers, and calendars are effective reminders of opportunities discussed with CVOE personnel and students.

## TECHNIQUES FOR USING PUBLIC RELATIONS VEHICLES

Because it would be too ambitious and because LEA policies and procedures regarding printed publicity pieces and other vehicles must be taken into account, only some general hints regarding several public relations vehicles can be given here.

## Newspaper articles

Tips from the West Virginia manual (84) are very thorough.

### NEWSPAPER-WRITING TIPS

*THE FIVE W'S FORMULA:* The lead paragraph of a news story should answer the basic questions: WHO, WHAT, WHEN, WHERE, and WHY. The sample below illustrates how the five W's are applied to a newspaper story.

WHO     —John A. Doe, State Supervisor of Vocational Education
WHAT   —will address the _____Club.
WHEN  —12 o'clock noon Friday
WHERE—the_____ Hotel
WHY     —to discuss "Area Vocational Schools—An Answer to Un-
            employment"

These facts (the five W's) could be used in the same order as shown above. However, in many cases, the WHY is more important in catching the reader's eye than the WHO. With the facts rearranged in attention-getting fashion, the story would read:

> Reducing unemployment through the establishment of area voca-
> tional schools will be discussed by John A. Doe during a meeting of
> the _____ Club at 12 o'clock noon Friday at the _____
> Hotel. Doe is State Supervisor of Vocational Education.

1. Get the most important facts right at the beginning of a story.
2. The following newsworthy things at meeting or events:
   — Action taken (officers elected, awards presented, etc.)
   — Something of interest said (capture the two or three main ideas from what was said).
3. Paragraphs should be kept short (from 20 to 50 words). If they run longer, just break into two paragraphs.
4. Get as much human interest into story as possible. (People like to see their names and the names of their friends in print.)
5. Make sure all facts and names are correct. When there is a question about the spelling of a word or name, put the word "correct" in parentheses following it.
6. Do not put your own comments, opinions, or judgments into a story unless they are used as direct quotes or paraphrasings.
7. Be sure adjectives and adverbs do not express personal opinion.
8. Use third person. Do not use "we," "us," "our," etc.
9. Use simple, accurate, and vivid words. Always take the reader into consideration when writing.
10. Avoid using gobbledygook (high-toned, involved, and technical words).
11. Avoid using flowery figures of speech and trite expressions.
12. Check local newspapers for style practices and then follow their style. Style includes such things as capitalization and abbreviation. How do

the newspapers use the word "street"—St., street, or Street? How do they indicate time? As 7 P.M. Friday, or 7 o'clock Friday evening?

13. Use the inverted-pyramid style of writing (below). The detail is developed in order of importance. Each paragraph should seem to be the end. This is done so the editor, who has space requirements to meet, can cut off portions of the story from the bottom without losing important facts.

Most Important Facts

Less Important

Least

14. Remember to answer questions posed by the five W's:
    WHO    —Who presided, who spoke, who became new members, who made proposals, who reported accomplished projects, etc.?
    WHAT   —What organization, what action took place, etc.?
    WHEN   —Be exact as to the time (give day, date, and hour).
    WHERE—Give the exact meeting place (building and even room number when it is important).
    WHY    —Purpose of meeting or event. If a special meeting, tell why it was called.

15. Alternate releases between evening papers and morning papers. Give different twist to the same story if there are two or more papers competing for the news.

16. *Fillers*—Newspaper fillers, the small statements used to fill a column of type, are another means of getting facts before the public.

17. *Pictures*—Talk picture possibilities over with news contacts. Pictures of one- or two-column width are more likely to be used than larger ones. Provide a list of names with the picture, identifying people as they appear. Plan a picture that tells a story; confine the group to three or four people so they can be identified.

18. Remember—*It is not news too long after it happens!*

It is entirely possible to work with a local newspaper toward the end of devoting the bulk of a Sunday-feature color section to CVOE. A natural structure for a major presentation is (1) an introduction on common features, (2) descriptions of several CVOE programs with emphasis on pictures of students at work, and (3) a summary which outlines advantages to employers and the larger community. Advisors and other contributors to the total program might be listed and perhaps pictured in such a feature.

**Radio and Television**

Some news items which are appropriate for release to newspapers should also be released to radio and television. Most local radio stations are very cooperative with LEA's which release stories with human interest. Most radio stations are eager to air human-interest programs. A very successful format is to have CVOE students answer questions asked by CVOE personnel. Another successful format is CVOE students who work at one establishment and their supervisor(s) answering questions asked by CVOE personnel. Question and answer sessions may be taped or live. (Similar formats may be used for releases to print media.) Television stations are seldom interested in educational affairs which affect primarily one community. In metropolitan areas, groups of LEA's can well approach television station managers to arrange publicity for vocational/occupational education in general, for CVOE in general, and for special events which affect large numbers, e.g., area-wide contests and awards and recognition banquets. Television stations should be provided pictures or charts and posters with each release.

Some of the events which deserve preparation of releases to newspaper and broadcast media are:

1. Initation of CVOE program(s).
2. Significant additions to facilities and equipment for the CVOE program.
3. Sizeable contributions to laboratory, scholarship fund, and other portions of the program.
4. Organization of an advisory committee.
5. Student club activities of many kinds.
6. Field trips and presentations by resource persons.
7. Awards and recognition banquet highlights.
8. Contest requirements and participation.
9. Contest results.
10. Student performance at work stations and permanent job placements.
11. Accomplishments on licensing examinations.
12. Results of evaluations.

LEA's should not fail to consider the benefits of advertising in newspapers and on broadcast media (Fig. 16-1). If budget limitations are severe, institution-supported papers and stations may carry appropriate messages to publics already in contact with the LEA. But new audiences usually require external vehicles. Most segments of the public now deem it proper for educational enterprises, private and public, to describe programs and enrollment procedures via paid announcements. New CVOE programs and programs which have less than capacity enrollment and which lead to good employment prospects may be advertised without reservation.

**CARBONDALE COMMUNITY HIGH SCHOOL DISTRICT 165**
**OPERATION REBOUND**

**STUDENT REGISTRATION**

**AUGUST 19, 1975—TUESDAY 9:00 A.M. TO 3:30 P.M.**
**AUGUST 20, 1975—WEDNESDAY 9:00 A.M. TO 3:30 P.M.**

STUDENTS WILL REGISTER AT:

**UNIVERSITY CITY**
606 EAST COLLEGE - THIRD FLOOR
BRENTWOOD BOULEVARD
CARBONDALE, ILLINOIS

FOR INFORMATION TELEPHONE 549-8232. IF NO ANSWER TELEPHONE 457-5626.

**Fig. 16-1. Typical newspaper advertisement.**

### Awards and Recognition Banquet

One of the most talked about and memorable occasions of CVOE students' experiences is the awards and recognition banquet.[1] (This is often called the employer-employee banquet.) Although local conditions and mores will have great implication for the planning and conduct of a banquet, several general suggestions will apply in most LEA's.

Students and advisors should be involved from start to finish, i.e., from planning through evaluation. The banquet serves both student and employer needs so they should be permitted to contribute ideas and other resources. A small group of student club officers, advisory counsel representatives, and CVOE personnel might plan a banquet and present plans to their parent groups for approval. These steps should be taken several months in advance of the event. The same group might follow through, dividing labor into (1) arrangements for a facility and food, (2) arrangements for the agenda, and (3) invitations and awards.

Several decisions should be made before arrangements are finalized. Many LEA's must decide whether to have one or more banquets. Number and type of CVOE programs and community size affect this decision. If more than a few community members are expected to attend several banquets, it may be best to hold one, if there is an appropriate

[1]Some LEA's find it difficult to foster banquets. A meal function is very desirable but, an awards and recognition ceremony alone can suffice.

facility. Funding is another variable. It is possible for student clubs to pay expenses from club funds. Some employer or employee groups insist on sponsoring the banquet. A banquet committee should be permitted to decide upon funding. Who shall be invited is another matter. Obvious invitees are:

1. CVOE students
2. CVOE personnel
3. Selected administrators and counselors
4. Governing board members
5. Advisory committee members
6. Immediate supervisors of student-learners
7. Special members of a platform party, such as a clergyman and a speaker
8. Several people from news media
9. An institution photographer
10. Community or LEA personnel who have done special things for CVOE

Students and employers should be permitted to decide upon the invitation list. Involvement in such decisions has learning values.

The following agenda includes typical items for awards and recognition ceremonies.

1. Invocation
2. Meal
3. Introduction of people at head table
4. Introduction of other people such as club officers, advisors, and board members, who are not at the head table
5. Special speaker, student speaker, or CVOE supervisor who summarizes year's accomplishments
6. Awarding of certificates to each student and of special awards to students, contest winners, honor students, officers, etc.
7. Awarding of certificates to each supervisor and special awards to selected employers, e.g., one with most work stations or ones retiring, or ones completing terms on an advisory committee.
8. Special thank-you to counselors, librarians, etc. who have made special efforts in behalf of CVOE students
9. Projections for coming years
10. Benediction

The agenda should be divided among several persons. A planning committee could decide upon responsibilities. A club officer(s) should share in platform responsibilities, e.g., employer awards. Employer and employee representatives and especially the advisory committee chairman should also have some responsibility.

### Institution Awards Presentations

Outstanding CVOE students should be observed at graduation or special awards programs, which are conducted for the total institution. State and national contest winners and/or local winners, e.g., "best CVOE boy student" and "best CVOE girl student" should be presented with commemorative plaques or certificates just as music contest winners and others might be recognized. CVOE student clubs (see Chapter 15) should be very much involved in this part of the total public relations program.

## CALENDAR OF PUBLIC RELATONS

CVOE personnel should prepare rather definite calendars for public relations. To assure continuity of the total public relations program, calendars should carry over from one academic year to the next. Public relations cannot wait "for things to settle down" after a new term is begun. Some newsworthy items are slighted if plans are not progressive. At the risk of not being applicable to given LEA schedules, the calendar in Fig. 16-2 is presented to show a year-long plan. Obviously, items in the

## Calendar of Public Relations Events

### Late August—September

Talk at Faculty Orientation Meeting
Orientation of Students and Parents
Releases regarding training station placements
Plan schedule of home visits
Plan student club program, especially involvement in public relations
Release regarding club meeting
Release regarding advisory committee schedule and purposes

### October

Release to school paper and broadcast media regarding club activities
Talk to parents group
Talk to Chamber of Commerce Education Committee
Update career information materials with counselors and librarians
Order new brochures
Invite administrators to related classes, field trips, etc.
New release regarding employer followup survey

Fig. 16-2. Sample calendar for public relations events. (Cont'd on next page.)

## November

Compliment LEA American Education Week activities
Redo bulletin boards and displays
Make special efforts on releases to broadcast media
Mail new brochures to all mailing lists
Distribute brochures internally and to Chamber of Commerce

## December

Student Club party
Release regarding special student work assignments during shopping season and semester break
End of term report to administrators, advisors, and SEA personnel

## January

Student Assembly Program
Brochures to potential students, especially withdrawls and dropouts
Work with counselors on career nights
Speak to Rotary Club, offer to talk to others
Release regarding progress of CVOE students
Display at City Hall

## February

Special presentations to register rooms in feeder schools
Parents and spouses night
Alumni group meeting
Release regarding student club work
Release regarding state contests
Begin banquet plans

## March

Renewed efforts at involving administrators in field-trips, entertaining re-source persons
Release regarding student participation in state convention
Release regarding advisory committee meeting
Release regarding planned evaluation
Release regarding evaluation review team

## April

Student demonstrations at assembly
Plan annual reporting
Awards and Recognition Banquet
Release regarding banquet
Plan exhibits
Talk at parent's night in feeder school

Fig. 16-2. Sample calendar for public relations events. (Cont'd on next page.)

May

Release regarding permanent job placements

Release regarding advisory committee contributions and membership changes

Release regarding evaluation efforts

Send annual report to administrators, etc., as planned

June—Early August

Student Club float in July 4 Parade

Student Club man CVOE booth at Country Fair

Release regarding summer work in industry

Release regarding need for several more training stations

Release regarding alumni group meeting and contributions

Visit prospective students and parents or spouses

Release regarding finalization of student-learner placements

Release regarding student attendance at leadership conference

Fig. 16-2.  Sample calendar for public relations events.

illustration are only examples. Something on the order of fifty distinct events in a normal CVOE year are worthy of news releases. Thus, there should be at least 70 to 120 distinguishable public relations efforts in a typical CVOE year. A calendar should provide long-range and short-range targets. Each week the plans should be specified by date and by who does what and how for the next several weeks.

### A PUBLIC RELATIONS PLAN

Because LEA policies re public relations vary a great deal, it is essential that CVOE personnel assess local policy and procedures, prepare a statement re CVOE public relations, and obtain approval from as many administrative levels as possible. A public relations plan should begin with a very brief statement concerning the importance of publicizing the accomplishments of students, employers, and advisors. Then a plan should indicate what channels will be followed in making releases, accepting speaking engagements, etc. The bulk of a plan should include a listing of types of events which will be publicized, a list of types of other public relations efforts which will occur regularly and upon request, a list of vehicles and techniques which will be employed, indications regarding who will be responsible for various aspects of the program, and information regarding special costs, e.g., printing and postage.

Because nearly all LEA's have either formal policies or well-established procedures regarding public relations, there is little likelihood that a carefully designed and tactfully presented plan will be disapproved. The greater likelihood is (1) that CVOE personnel will be slightly overambitious re the number of public relations events which can be accomplished because of time and (2) that secretarial and clerical time and operating expenses such as printing and postage will be more than a little restraining.

## Summary

Public relations are inevitably a function of CVOE programs and personnel. Positive reasons are far and away adequate justification for careful planning and judicious execution of a great many public relations events. The fact that interfaces with internal and external publics are impossible, that is, the fact that a public relations program exists, even if by default, is also ample reason to plan and execute a multifaceted program which satisfies the six principles which introduced this chapter. Public relations:

1. Must be positive in nature.
2. Must be a continuous program.
3. Must be honest in both intent and execution.
4. Should be comprehensive in character.
5. Must be simple in meaning and conception.
6. Should be sensitive to the attitude and level of understanding of the public.

## Activities

1. Design a brochure for a CVOE program in your occupational area. Assume that the brochure may be used as a mailing piece. Indicate in outline form, what is to be contained on each panel of the brochure.
2. Prepare an outline for a ten-minute presentation to potential CVOE students and relatives.
3. Prepare a script for a twenty-minute presentation to a service club or chamber of commerce or union meeting.
4. Write news releases concerning a/an:

   a. Advisory committee meeting or advisory committee-related event
   b. Student club meeting or party
   c. New equipment acquisition
   d. New CVOE staff appointment
   e. CVOE banquet
   f. Year-end statistical and descriptive report

5. Prepare a script for a ten-minute radio spot for a teacher-coordinator and two student club officers. List questions an interviewer might ask and outline answers for the three participants.

6. Collect pictures, posters, and slides which might be used to illustrate various public relations efforts.
7. Prepare a month-by-month or week-by-week calendar of public relations events for an actual CVOE program or interview a CVOE supervisor or teacher coordinator to reconstruct a calendar of public relations events for the previous year.
8. Prepare a public relations plan, including the sections described in the final section of this chapter.

Section **Five**

# *Evaluation and Program Change*

# Chapter 17

# Evaluation

*Evaluation* in many forms is very much in vogue in educational and other enterprises which are supported in various ways by agencies of government. To vocational/occupational educators, the imposition of accountability measures is welcome because their work is very much in the interest of various segments of the citizenry and the general welfare. Cooperative Vocational/Occupational Education (CVOE) personnel are especially appreciative of evaluation because viable programs entail checks and balances which assure that they can only be benefited by fairly and thoroughly done assessments of strengths and weaknesses.

This chapter is neither a theoretical nor a broad treatment of evaluation. Furthermore, it does not describe the full range of selected evaluation techniques, such as student followups.[1] Rather, this chapter is a somewhat detailed description of (a) how to plan a system for evaluating CVOE and (b) of three particular techniques. Features of this chapter have been developed in light of the peculiar evaluation requirements of cooperative education and with knowledge regarding the effectiveness of various major approaches to improving vocational/occupational education.

Some of the outcomes of reading this chapter are:

1. Understanding major considerations which must be made by evaluation planners.
2. Ability to plan a calendar of evaluation events.
3. Ability to conduct student followups.
4. Ability to conduct employer followups.
5. Ability to manage team assessments of CVOE programs.
6. Understanding of several uses of checklists.

## PLANNING AN EVALUATION SYSTEM

The first principle of evaluation is that it must be done according to elements of an evaluation system. The elements of an evaluation system

---

[1]For extensive treatment of such matters as student and employer followups and team reviews, with emphasis on vocational/occupational education, see Wentling and Lawson (83).

cannot be well designed without careful consideration of a rather large number of matters which impinge upon CVOE programs in various ways.[2]

### Considerations for Evaluation System Planning

At least three categories of matters which relate to evaluation should be studied. First, it is essential to examine constraints which might be imposed by and assistance which might be provided by state education agencies. Many SEA's have evaluation systems for various components of education at various levels. CVOE personnel should acquire documents such as master plans for higher education, one- and five-year plans for vocational-technical education, requirements and guidelines for SEA approval and recognition of LEA's and LEA programs, guidebooks for evaluation of vocational/occupational programs, and policy and priority statements of state governing boards and councils which relate to vocational/occupational education. Such documents may impose requirements concerning types and timing of local evaluation activities, e.g., the SEA may require periodic followup studies of graduates. They are certain to describe evaluation activities which are managed by SEA's, e.g., several kinds of periodic on-site evaluations of programs, facilities, and personnel. Knowledge of such matters may help evaluation system planners define the scope and timing of certain system elements: (a) so that SEA requirements re local evaluation activities are satisfied and (b) so that data from and improvements which ensue from evaluation activities may be examined by SEA evaluators. (See Calendar of Major Evaluation Events later.)

Second, it is essential to examine LEA matters concerning evaluation. CVOE personnel must make determinations such as whether prime responsibility for research and evaluation has been assigned to an administrator; how many levels of approval must be sought for contemplated evaluation activities; and what secretarial, printing and duplicating, mailing, data processing, and other services central offices might provide. More important to system design decisions are such matters as LEA evaluation plans; reports of previous and schedules of future SEA visitations, regional accreditation visitations, and professional accreditation visitations; LEA policy and procedure statements which relate to evaluation; minutes or other reports of the work of bodies such as a citizens' advisory council, which might describe previous evaluations or concerns which could be pursued in future evaluations; differential cost studies; and reports of government, fire, safety, and sanitation inspections.

[2] That an LEA will be subjected to various evaluation activities and that various personnel will utilize voluntary evaluation techniques are given. Thus it is better to devise an evaluation system, i.e., to relate ongoing and new evaluation activities in meaningful ways.

Third, it is essential to examine documents relating to planning and evaluation of vocational/occupational education. Some kinds of these are: one- and five-year plans and related documents which are submitted to SEA's, reports of previous and schedules of future visitations by external agencies such as the state vocational-technical education agency or the *American Dental Hygienists' Association,* contractual agreements with other LEA's, contractual agreements with SEA's and other agencies for such things as CVOE programs for special needs students, vocational/ occupational education general and special advisory committee minutes and reports, summations of student learning in related classes and progress at training stations, monthly and annual teacher-coordinator reports of student work and coordination activities, and summations of relevant evaluation activities such as supervisor's ratings of teachers and student evaluations of instruction.

These kinds of documents will be useful to system designers and to the several kinds of internal and external evaluators, which are certain to be involved in any well-designed, multifaceted evaluation system.

### Working With a Design Task Force

In most LEA's, it is well to define an evaluation system design via a task force. A task force may consist of only internal people. But, experts, such as employers, SEA consultants, private consultants, and professors should be considered. Especially, if indecision or unresolvable controversy is likely to result during the work of a task force and, obviously, if an LEA has no competent evaluation specialist, an external expert can help to expedite good planning in a consultant's role. A consultant should be knowledgeable about vocational/occupational education, cooperative education, evaluation, tests and measurement, and LEA governance and decision making. A task force should be restricted to seven or less members, representing at least two levels of administration, the LEA's research and evaluation unit, and the CVOE program(s) for which an evaluation system is being designed. A written description of a task force's responsibilities, probable duration, membership, and requirements, such as secretarial services and access to LEA documents should be approved, preferably in writing, by appropriate levels of administration.

At minimum, the work of a task force should entail two meetings with assignments to be accomplished between the two meetings. The first meeting should accomplish the following:

1. Clear description of the need for a CVOE evaluation system design.
2. At least tentative definition of the scope of the system, e.g., all aspects

of three specific CVOE programs and relationships with but not details of ancillary services such as guidance, library, and learning resources.
3. Distribution of copies and/or explanations of provisions for accessibility of various documents described in the previous section. (Sections of documents especially pertinent to evaluation should be underscored or identified in some way.)
4. Distribution of lists of :
    a. Required planning and budget-related deadlines.
    b. Required evaluations and inspections and known and probable dates.
    c. Voluntary evaluations and inspections and known or approximate dates.
5. Description of kinds of evaluation activities which might be appropriate to CVOE. (Some of these are: student followup, employer followup, assessment of guidance services, assessment of services to special needs students, cost-effectiveness analysis, utilization of community resources, and provision of internal resources.) Written descriptions and sample evaluation instruments should be provided. Descriptions should indicate what evaluation outcomes respective instruments provide. (See below.)
6. Assigning responsibility for examining documents and considering possible evaluation activities in light of program objectives and assessment needs and constraints—external and internal. Task force members should be asked to consider the need for the kinds of information listed in Fig. 17-1.

The second task force meeting should accomplish the following:
1. Review of responsibilities.
2. Questions and answers regarding matters treated in distributed documents.
3. Questions and answers regarding various ongoing and potential evaluation activities.
4. Proposals from task force members for making evaluation more systematic by:
    a. deleting unnecessary ongoing evaluation activities.
    b. modifying ongoing evaluation activities.
    c. changing the schedules of ongoing activities.
    d. adding new evaluation activities to the system to acquire information for specified needs.
5. Discussion of proposals.
6. Decisions, via conference leadership and/or voting techniques, regarding a group proposal.
7. Explanation of the task force's future.

## Information Needs for CVOE Evaluation

A.  Employment in occupation(s) for which prepared.  _____
B.  Employment in related field.  _____
C.  Unemployment history.  _____
D.  Income and benefits.  _____
E.  Working conditions.  _____
F.  Job advancement and mobility.  _____
G.  Geographic mobility.  _____
H.  Educational history.  _____
I.  Reasons for continuing education.  _____
J.  Impact upon unemployment.  _____
K.  Similarities and differences of program leavers and graduates.
    _____

L.  Labor market trends.  _____
M.  Employer evaluations of job performance.  _____
N.  Employer comparisons of graduates of similar programs.  _____
O.  Adequacy of preparation for immediate employment.  _____
P.  Adequacy of preparation for advancement.  _____
Q.  Adequacy of preparation for continuing education.  _____
R.  Adequacy of specific program components.  _____
S.  Adequacy of ancillary services, such as guidance and learning
    resources.  _____

Fig.17-1.    List of information needs for CVOE evaluation.

The task force might be disbanded or asked to serve as the first members of a standing committee with responsibilities such as annual review of the evaluation system. In any event, the members should be led to understand what use will be made of their decisions. Typically, this will entail steps approximating the following:

1. CVOE supervisor(s) and/or vocational/occupational education director/dean prepare a proposal for submittal to chief administrative officer.
2. Chief administrative officer either approves the proposal with no or minor modification or returns it with suggestions for making it more acceptable. (In the latter case, CVOE leadership may wish to reassemble the task force.)
3. Chief administrative officer apprises other administrators and governing board of major features of the evaluation system.
4. CVOE leaders proceed at appropriate times to modify existing and implement new evaluation activities.

### Scheduling Evaluation Events

Evaluation activities will be poorly done if they occur in close time proximity. Evaluation activities will have little impact upon future learning experiences if they are done long after, rather than prior to, planning activities. Therefore, it is essential that CVOE, vocational/occupational, and LEA leadership maintain calendars of planning, budget-related, and evaluation events. Calendars should be updated continuously and should be available to all personnel, advisors, and consultants. It is well to devise a code system for indicating which events are certain to occur at specified times and which events may be rescheduled to accommodate local conditions. Professional personnel should be encouraged to schedule self-initiated evaluation activities when there will be adequate time and so that results may have maximum impact on planning and other evaluation activities.

The Sample Calendar of Planning, Budgeting, and Evaluation Events (Fig. 17-2) illustrates several kinds of decisions which an evaluation system design task force and CVOE leadership might make. Notations at the left-hand side depict various events which will occur during given months. Notations at the right-hand side of each of the five calendar pages depict modifications and additions which a task force might make to systematize existing evaluation activities. In sum, these entail: (1) Expansion of compulsory followup studies so that one- and three-year leavers and graduates of CVOE programs will be surveyed.[3] Note that only three of five programs will be studied in LEA year 2 (see Fig. 17-2). Cosmetology was scheduled so that data from both student and employer followup studies would be available to a review team later in the year. (2) Addition of employer followup studies, which parallel student followup studies by CVOE programs but occur several weeks later to avoid overloading clerical personnel. (3) Addition of team reviews of one or more programs each year, excepting the year (LEA year 3) when the SEA will be conducting a special on-site evaluation of vocational/occupational programs. Note that decisions regarding which CVOE programs to review each year are not indicated. Typically, such decisions cannot be made as long as four years in advance. Team reviews should be made when conditions have had time to stabilize, e.g., when leadership, facilities, and most employers have been associated with a program for several years or more. Thereafter, reviews should be made when matters such as competency demands or results of followup studies suggest that learning experiences need to be realized with demands of the occupation(s).

---

[3]As was indicated in Chapter 4, the authors are skeptical of the widespread recommendation that followup surveys be done one, three, and five years after graduation. Too many things change in five years. It is doubtful that many who recommend five-year followup have done one.

## Calendar of Planning, Budgeting, and Evaluation Events

LEA Year 1

MODIFICATIONS
AND ADDITIONS

August
  Compulsory followup of one- and three year
  graduates

September

October
  City fire marshall inspection
  Quarterly safety committee inspection

November
  Boiler and controls inspection

December
  Annual program description revisions

January
  Quarterly safety committee inspection

February                                       TEAM REVIEW OF 1
  Departmental budget proposals                CVOE PROGRAM,
                                               PREFERABLY
March                                          COSMETOLOGY
  1- and 5-year vocational-technical education
  plan

April
  Supply requisitions deadline
  Quarterly safety committee inspection
  Governing board deadline for contractual
  agreements for next year
  Governing board facilities inspection

May
  SEA special grants and projects proposal
  deadline
  Equipment requisition deadline
  Annual CVOE report
  Governing board budget meeting

June
  Annual SEA audit

July
  Special needs project audit

**Fig. 17-2. Sample calendar of planning, budgeting, and evaluation events. (Cont'd on next page.)**

LEA Year 2

August
   Compulsory followup of one- and three-year
   graduates

September

October
   City fire marshall inspection
   Quarterly safety committee inspection

November
   State Cosmetology licensing board visitation
   Boiler and controls inspection

December
   Annual program descriptions revisions

January
    Quality safety committee inspection

February
   Departmental budget proposals
   SEA recognition visitation (every 3 years)

March
   1- and 5 year vocational technical education plan
   Supervisory evaluate instruction

TEAM REVIEW OF
2 CVOE
PROGRAMS

April
   Supply requisition deadline
   Quarterly safety committee inspection
   Governing board facilities inspection

May
   Equipment requisition deadline
   Annual CVOe report
   Governing board budget meeting

June
   Annual SEA audit (semiannual
   vocational/technical audit)

July

**Fig. 17-2. Sample calendar of planning, budgeting, and evaluation events. (Cont'd on next page.)**

LEA Year 3

MODIFICATIONS
AND ADDITIONS

August
  Compulsory followup of one- and three-year
  graduates

September

October
  City fire marshall inspection
  Quarterly safety committee inspection

November
  Regional Accreditation Visitation (every 5-7
  years)
  Boiler and controls inspection

December
  Annual program description revisions

January
  Quarterly safety committee inspection

February
  Departmental budget proposals
  SEA vocational/occupational program approval
  visitation (every 5 years)

March
  One- and five-year vocational-technical
  education plan
  Supervisors evaluate instruction

April
  Supply requisitions deadline
  Quarterly safety committee inspection
  Governing board facilities inspection

AND SAFETY COMMITTEE
HOSTS VOCATIONAL/
OCCUPATIONAL EQUIPMENT
COMMITTEE REVIEW OF
FACILITIES AND EQUIPMENT

May
  Equipment requisition deadline
  Annual CVOE report
  Governing board budget meeting

June
  Annual SEA audit

July

**Fig. 17-2. Sample calendar of planning, budgeting, and evaluation events. (Cont'd on next page.)**

LEA Year 4

August
  Compulsory followup of one- and three-year
  graduates

September

October
  City fire marshall inspection
  Quarterly safety committee inspection

November
  Boiler and controls inspection

December
  Annual program descriptions revisions

January
  Quarterly safety committee inspection

February
  Departmental budget proposals

TEAM REVIEW OF
2 OR 3 CVOE
PROGRAMS

March
  One- and five-year vocational-technical
  education plan
  Supervisors evaluate instruction

April
  Supply requisitions deadline
  Quarterly safety committee inspection
  Governing board facilities inspection

May
  Equipment requisition deadline
  Annual CVOE report
  Governing board budget meeting

June
  Annual SEA audit (semiannual)
  vocational/technical audit)

July

Fig. 17-2. Sample calendar of planning budgeting, and evaluation events. (Cont'd on next page.)

LEA Year 5

**MODIFICATIONS
AND ADDITIONS**

August
  Compulsory followup of one- and three-year
  graduates

September

October
  City fire marshall inspection
Quarterly safety committee inspection

  November
Boiler and controls inspection

  December
    Annual program description revisions

January
  Quarterly safety committee inspection

February
  Departmental budget proposals
  SEA Recognition Visitation (every 3 years)

March
  1- and 5-year vocational-technical education
  plan
  Supervisors evaluate instruction

April
  Supply requisitions deadline
  Quarterly safety committee inspection
  Governing board facilities inspection

May
  Equipment requisition deadline
  Annual CVOE report
  Governing board budget meeting

June
  Annual SEA audit

July

FOLLOW-UPS OF 1 & 3
YEAR LEAVERS AND
GRADUATES OF 5
CVOE PROGRAMS

EMPLOYER
FOLLOW-UP
(SAME AS ABOVE)

TEAM REVIEW OF
? CVOE
PROGRAMS

**Fig.17-2.  Sample calendar of planning, budgeting, and evaluation events.**

The following sections of this chapter deal with four evalution activities which are potentially very beneficial to CVOE. Most of the evaluation outcomes described in this section can be secured through three of the activities which were added to the sample calendars, i.e., student followup studies, employer followup studies, and team reviews.

### STUDENT FOLLOWUP SURVEYS

Chapter 4 dealt with followup surveys from the standpoint of determining needs prior to initiating CVOE programs. The present concern is to evaluate ongoing programs. Student followup surveys (Figs. 17-3 through 17-6) are especially useful for gathering necessary information regarding items A to J and some information regarding items N to R of the list of information needs in the previous section. (See Fig. 17-1.) In keeping with the recommendation for CVOE program planners given in Chapter 4, evaluation system and component designers are admonished to become familiar with the literature of survey research. Wentling and Lawson (83) are especially important in this regard because they give chapter-length treatment of both student and employer followup surveys.

The following sample documents have been adopted from ones prepared via steps outlined in Chapter 4 and in accord with principles of item and questionnaire format. They have been found to be effective in LEA's.

### Cover Letter for Student Followup

(school letterhead)

(name)
(street)
(city)

Dear (use first name if appropriate):

We are conducting a survey of people who attended the _____ program. The enclosed form requires only a few minutes of your time and will help us to improve the program. Your responses will be held in strict confidence.

Please complete the form and return it in the self-addressed envelope.

I shall be personally grateful to you.

Sincerely,

(name)

Coordinator

Enclosure

**Fig. 17-3.   Sample cover letter for student followup survey.**

## Student Followup Form

(Name of CVOE Program Here)

## Background Information
1. Name _____ (type name before mailing) _____
2. Address Street _____
   City _____ State _____ Zip Code _____
3. Telephone number _____
4. Person who will always know your address
   Name _____
   Street _____
   City _____ State _____ Zip Code _____
5. Marital Status       5. Military Status
   single _____    active _____
   married _____    reserve _____
   divorced _____    veteran _____
                   does not apply _____
6. Employment Status (check one)
   _____ working
   _____ working and looking for a different job in my line of work
   _____ working and looking for a job in a new line of work
   _____ not working and not looking for work
   _____ not working and looking for work
7. Employment history (complete appropriate blanks)

| month & year | employer | job title | hourly or monthly (pay optional) |
|---|---|---|---|
| | | | |
| | | | |
| | | | |
| | | | |
| | | | |
| | | | |

8. Employment expectations (check one)
   _____ remain in present job
   _____ remain in present occupation but change employers
   _____ advance in my line of work
   _____ change lines of work
   _____ discontinue working
   _____ return to working as soon as I can

Fig. 17-4. Sample student followup form. (Cont'd on next page.)

Educational History and Plans

9. Since attending                              10. In future I plan to attend

_____
(name of program here)

I attended

_____trade school      _____
_____technical institute   _____
_____community college  _____
_____four year college   _____
_____military school    _____
_____adult classes     _____

11. Relevance of High School (Community College, Institute, Whatever) Training (will the response which best describes your opinion)

SA strongly agree          D disagree
A agree                    SD strongly disagree
N neither agree nor disagree

| SA | A | N | D | SD | |
|----|---|---|---|----|--|
| SA | A | N | D | SD | name of program here was the right one for me. |
| SA | A | N | D | SD | a counselor helped me get a job. |
| SA | A | N | D | SD | a teacher helped me get a job. |
| SA | A | N | D | SD | getting a job was easy. |
| SA | A | N | D | SD | my job skills were good enough to g get me started. |
| SA | A | N | D | SD | coop experiences were important. |
| SA | A | N | D | SD | related class experiences were good. |
| SA | A | N | D | SD | English was relevant to my work. |
| SA | A | N | D | SD | _____ was relevant to my work. |
| SA | A | N | D | SD | (List vocational/occupational) was relevant to my work. |
| SA | A | N | D | SD | courses or was relevant to my work. |
| SA | A | N | D | SD | course units was relevant to my work. |
| SA | A | N | D | SD | such as human was relevant to my work. |
| SA | A | N | D | SD | relations and was relevant to my work. |
| SA | A | N | D | SD | safety here was relevant to my work. |

12. Suggestions for improving name of program here
(circle one response for each item)
It would be better to

| SA | A | N | D | SD | |
|----|---|---|---|----|--|
| SA | A | N | D | SD | begin classroom experiences earlier. |
| SA | A | N | D | SD | begin laboratory experiences earlier. |
| SA | A | N | D | SD | begin coop experiences earlier. |
| SA | A | N | D | SD | vary coop experiences more. |
| SA | A | N | D | SD | deal more with manuals and reference books. |
| SA | A | N | D | SD | deal more with job information and advancement. |
| SA | A | N | D | SD | deal more with educational opportunities. |

Fig. 17-4. Sample student followup form. (Cont'd on next page.)

| SA | A | N | D | SD | provide more job placement services. |
|----|---|---|---|----|--------------------------------------|
| SA | A | N | D | SD | provide more information about scholarships. |
| SA | A | N | D | SD | provide more individual instruction. |
| SA | A | N | D | SD | provide more leadership training. |
| SA | A | N | D | SD | provide more decision making experiences. |

13. Comments

The one most valuable feature of the program was _____

because _____

_____

_____

The one best way to improve the program would be to _____

_____

_____

_____

**Fig. 17-4.   Sample student followup form.**

## Reminder Card for Student Followup

Dear_____,

Recently, we mailed a survey form, asking you to help us improve the _____ program. Because the mailing has not been returned to us, we assume you are going to complete the form and return it. Please do so at your earliest convenience.

Sincerely,

Coordinator

**Fig. 17-5.   Sample reminder card for student followup survey.**

They illustrate (1) a survey form (see Fig. 17-4) which might result from efforts of CVOE personnel and others to design items which elicit information appropriate to selected objectives and (2) a cover letter (see Fig. 17-3), a reminder card (see Fig. 17-5), and a reminder letter (see Fig. 17-6).

They also illustrate certain practices which CVOE personnel are usually somewhat better able to utilize than are others, such as research directors. Some of these practices are:

1. Using first names in the salutation because of familiarity with the previous student.
2. Using identical documents for early leavers and graduates.
3. Being somewhat terse and rather insistent, in keeping with previous coordinator-student relationships.
4. Expressing personal gratitude.

## Reminder Letter for Student Followup

(letterhead)

(name)

(street)

(city)

Dear (use first name if appropriate):

We are anxious to summarize results of our survey and note that we do not have your response to an earlier mailing. Please use the enclosed form and envelope so that we may have your valuable input.

I shall be personally grateful for your immediate response.

Sincerely,


Coordinator

Enclosure

**Fig. 17-6.   Sample reminder letter for student followup survey.**

5. Obtaining ratings of CVOE program components, ancillary services, and vocational/occupational courses and units.

In given situations, it would be wrong to utilize all or parts of the sample survey form. Rather, CVOE and related personnel should go through all of the well-established steps for assuring an effective survey, e.g., locating previous students, deciding what to accomplish by mail, telephone, and personal interview, and constructing items in accord with information needs. Special efforts should be made to construct items which will elicit judgments regarding the relevance of CVOE experiences to employment realities. Items which deal with the relevance of CVOE and related experiences should be constructed with the respective CVOE program uppermost in mind and with terms which previous students will understand. (This is reason enough for local design of survey forms.)

It is well to devote every necessary effort to development of a valid instrument so that it can be used for several years. It will be more than interesting to compare and contrast (1) responses of different groups of graduates, (2) responses of early leavers and graduates, and (3) responses of given individuals two years apart.

### Collating and Presenting Results

Student surveys will entail fewer than 100 returns per CVOE program, excepting instances wherein several attendance centers use the same survey form (see Fig. 17-4). Therefore, it will seldom be appropriate to use computer or machine tabulation. With the exception of item 7, items 5-12 on the sample form can best be collated and presented as percentages. Copies of the instrument will do nicely for tallying and then indicating percentages for each response. Responses to item 7 should be examined to see what format might best summarize responses. A bar graph of months prior to advancement, a frequency listing of job titles, and a frequency listing within income levels might be useful. Item 13 usually results in a wide range of responses, which can best be summarized by listing several common compliments and several frequent and meaningful recommendations for improvement.

Results should be disseminated to a predetermined list of personnel, e.g., administrators, counselors, CVOE supervisor, respective coordinators, and to advisory committee members. The chief administrator may wish to distribute copies to governing board members. It may be appropriate to attach a copy to an annual report to the SEA. Especially, if student organization leaders have been involved in designing and conducting the study, they should be privileged to examine results. (See Chapter 18 regarding utilization of results.) The general publicity value of student followup surveys should be realized by disseminating positive summary information to the media. (See Chapter 16, Public Relations.)

## EMPLOYER FOLLOWUP SURVEYS

Employer followup surveys (Figs. 17-7 through 17-9) should be companions to student followup surveys. The two kinds of surveys provide checks and balances on similar kinds of information and information which can only be gotten via one or the other. Evaluators must make essentially the same decisions regarding employer followup as regarding student followup. The major ones of these are:

1. What evaluation system information needs should be satisfied by this evaluation activity?
   Information needs K-N which were listed early in this chapter can be satisfied rather completely by employer followup surveys (see Fig. 17-1). Needs O-R can be partially satisfied.
2. What data collection method(s) will be effective and manageable?
   Three should be considered: face-to-face interview, telephone interview, and mailed questionnaire. Community size, distance, familiarity with sponsors and supervisors, degree of detail of the survey, and other factors govern this choice. In most instances, the mailed questionnaire technique will be most manageable and productive.
3. What categories of information, item types, and format should be used?

## Cover Letter Employer Followup

(school letterhead)

(name)
(street)
(city)

Dear_____:

We are conducting a survey of employers or supervisors of people who attended the _____program. The enclosed form takes only a few minutes to complete. We would like the immediate supervisor or someone who is familar with the performance of (graduate's name) to complete the form and return it in the enclosed envelope.

Please be assured that responses will be held in absolute confidence.

Results of this survey will be used to improve the _____ program and related services.

I shall be personally grateful to you.

Sincerely,

Coordinator

Enclosure

**Fig. 17-7.  Sample cover letter for employer followup survey.**

As was indicated in the treatment of student followup surveys, matters such as these are critical but beyond the scope of this book.

4. Who should be involved in survey design, collation of findings, and utilization of results?

Obviously, members of an evaluation system design task force, several levels of administration, CVOE personnel, guidance and placement personnel, should have various inputs. Student organization leaders might also play positive roles (but not be privy to confidential information).

The following sample documents have been adopted from ones which have been prepared via steps outlined for student followup surveys in Chapter 4 and in accord with principles of item and questionnaire format. They have been found to be effective with supervisors in many kinds of establishments. They illustrate (1) a survey form (see Fig. 17-8) which might result from efforts of CVOE personnel and others to design items appropriate to selected objectives and (2) a cover letter (see Fig. 17-7), and a reminder letter (see Fig. 17-9).

## Employer Followup Form

(name of CVOE program here)

1. Name of Employer or Supervisor _____
2.          Establishment _____
3. Name of Employee _____
4.          Employee's graduation date _____
5. What is your job title? _____
6. What is this employee's job title: _____
7. In what capacity are you related to this employee? _____
8. Employee Characteristics:

(Circle the response which best describes your opinion)

| | | | |
|---|---|---|---|
| SA strongly agree | | D disagree | |
| A agree | | SD strongly disagree | |
| N neither agree nor disagree | | | |

### This employee is

| SA | A | N | D | SD | |
|----|---|---|---|----|---|
| SA | A | N | D | SD | punctual. |
| SA | A | N | D | SD | reliable and dependable. |
| SA | A | N | D | SD | eager to get along with others. |
| SA | A | N | D | SD | well mannered. |
| SA | A | N | D | SD | better prepared than people from other preparatory programs. |
| SA | A | N | D | SD | thorough and accurate. |
| SA | A | N | D | SD | doing high quality work. |
| SA | A | N | D | SD | competent with planning and mental tasks. |
| SA | A | N | D | SD | competent with manual tasks. |
| SA | A | N | D | SD | willing to be supervised. |
| SA | A | N | D | SD | pleased to take suggestions. |
| SA | A | N | D | SD | adaptable. |
| SA | A | N | D | SD | able to make good judgments. |
| SA | A | N | D | SD | likely to be promoted in average time. |
| SA | A | N | D | SD | likely to benefit from additional education and training. |
| SA | A | N | D | SD | likely to get ahead. |
| SA | A | N | D | SD | safety conscious. |

9. Comments

The one outstanding strength of this employee when he/she came to work here was _____

The one outstanding weakness of this employee when he/she came to work here was _____

The two skills or personal qualities which I value most in new employees are _____

Fig. 17-8.  Sample employer followup form.

## Reminder Letter For Employer Followup

(letterhead)

(name)
(street)
(city)
Dear_____    _____

   We are anxious to summarize results of our survey of people who
attended the _____ program and note that we do not have a
response from the supervisor of (graduates name). We hope that the
supervisor or someone who is familiar with this employee's performance will complete the enclosed form and mail it in the enclosed
envelope before week's end.

   I shall be personally grateful for your attention to this important
matter.

Sincerely,


Coordinator

**Fig. 17-9.   Sample reminder letter for employer followup form.**


### Sample Reminder Card

   LEA personnel should judge whether to use reminder cards and/or
telephone calls and/or reminder letters to ask nonrespondents to respond.
If a card is used, the wording used on the sample reminder card student
followup would do nicely. Reminders need not take the same form for
each nonrespondent.

   Employer followup survey instruments can be made more specific if
CVOE personnel want to assess the appropriateness and effectiveness of
various program components. Opinions regarding the scope and rigor of
knowledge, mental skill, and manual skill development activities in related classes and at training stations can be assessed by instrument items
which are designed for a specific CVOE program. For example, typing,
filing, customer relations, and personnel relations components of a particular office occupations program could be evaluated by adding four or
more items to the sample followup form.


### Collating and Presenting Results

   Statements regarding student followup surveys apply here as well. In
most instances, employer followup studies result in information which is
especially newsworthy. Releases which entail charts which result from

collating responses to selected survey items and representative (positive) statements made in response to open-ended questions are very well received by many publics. (See Chapter 16, Public Relations.)

(See Chapter 18 regarding utilization of results.)

## TEAM REVIEWS

Educators have long made good use of evaluations done by teams of educators. Especially in recent times, in vocational/occupational education, laymen, employer and union representatives, and students have served on review teams. There are a number of good designs for team reviews. The design which is described here is only a little more sophisticated than typical reviews which good CVOE personnel have utilized for many years. Serious students of evaluation should study the literature of evaluation and accreditation to discover types of team reviews which might serve special evaluation goals. Following are the major steps in a procedure for planning and conducting a team review of a CVOE program or several programs.

### CVOE Staff Define Review Goals

By definition a team review takes a global view of selected aspects of a program or programs and related services. Team review collects information from various sources and results in recommendations for improving program components. The first substantial step which CVOE staff members must take after LEA leadership have approved pursuit of this evaluation activity is to define review goals. A subcommittee of an advisory committee might well be involved in defining review goals and other aspects of a team review.

Goals should be defined very specifically along three dimensions. The *first* dimension has to do with number of CVOE programs. Unless vocational/occupational CVOE leadership personnel have a great deal of experience with review teams, it is well to review one CVOE program at a time.

After various personnel have at least minimal experience with team reviews, several CVOE programs can well be reviewed simultaneously. For example, all business and office-related programs or all agriculture and ag-related programs might be reviewed at one time. Similarly, a technical institute serving a rather distinct number of employers via three or four medical-related programs might be wise to conduct a team review of all programs—the better to benefit all programs with information from employers and the better to minimize LEA expense and time which employers must give to interviews.

The *second* dimension has to do with level on the education ladder. Even LEA's in the private sector may wish to evaluate articulation with secondary schools. Relationships with counselors and articulation with certain secondary school subjects are very important to matters such as entrance requirements, prerequisites, and the design of initial learning experiences in any LEA. Similarly, CVOE personnel may wish to know how graduates fare in subsequent preparatory programs. If significant numbers of graduates pursue related advanced study soon after graduation, it is well to assess the degree to which a CVOE program prepares people for such study.

The *third* dimension has to do with areas of concern.[4] Checklist and interview items listed in the next section of this chapter are categorized as follows:

administration,
objectives,
internal resources,
external resources,
student ingression and placement,
classroom instruction and learning,
training stations,
program management,
youth organizations,
guidance services, and
public relations.

CVOE staff should determine which of these areas of concern should be investigated by an evaluation team. Definition of evaluation goals along this dimension will have implications for approvals of the team review design, team makeup, and team interview schedules.

Review goals should be written as specifically as possible. After consideration of many matters, a CVOE staff might state goals as follows:

1. To review the associate degree automotive technology program and related, supportive courses such as physics and mathematics.
2. To assess quality of relationships with professionals and potential students in "feeder" institutions.
3. To assess quality of student matriculation and performance in industrial training and baccalaureate programs.
4. To assess objectives, internal resources, external resources, training stations, program management, and youth organizations.
5. To utilize reports and other inputs from previous assessments of guidance services, student ingression and placement, classroom

[4]The term *areas of concern* is taken from the Illinois Division of Vocational Technical Education's on-site evaluation system, which deals with eight areas of concern similar to, but by no means identical to, the eleven listed here.

instruction and learning, and administration and public relations functions.

**Define Team Makeup and Schedule**

Review teams must consist of people who represent various interests. At minimum, a CVOE program review team should have representatives of (1) employer, (2) employee, (3) educator, and (4) student viewpoints. (Sometimes a recent graduate can represent both student and employee viewpoints.) Decisions regarding the makeup of a team should begin with identification of a review team leader. The team leader should have experience on evaluation teams, more than simple familiarity with the kind of program(s) to be evaluated, facility for supervising others, and writing ability. In most instances, the team leader should be from outside the LEA. A CVOE leader from another attendance center or a neighboring LEA is often appropriate. Sometimes an employer who has had various associations with educational enterprises can perform the team leader functions.

If only one CVOE program is to be reviewed, one or two employers should serve on the team. In the case of an automotive technology associate degree program, a service manager from a dealership and an independent garage owner would be appropriate. An officer of an association of service station owners and managers would also be appropriate. The major kinds of establishments which provide work stations and employ graduates should be represented — not necessarily by one team member for each type of establishment. Team members may come from the immediate service area or from a neighboring LEA. People from some distance away are more apt to make unbiased assessments. (But, LEA's will incur more travel and lodging expense.)

Employees should be represented by an association officer or business agent if an organized labor group(s) serves workers in respective occupations in the community. If there is no organized employee group, one or two people with varied and successful experience should serve on the team.

Educators should be selected according to familiarity with the areas of concern which will be assessed. In the example which is being used here, one or two people with CVOE experience in automotives would do nicely. In other instances, an administrator at the principal/dean or superintendent/president level and a counselor or placement officer would be needed to make judgments regarding the respective areas of concern to be assessed.

A student team member(s) can help other team members focus upon matters important to enrolled students. An officer of a youth organization in a neighboring LEA is a good selection. The student should be enrolled in or be a recent graduate of a cooperative program but need not be from the occupational area which is under review.

The size of a review team should depend primarily upon the number of people to be interviewed and secondarily upon matters such as accessibility of people to be interviewed, quantity of documents a team may be expected to examine, and number of areas of concern about which recommendations may be given. Table 17-1 indicates how many people of various kinds might be interviewed regarding the automotive program. Assuming that actual interviews and travel between interviews will average one hour, and realizing that some people will be interviewed in groups, it is well to estimate 36-40 hours of interview time. Assuming further that interviews are to be conducted during one working day (and that an evaluation report will be drafted that evening and the next day) it is apparent that six team members, conducting six or seven interviews each, can make the necessary contacts. Thus, the review team might consist of a/an:

CVOE supervisor serving as team leader,
service manager from a dealership,
independent garage owner/mechanic,
union business agent,
teacher-coordinator from a similar program, and
Vocational Industrial Clubs of America president.

## Table 17-1. People Interviewed by a Review Team

| | Individuals | Contacts | |
|---|---|---|---|
| Administrators | 2 | 2 | |
| Counselors | 2 | 2 | |
| Academic Teachers | 2 | 2 | |
| Occupational Teachers | 2 | 2 | |
| CVOE Personnel | 2 | 2 | |
| Employers and Supervisors | 16 | 10 | (establishments) |
| Coop Students at Work | 12 | 10 | (establishments) |
| Coop Students in the LEA | 8 | 2 | (groups) |
| Counselors and Others in "Feeder" Schools | 6 | 3 | (schools) |
| Placement Service, Chamber of Commerce, and Other Advisory Committee Members | 4 | 1 | (at a coffee) |
| Total | 56 | 36 | |

Potential team members should be identified from among their peers on the basis of experience or background in or with the CVOE, familiarity in relating to people, and ability to express viewpoints.

The following is a typical schedule which has worked well for team reviews of the type being developed here.

*DAY 1*

| | |
|---|---|
| 4:00 P.M. | Team assembles in motel meeting room. |
| | Team leader orients team to evaluation goals, schedules, etc. |
| 5:00 P.M. | Dinner with CVOE personnel, advisory committee, and chief administrator(s). |
| 5:45 P.M. | Chief administrator and CVOE personnel describe program, identifying strengths, weaknesses, problems, etc. as they view them. |
| 6:30 - 8:00 P.M. | Tour of in-house facilities and orientation to community. |

*DAY 2*

| | |
|---|---|
| 8:00 A.M. - 3:00 P.M. | Interviews |
| 3:00 - 5:00 P.M. | Team review of documents, interview notes and sharing of observations. |
| 5:30 P.M. | Team dinner. |

*DAY 3*

| | |
|---|---|
| 8:00 - 9:00 A.M. | Special interviews. |
| 9:00 A.M. - Noon | Finalize Report. |
| 1:30 P.M. | Oral report (team leader only). |

### Obtain Necessary Sanctions for Review Plan

This important step should be completed by CVOE and/or vocational/ occupational program leadership. One or more levels of administration and, in some instances, the governing board should approve the review plan, including team makeup (not by name), general schedule of events, and specific dates. Sanction should include approval of procedures for reimbursing lodging, meals, and travel expenses of team members. It should also include approval of group meal functions and incidental costs, such as printing evaluation reports.

### Invite Team Members

Team members should be invited by the CVOE supervisor or the chief administrative officer, depending upon acquaintanceships, etc. Initial contact by telephone or face-to-face requests should be followed by confirming letters. Following is an outline for telephone contact (Fig. 17-10) and a confirming letter to an evaluation team member (Fig. 17-11).

## Sample Outline for Telephone Invitation of Potential Team Member

1. "Hello. This is _____ from _____. How are you today?"
2. Recall some positive experience, e.g., a good student, service on an advisory committee, support of school's victory at interscholastic event.
3. "You have been recommended by _____ for a job we think you can do better than anyone else can do it."
4. "I am calling to enlist your help in a project which will improve our cooperative program. We would like you to serve on an evaluation team. We are going to assemble a team to review the Automotive Technology program.
5. "Do you think you could help us to learn what we can do to improve? Before you say yes or no, I would like to tell you what is involved.
    A. "Because of your background, you would have no preparation other than looking at a few things we would send you.
    B. "But the job would consume some of your valuable time. Approximately two evenings and two days (adjust if review is to be shorter or longer) are involved. But you might like the fact that it would be a one-shot deal. You would be over and done with the job quickly.
    C. "You would work with five other people and interview people in the school (college) (whatever) and the community. On the afternoon of the first day and the morning of the second and last day, you would help the team leader draft an evaluation report.
    D. "You would have dinner one evening, work through the next day and early evening, and finish on the second morning."
6. "Could you help us with this important job?"
   Assuming Agreement:
7. Letter will follow.
8. Reimbursement for:
9. Materials will be sent.
10. Thank you/we'll be in touch.

Fig. 17-10. Outline for telephone invitation to a potential evaluation team member.

## Sample Confirming Letter to Evaluation Team Member

(letterhead)

Dear Mr. Siegfried:

This is to confirm the salient features of our conversation re the team review of the Automotive Technical program. As indicated, the schedule for the evaluation will be:

1st Day _____3, 19\_\_\_\_    4:00
Orientation Meeting
5:00 P,.M.
Dinner and Orientation to Program
and Personnel

2nd Day_____4, 19\_\_\_\_    8:00 A.M.
Interview people and collect data.
3:00 P.M. to 5:00 and 7:00 P.M. to
8:30 P.M.
Share observations and draft report.

3rd Day _____ 5, 19\_\_\_\_    8:00 A.M. to noon
Collect necessary additional data
and finalize report.

We shall be sending a packet of materials about the program(s) in a few days. You should study these before coming to the orientation meeting at 4:00 P.M. on _____at the _____ Motel.

Please be assured that we shall do everything possible to make you comfortable.

You will be reimbursed for the travel, room, and meal expenses.

Sincerely,

Supervisor, Automotive Technology

**Fig. 17-11.  Confirming letter to evaluation team member.**

### Send Materials to Team Members

Review team members should be provided with materials which will help them understand various aspects of the ongoing program(s). Items which should be provided include:

State education agency regulations and evaluation requirements,
The local education agency's general program and student guidebooks,
Plan documents for vocational/occupational programs,
Program and course outlines,
Reports from evaluations or accreditation visits during the past several years,
Results of student followup studies,
Results of employer followup studies,
Program reports and records,
Assessments of student progress in related classes,
Assessments of student progress at training stations,
Results of student evaluations of instruction,
Sample training agreements,
Sample training plans, and
Advisory committee reports.

CVOE personnel should use judgment in deciding which items to mail to team members for study prior to the visitation. Obviously, large documents which bear only indirectly upon the visitation need not be duplicated. Some things should be made available for the team's use during the visitation. Some LEA's have been pleased with the decision to send all but evaluation reports to team members and to provide several copies of relevant evaluation reports for use in the team's meeting room.

### Provide for Team Accommodations

Review teams should be provided a number of things to assure comfort and convenience. Those who do not reside nearby should have reserved motel/hotel rooms. The team should have a comfortable meeting room with a large work table in the motel/hotel or in the LEA. The meeting room should have coffee/tea and snacks. Plans should be made for scheduled meal functions and restaurants should be recommended for other meals. Parking permits, maps, building layouts and other courtesies should be extended.

### Meet With Team Leader

The CVOE supervisor should meet with the team leader at least several days prior to the visitation. The team leader should be provided with relevant materials which might not have been sent to team members and with items such as parking permits for the team. Together, the supervisor and the team leader should make up interview schedules for each of the team members. Insofar as possible, each team member should interview several kinds of people on the interview list. For example, an employer should see employers *and* some people in the LEA.

### Orient Team Members

The team leader should orient team members. He should provide name tags, engage in casual conversation, assure that team members have accommodations, answer questions, and allay apprehensions as team members arrive. After all have arrived and been made comfortable, the team leader should deliberately and thoroughly complete the following orientation steps:

Define the team review goals. (See five review goals stated early in this chapter.)

Distribute and describe uses of checklists (see next section of this chapter) for each area of concern.

Describe the overall time schedule.

Distribute and discuss individual interview schedules.

Distribute and discuss Principles of Interviewing (See illustration).

Discuss again the team members' time commitments and interviewing schedule.

Describe procedures which will be used in report-writing sessions, allaying concerns about writing abilities by indicating that the team leader will be responsible for rhetoric.

Describe the oral report, explaining that team members are not expected to attend.

The Illinois handbook (30) provides the following information on principles of interviewing.

### Principles of Interviewing

Interviewing is a basic method — a machine — of the Three Phase Evaluation System. An interview, then, is not just a conversation; it is, rather, a carefully thought out technique for finding out from respondents (the people we interview) how things are and how people feel and think. The interview itself is not intended to change or influence the respondent. The interviewer, therefore, must be an understanding person, capable of accepting what the respondent says without judging or rejecting him.

We know that in order to understand a person we must know what some of his needs are. A respondent in an interview situation has needs which the interviewer must understand and try to meet:

\_\_\_\_\_the respondent needs to see the interviewer as someone who is not a threat to his immediate or future well-being, nor to his self-esteem;

\_\_\_\_\_he needs to see the evaluation itself as not posing a threat;

\_\_\_\_\_he needs to understand, even in a limited way, the purpose of the evaluation, the reason he was selected and why his cooperation is required;

\_\_\_\_\_he needs to see the interview situation as a pleasant way of spending some time;

\_\_\_\_\_he needs to feel, after the interview is completed, that he has had a real opportunity to express himself freely on the subject.

To meet these needs of the respondent, the interviewer must be very conscious of what he is doing and how he is doing it. Certain techniques should be followed to help insure a good interviewing relationship, as well as to obtain an accurate, unbiased interview. Let us now turn to a discussion of some of those techniques and procedures.

A good interviewing relationship requires that the respondent feel relaxed and at ease with the interviewer—to the point where he feels free to say what he *really* thinks or feels about a given subject, without fear of criticism or disapproval. To maintain an atmosphere of this kind, the interviewer must have a sympathetic interest in people and the ability to recognize and understand their feelings. He must respond in both an encouraging, reassuring or supportive way. But support should not influence or bias the content of what they say. Assuming you have the basic conviction and sincerity necessary to good interviewing, you will rapidly become sensitive to the moments in an interview where encouragement or reassurance is needed, but some standard professional procedure will help you both to minimize the need and to deal with it when it arises.

Generally, keep the following points in mind while conducting an interview:

a. Be *friendly and informal* but, at the same time, *professional* in your manner. Remember that you are a stranger, and everything you say or do should help to gain the respondent's confidence in you as well as in himself.

b. Be a *sympathetic, interested* and *attentive* listener. Encouraging nods, "uh-huh's," "I know how you feel," and similar gestures will convey to the respondent that he is understood and that his opinions are valued and appreciated. But don't overdo it! There is nothing quite so distracting to the average person as the listener who keeps up a running stream of "uh-huh," "is that so," when it's not needed. A nod of the head is usually a much more articulate way of showing your interest than a constant clucking in the background, which many respondents will feel is a camouflage for a lack of genuine interest in them and their problems.

c. Be *neutral* with respect to the subject matter. Do not express your own opinions either on the subjects being discussed by the respondent or on the respondent's ideas about those subjects. You must never betray feelings of shock, surprise, indignation or disapproval at what the respondent is saying either by word or involuntary gesture. Your job is to understand and accept what he is saying, not to approve or disapprove of it, nor to agree or disagree with it.

d. Be *observant*. Be alert to the way in which the respondent expresses himself and to the gestures he uses. These signs may serve as cues that the respondent is becoming uncomfortable and ill at ease or that he is not expressing what he really feels.

e. Last but not least, *be at ease yourself*, in the interview situation. If you feel hesitant, embarrassed, hurried, or awkward, the respondent will soon sense this feeling and behave accordingly.

Beyond these standard points applicable to all interviews, there are some respondents or situations that require encouragement or reassurance either in getting the interview started or during its course. The cardinal principle in all of these cases is to put the respondent at his ease and to get him interested in the interview, so frequently you will know what to do simply by putting yourself in the respondent's position, and asking yourself how you would be feeling under those circumstances. See the Illinois handbook (30).

These steps in the orientation should be accomplished by the team leader prior to dinner. At dinner, the team leader should introduce team members and the chief administrator should introduce LEA personnel and advisors. After dinner, LEA personnel should talk about program strengths, felt weaknesses, problems, etc. The bulk of the time should entail a tour of relevant LEA facilities and orientation to the community, with emphasis on how to travel to appointments for the next day.

### Assist Team Members

LEA personnel should provide guides for team members for at least part of day two. One way to assure team members good starts on their interviews is to assign a student to each team member. The student can be interviewed by the team member at breakfast and can then escort the team member to the first two or three interviews. LEA personnel should also assure that special groups, such as advisors, are assembled for planned group interviews. At the end of the last report-writing session, someone from the LEA should review reimbursement procedures and thank team members as they leave.

### Report Writing

LEA personnel should be on call to answer questions and give assistance if requested during report-writing sessions. But, only team members should attend writing sessions. The following illustrations describe a suggested report format (Fig. 17-12).

Title Page


TEAM REVIEW


Automotive Technology


Midtown Community Schools

May 1978


*Notes:*
1. Title page and back cover of heavy stock.
2. Use plastic or theme binders.

**Fig. 17-12. Sample evaluation report format. (Cont'd on next page.)**

Team List Page

Team Leader

_____

_____

CVOE Supervisor
Providence Community College

Team Members

_____

_____

Service Manager
Xalto Dealership

_____

_____

Manager
Ajax Independent Garage

_____

_____

Business Agent
Local 1057

_____

_____

Student
Ralston Community Technical Institute

_____

_____

Teacher-Coordinator
Xalto Community College

**Fig. 17-12. Sample evaluation report format. (Cont'd on next page.)**

## SUMMARY OF CONCLUSIONS AND RECOMMENDATIONS

*Note:*

One to three paragraphs which (1) summarize findings regarding status of CVOE program within the defined parameters of the evaluation and (2) summarize recommendations for improvement. This page introduces the detailed body of the report.

### Objectives

| Conclusions | Recommendations | Suggested Solutions |
|---|---|---|
|  |  |  |

Note: One or more pages for each area of concern identified in the review goals.

### Internal Resources

| Conclusions | Recommendations | Suggested Solutions |
|---|---|---|
|  |  |  |

### External Resources

| Conclusions | Recommendations | Suggested Solutions |
|---|---|---|
|  |  |  |

### Training Stations

| Conclusions | Recommendations | Suggested Solutions |
|---|---|---|
|  |  |  |

### Program Management

| Conclusions | Recommendations | Suggested Solutions |
|---|---|---|
|  |  |  |

### Youth Organizations

| Conclusions | Recommmendations | Suggested Solutions |
|---|---|---|
|  |  |  |

Fig. 17-12. Sample evaluation report format. (Cont'd on next page.)

Back Cover

Same sheet stock as

title page or front cover.

**Fig. 17-12.  Sample evaluation report format.**

**Report Writing Hints**

The suggested format begins with a summary of conclusions and recommendations. This part of the evaluation report should be written last. It consists of a general overview of the occupational program evaluated by the team. It should reflect the findings of the on-site visitation. The intent of the summary is to highlight exemplary characteristics and to recommend how the LEA may concentrate efforts to overcome identified deficiencies. It may be well to list recommendations for improvement in priority order. Some other suggestions for developing this statement are:

1. Be precise but include enough information to avoid misinterpretation.
2. Utilize data collected from written materials as well as information gathered during interviews.
3. Use terminology which will help the LEA select means for improving program components.

The body of the report format has spaces for three kinds of statements: conclusions, recommendations, and suggested solutions. The conclusions column of the evaluation report is for statements which note exemplary characteristics and deficiencies for respective areas of concern. The following questions should be considered when these statements are developed:

1. Is there sufficient evidence to support each statement?
2. Does each statement reflect total team's view?
3. Is each statement compatible with the major objective of the area of concern?
4. Is each statement precise and pertinent to a characteristic of the program?

The recommendation column of the report is for statements which encourage the district to continue exemplary characteristics and/or to improve or correct deficiencies. The following should be considered as recommendations are developed.

1. Does each statement provide direction and suggest meaningful action(s)?
2. Does each recommendation include terminology which encourages the LEA to react to the respective conclusion?

The suggested solutions column is for statements which describe specific things the LEA can do to improve program components. The following questions should be considered when offering suggested solutions:

1. Are written statements specific?
2. Does each leave no doubt as to action required?
3. Will suggested action eliminate program inequities?
4. Have alternative suggested solutions been discarded at the expense of what has been written?
5. Are suggested solution statements measurable?
6. Will suggested solutions remove faults noted in the conclusion column?
7. Is each statement written in realistic terms, considering economics, human variables, etc.

## Oral Report

Because no written report can reflect all the thinking of each of the team members and because no team can discover all that might be known about a program, it is well to present the evaluation report orally. The oral report should have two basic goals: (1) To accuratize the report by aligning statements with information the team may have missed or misinterpreted, and (2) To improve understanding by changing phraseology, word usage, etc. The oral report should be given by the team leader. Other members of the team need not attend. But, if LEA personnel feel that particular benefits might accrue, one or more members of the team might be asked to remain.

The oral report should be attended by CVOE personnel, LEA leadership, professionals responsible for various of the areas of concern, at least some members of the advisory committee, a representative(s) of the governing board, and a student leader(s). The chief administrative officer should make introductions and serve as moderator. The team leader should read the report, stopping for questions, points of clarification, etc. When appropriate, statements should be redrafted and then read to assess clarity. Needless to say, findings and decisions of the team should not be altered. The team's intentions should be made more clear and precise if need be. The oral report should end on a positive note with the chief administrative officer thanking all who attended.

## Publish and Disseminate Report

LEA personnel should assume responsibility for copy editing, publication, and dissemination of the report. All the people who attended the oral report, members of the groups they represent, and others deemed appropriate by CVOE and CEA leadership should receive copies. As has been indicated several times previously, evaluation activities are especially newsworthy. The summary of conclusions and recommendations part of a review team report is usually an excellent outline for a news release. An article featuring summary statements, plans for utilizing results, and a picture of people at the oral report is very easy to prepare. (Earlier, an article about evaluation goals, featuring a picture of the team is entirely appropriate.) See Chapter 16, Public Relations. (See Chapter 18 regarding utilization of results.)

CHECKLISTS

The most common evaluation activity in CVOE involves the use of checklists, usually by advisory committee members at year's end. The following lists are the result of collating, rephrasing, unifying, and culling a large sample of checklists from varied and unknown sources—many of them former CVOE leadership students.

Selected checklists can be used meaningfully by teacher-coordinators, CVOE supervisors, vocational/occupational educational leadership, ancillary services leadership, and institution leadership to assess self-performance and program components within respective spans of responsibility. It is well for various kinds of personnel to use checklists which pertain to their level and subordinate levels of responsibility. This should be done annually or semiannually. Checklists may also be used to assess quality of relationships with relevant units at one's level or above.

Checklists have been used with much success by advisory committees. An advisory committee review of a CVOE program(s) has many of the features of a team review (see previous section.) But, because advisors from the community cannot be expected to devote parts of several days to a review, the scope and depth of a committee's review cannot be as thoroughgoing as a more formal team review. Especially on areas of concern such as objectives, internal resources, external resources, training stations, program management, and youth organizations, advisors who are continuously apprised of CVOE events and activities can make judicious judgments on checklist items.

As was indicated in the previous section, review teams should have checklists for areas of concern which relate to review goals and should use them to guide interview efforts and to outline at least some features of review reports.

Many CVOE people ask advisory committee members to mark checklist items either "yes" or "no." Because a great many items on the following lists are matters of degree and not subject to either/or answers, it is better to use a *rating scale response*. Items have been phrased positively so that *SD, D. N, A,* and *SA* responses (for *strongly disagree* to *strongly agree),* like the ones shown in previous sections regarding followup surveys, may be used.

## Suggested Checklist for CVOE Program

### Administration

The governing board is informed about CVOE.
The governing board is supportive of and has positive attitudes toward CVOE.
The administration is informed about CVOE.
The administration is supportive of and has positive attitudes toward CVOE.
The administration assures that academic teachers, counselors, librarians, and other student-contact personnel are informed about and supportive of CVOE.
Written LEA policies and procedures relate to CVOE as well as to other programs.
There is a defined, understood, and functioning chain of command for CVOE.
The leadership of vocational/occupational programs are the equal of the leadership of other programs.
Vocational/occupation leadership report to the same administrative officer as do other program leadership.
Coordinators report to a designated supervisor.
The supervisor minimizes overlapping and confusing community contacts.
Horizontal communication regarding CVOE is effective.
Vertical communication regarding CVOE is effective.
Authority and responsibility are correlated.
The organization structure is functional.
The organization structure is understood by;

administrators.
CVOE personnel.
counselors.
advisors.
employers.

### Objectives

Objectives for the LEA, vocational/occupational education, and CVOE programs are:
written.
measurable.
compatible.
widely disseminated.
understood by personnel and students.

Objectives and short- and long-term goals are reviewed and modified annually.
Objectives are developed for CVOE cooperatively by employers/employees, educators, and students.
Student and community needs are reflected in objective statements.
Each student has a realizable occupational objective.
Program and course objectives are realistic.

Objectives obligate the LEA to serve identified groups.

At the program level, objectives provide for:

training for jobs within the designated cluster.

student development beyond the immediate job.

individualized learning.

At the program level, objectives provide standards for operation and continuous assessment.

## Internal Resources

1. *Personnel*

Job descriptions and roles correspond with the organization chart.

Each CVOE professional satisfies requirements in the state plan and the LEA's personnel qualifications statement for both professional preparation and employment experience.

Personnel participate in educational, occupational, and community groups.

Personnel make use of professional and occupational publications.

Personnel have close, working relationships with:

students.

other vocational/occupational teachers.

academic teachers.

guidance personnel.

administrators.

government agency personnel.

employers.

employees.

community groups.

CVOE personnel are involved in in-service training of other student-contact and administrative personnel.

Personnel have groups and individual plans for updating:

professional education competencies.

cooperative education competencies.

occupational competencies.

No coordinator is assigned too many student-learners.

All coordinators have sufficient time for coordination, preparation, and evaluation.

All CVOE personnel have time for counseling.

Clerical/secretarial personnel are provided.

2. *Facilities and Equipment*

Classroom and laboratories are comparable to others in the LEA.

The classroom is in rather than isolated from major LEA learning areas.

Classrooms and laboratories are comfortable and pleasant.

Classrooms and laboratories are orderly and businesslike.

Classrooms and laboratories have adequate and flexible general and specialized equipment and supplies.

Seating is easily modified to accommodate group work and special events.

Chalkboards, bulletin boards, audiovisual equipment and other teaching aids are readily accessible to staff and students.

Career information, supplementary texts, and other materials are readily accessible to students.

Offices, counseling, filing, and storage facilities are in close proximity to the classroom, adequate in size and quantity, and comparable in quality to other facilities of the LEA.

There is adequate reference material for each student job.

Student belongings and learning supplies and projects are secured systematically.

Washroom facilities are nearby and adequate.

Facilities satisfy statutory and reasonable safety standards.

3. *Adequate Budgeting*

Financial resources are allocated equitably.

Finances are provided for:

instructional materials.
travel to work stations.
other professional travel.
updating equipment.
basic student club needs.
field trips.
secretarial services.
ten or eleven months' pay for coordinators.
telephones.
meeting expenses.

## External Resources

1. *Employers and Employees*

Employers and employees cooperate with the LEA.

Employers want the LEA to solve selected personnel supply and training problems.

Employee unions are supportive of CVOE.

2. *Advisory Committees*

Committees are broadly representative of employers, employees, and communities and government agencies.

Committees are well-organized and understanding of terms of office, functions, etc.

Committees have yearly plans of events.

Committees are not dominated by LEA personnel.

Members are well informed of LEA and CVOE objectives and programs, via a variety of vehicles.

Meetings and other functions are well planned and conducted according to plan.

Members offer advice via several vehicles and on numerous matters.

Members are informed of use and nonuse of recommendations.
Committee minutes are disseminated to appropriate people.
Committee members are involved in:

selecting work stations.
selecting CVOE personnel.
selecting students.
evaluating program components.
publicizing CVOE programs.
procuring resources.

3. *Facilities and Equipment*
External facilities utilized include:
training stations.
leased facilities.
special demonstration equipment.
surplus properties.

Contributions to CVOE programs include:

appropriate pieces of equipment.
materials and supplies.
cash.
speakers.
resource persons.
well-conducted field trips.

4. *External Agencies*
Resources of state education agencies are utilized.
Resources of department of labor and other government agencies are utilized.
Federal and state employment security offices support the cooperative plan in
several ways.

## Student Ingression and Placement

Potential students are contacted in various ways.
Applicants are fully informed regarding program components and outcomes.
Selection criteria are in accord with occupational requirements and legal con-
straints.
Advisory counsel members are involved in recruitment, selection, and placement.
Placement is in accord with career objectives and previous employment.
Teacher-coordinators make final selection and placement determinations.
Parents may easily become involved in selection and placement.
All who need, want, and can profit from CVOE are enrolled.

## Classroom Instruction and Learning

A syllabus is updated at least annually.
Both general and specific experiences are provided, according to class and
individual study plans.
Preemployment orientation prepares students for interviews.

Materials for group and individual study are modern and varied by occupation, level, and type.

Texts and supplementary materials are utilized.

Presentation techniques vary according to principles of pedagogy.

Learning outcomes are assessed via a variety of means, including student evaluation of instruction.

There is a balance of theoretical and practical experiences.

Classroom experiences are student-centered.

Classroom experiences are individualized.

Employers help in selecting special study and research problems.

Employers are informed of in-school performance.

Employers and other resource persons are utilized.

Students report and discuss actual job activities.

Students are responsible for much of the classroom experience.

Students maintain classroom appearance and utility.

Tests and other evaluative techniques are planned and known to students.

Standards are realistic, fair, and related to occupational standards.

Evaluative devices are objective and related to group and individual learning.

Evaluation results are used to guide future performance rather than to devalue previous performance.

Classroom conduct is businesslike.

Students are serious and begin working as early as possible and finish working as late as possible.

Classroom experiences stress:

attitude development.

personality development.

human relations at work.

safety knowledge and consciousness.

positive thinking and planned action.

leadership characteristics.

Assignment sheets and other teacher-prepared materials are distributed at proper times and are clear and concise.

Outside preparations, such as reading, observing work sites, questions and problems, are assigned and evaluated.

Some experiences are related to student's other subjects.

## Training Stations

Training stations are selected according to written criteria.

A file of potential training stations is updated several times each year.

Individual training agreements include plans for job progression.

CVOE personnel have regular and special conferences with students and supervisors, indvidually and together.

Problems are identified as early as possible.

CVOE personnel record regularly scheduled assessments of student performance by type, quality and quantity.

All training stations satisfy child labor law, minimum wage, and other statutory requirements.

All employers satisfy reasonable and proper moral and legal standards of treatment of employees.

There is a functioning system for relating classroom experiences to job experiences.

Employers understand their several roles in work station and in-school education.

Special efforts are made by CVOE personnel and employers to assure student-learner:

job adjustment.
job safety.
job performance according to written agreement.

Evaluation of student-learner performance involves consideration of:
ability to work with others.
response to supervision.
response to unexpected.
progress according to items in written agreement.
job decision making.
job initiative.
solution of daily problems.
student expectations.
employer expectations.

Employers, supervisors, and employees are satisfied with student and graduate:
abilities.
attitudes.
appearance.
personalities.
citizenship.

## Program Management

Written training agreements are agreed upon by employees, sponsors, and coordinators.

Written training plans for individuals are agreed upon by employers, sponsors, and coordinators.

Work permits are acquired before employment.

Social security numbers are acquired with ease.

Employers satisfy statutory requirements, including OSHA.

The LEA and employers satisfy responsibilities for insurance which protects student-learners.

Students receive pay.

Personnel maintain files of current legislation, interpretations, and agency regulations regarding student and minor employment.

CVOE programs are integral parts of the total curriculum.
LEA schedules accommodate CVOE rather than vice versa.
Schedules are in the best interest of students and employers.
Credit is awarded for related classes.
Credit is awarded for work experience.
CVOE personnel have ample time for:
  student selection and placement.
  record keeping.
  coordination.
Coordination time is actually used at:
  work stations.
  potential work stations.

Program records indicate:
  hours worked.
  related-class progress.
  training station progress.
  observance of labor laws.
  observance of safety laws.

Reports are made according to schedule to:
  administrators.
  the governing board.
  advisors.
  SEA's.


## Youth Organizations

Eligible students are apprised of the benefits and their responsibilities of club membership.
Members learn communication skills.
Members learn social skills.
Members learn how to conduct meetings.
Members learn how to plan year-long programs.
Members learn how to plan and conduct special events.
Members learn how to cooperate with advisory committees and other groups and individuals.
Members learn how to participate in state and national affiliate meetings and contests.
Members participate in community service activities.
Youth organizations are a CO—curricular phase of instruction and learning.
Class periods are set aside or designated for respective club activities at least once each month.
Financial resources are provided by the LEA for youth group activities above the local level.
Youth groups participate in regional, state, and national contests, observances, and other events.

## Guidance Services

Guidance personnel interview students at regular intervals and as special needs arise.

Student progress is discussed.

Future development is discussed and itemized.

Guidance personnel interview parents.

Guidance personnel discuss student needs and progress with other student contact personnel.

CVOE and guidance personnel work together to:

inform potential students about CVOE.

make recommendations regarding occupational awareness programs.

refer students for group and individual testing.

refer students with special needs to various remedial services within and without the LEA.

refer students for permanent employment.

select students for various programs.

refer students for individual counseling.

conduct in-service programs for CVOE staff regarding services available to students.

Guidance personnel are understanding of and supportive of CVOE.

Guidance personnel work effectively at recruitment.

Guidance personnel serve on CVOE advisory committees.

Guidance personnel manage and control job placement services (other than cooperative education) for:

vacation periods.

part-time jobs.

full-time jobs.

new jobs long after graduation.

Guidance personnel contribute to or manage conduct of:

student followup surveys.

employer followup surveys.


## Public Relations

Brochures and other descriptive materials are made available to several publics.

Regular reports and records are disseminated to administrators and counselors.

All student-contact personnel are informed about CVOE programs via printed and face-to-face vehicles.

There is a public relations plan and calendar.

Printed and broadcast media are involved in a variety of public relations efforts and are invited to selected CVOE events.

Personnel have close, working relationships with the LEA's public relations officer(s).

News releases are prepared and disseminated in accord with principles of good practice.

Personnel are available for presentations to community groups.
Personnel are available for presentations to potential students and their relatives.
Public relations efforts are coordinated with youth clubs.
Special public relations events occur during American Education Week and American Vocational Education Week.
Outstanding student and employer performance and contributions are recognized.
Public relations reaches various publics:
Eligible enrollees.
Community groups.
Media personnel.
Employers/employees.
Parents and parent groups.
LEA personnel.

### Collating and Presenting Results

Statements made earlier in this chapter regarding student and employer followup studies are applicable here. Whether they are generated by LEA personnel, or by special review teams, checklist responses should be collated, presented in meaningful form, and disseminated to appropriate internal and external people. For example, results of evaluation activities utilizing checklists may be appended to advisory committee minutes and to annual and interim reports to SEA's. If checklists are used by advisors in a formal evaluation activity, such as an annual program review, results are newsworthy. (See Chapter 16, Public Relations.)

(See Chapter 18 regarding utilization of results.)

### Summary

It is important to have an evaluation system for CVOE. A system of evaluation activities should be designed with full knowledge of SEA, LEA, vocational/occupational education, and CVOE policies, procedures, constraints, etc. Real world constraints, such as competency requirements, also bear heavily upon system design. Design is best done by a task force which establishes relationships among several kinds of major and minor evaluation activities. Because evaluation of CVOE entails many activities—if only those which are mandatory—a calendar must be kept. The four most commonly used and effective evaluation activities are student followup survey, employer followup survey, team review, and checklists. These have been used with good success, primarily without relationships one to another. In a functioning evaluation design, they serve as inputs to each other and result in improvements to various program components, individually and collectively. CVOE programs which incorporate all four are certain to experience salutary and synergistic effects, which are far too uncommon in education.

**Activities**

1. Interview a CVOE supervisor regarding the chronology of evaluation activities in his/her program. Discover which activities are imposed, self-imposed, reported to SEA's, reported to the media. Discover what kinds of people are involved in each of the activities.
2. Read one or more of the references regarding surveys. Prepare a student and/or an employer followup instrument which is more specific in some respects than sample instruments in this chapter.
3. Pilot the instrument(s) with four or five CVOE students or employers.
4. Serve on an on-site evaluation team.
5. Prepare ten checklist items which deal more specifically with one area of concern than do items in this chapter.
6. Prepare a sample news release for one of the evaluation activities described in this chapter. (See Chapter 16.)

# Chapter 18

# Program Change

Cooperative vocational/ occupational education (CVOE) has natural checks and balances. Students, supervisors, and coordinators learn from one another and make many minor and some major adjustments in program components. The ongoing work of advisory committees and student organizations also modifies program components gradually. This chapter deals with a more formalized method for planning and implementing change which is indicated by evaluation activities, especially those which were described at length in the previous chapter.

Some of the outcomes of reading this chapter are *understanding:*

1. The role of CVOE program leadership in planning and implementing change.
2. A group approach to deciding upon alterations in program components.
3. The importance of scheduling and assigning tasks associated with change.
4. Special uses of selected evaluation activities.

## PLANNING AND IMPLEMENTING CHANGE

The products of evaluation activities are of little consequence unless they are (1) in a form which lends itself to action decisions and (2) are used during various planning activities to schedule changes in what some individual or group does. Such things as survey data and evaluation reports are not useful in raw form.

### Unifying Evaluation Results

The first step toward utilizing evaluation results is to translate the products of evaluation activities into manageable form. The goal is to define as precisely as possible (within reason) who will do what during what time frame to what performance standard. It is strange but true that there is not a sizeable literature regarding translation of evaluative data into plans for change.

The authors recommend that CVOE personnel use the format which was provided in the previous chapter for the body of team review reports. That is, data from evaluation activities should first of all be converted into conclusions, recommendations, and suggested solutions. Collated data from such instruments as student evaluation of instruction, student and employer followup surveys, and checklists should be interpreted in the same fashion as was described for team reviews. Interpretations should be done by groups of individuals, excepting, perhaps, in the case of student evaluation of instruction. Even then it is well for a teacher to discuss plans for change with a peer or an immediate supervisor.

The principle for selecting people who will interpret results into an action plan is to select those who are responsible for the areas of concern which are most likely to be affected or which will be most affected. For example, in the previous chapter, the team review of the associate degree program in automotive technology assessed objectives, internal resources, external resources, training stations, program management, and student organizations. Thus, consideration should be given to naming the following to a change planning group:

1. the CVOE program leader,
2. one of his superiors who is responsible for budget allocations,
3. an advisory committee member,
4. a supervisor from one of the training stations,
5. a teacher-coordinator, and
6. a student organization leader.

Six people may be too many. But, three LEA professionals and a student would probably do most of the work with guidance from one or two people from the community.

In the case of team review, a planning group would begin by examining conclusions, recommendations, and suggestions. In the case of other evaluation activities, a planning group should meet several times to draft such statements. At the first meeting, the CVOE program leader should orient the planning group to the nature of these statements and how to generate them. (See chapter 17.) In every instance, conclusions should relate to (1) goals of the evaluation activity, e.g., student followup survey, and (2) one of the eleven areas of concern. Operationally, a planning group should proceed as follows. (1) Examine collated data from the respective evaluation activity and write conclusions appropriate to areas of concern. (2) Continue writing conclusions as they come to mind until all data have been examined. (3) Then sort conclusions into areas of concern and order them in some logical pattern within each area of concern, e.g., by grade level, chronologically, by occupation, by significance. (4) Write recommendations and suggested solutions working as a group, and/or subgroups, and/or individuals. (5) Review and discuss recommendations and suggested solutions as a group. (6) Review the total report to assure (a) that conclusions appear in the correct area of concern and (b) that conclusions within an area of concern appear in logical order. (7) Within each area of concern, rank recommendations in order of priority from the recommendation which is most important to improvement of that area of concern to the recommendation which least needs immediate attention. Numbers in parentheses after each recommendation statement are a good way to indicate priority ranks.

### Obtain Sanction(s)

When a planning group is satisfied with recommendations and suggested solutions, CVOE leadership should seek approval from one or more levels. Sanction should be sought for the substance of the document and for proceeding to schedule change. In most cases, institution leadership will provide additional information, indicate which recommendations can be implemented only with great difficulty, and indicate which recommendations cannot be implemented for various reasons. It is well for administrators to meet with change planning groups to explain barriers and constraints. Many times trade-offs and cost-saving measures can result.

### Modify, Adapt, Adopt

Attempts to obtain sanction nearly always result in information which suggests alterations, recommendations, and suggested solutions. Whenever possible, recommendations should be left unchanged and suggested solutions should be adjusted to facilitate planned change. A planning group should deal with recommendations which require change. Each should be adopted, adapted, or rejected. Rejection should occur only with good cause. Recommendations should not be rejected only because resources cannot be allocated immediately.

Suggested solutions should be reevaluated after administrative approval and suggestions have been forthcoming. They should be adopted, modified, or replaced with alternatives which will be more manageable. Solutions may also be added.

**Schedule Solutions**

After evaluative data from surveys, checklists, etc. have been translated into conclusions, recommendations, and suggested solutions; and after they have necessary sanctions and alterations, solutions should be scheduled for implemention. A sample form for scheduling program change is in Fig. 18-1. A planning group should complete a sheet for each recommendation. The *who* column should be used to indicate the one or more people who will be responsible for actualizing respective solutions. The *when* column should specify a deadline, a specific date, or a time span as appropriate. The *comments* column should be used for special hints, such as who may assist in the solution, what other solutions might be

## Change Implementation Schedule

| Conclusion | Recommendation | | |
|---|---|---|---|
| Solution | who | when | |
| 1. | | | |
| 2. | | | |
| 3. | | | |
| 4. | | | |

Fig. 18-1.   Sample change implementation schedule.

related in some way, what special resources might be employed, and what performance standard is necessary.

### Additional Sanction

Several kinds of solutions will require additional sanction. Nearly all solutions which entail expenditures will require approvals on standard requisitions, travel vouchers, etc. and/or prior approval by administrative offices and perhaps the governing board. In most instances, it is well to share evaluative data and planning documents with those who must approve specific solutions. Solutions which require additional personnel will require high-level approval. Solutions which involve cooperation from several administrative units should normally be approved by the next higher level of administration.

### Incorporation in Other Documents

Many solutions should be referred to other documents. Some examples are: changes in personnel and student handbooks; sections in one- and five-year program plans; modifications in courses of study, new items in calendars for evaluation, public relations, recruitment, etc.; modifications to brochures and other publicity pieces; modifications to standardized procedures in the LEA's internal and external affairs. Solutions, i.e., implemented change, must be woven into every fabric of the institution. Changes must be internalized and not forgotten.

## UTILIZING RESULTS OF FOLLOWUP SURVEYS

Some special hints are in order regarding the use of results from followup surveys and other evaluation activities which are especially important to CVOE. The use of followup survey results should follow the procedure outlined in the previous section. Conclusions should parallel prestated objectives. Obviously, results may suggest solutions to satisfying reporting requirements; preparing public relations pieces; identifying program components which should be studied in depth; and determining learning experiences which should be deleted, modified, added, emphasized, expanded, etc.

### Student Followup Surveys

By itself, a student followup survey will seldom provide adequate information for decisions regarding major shifts in program purpose and experiences. Student followup surveys provide (1) information adequate to adjustments which should be made from year-to-year or term-to-term, and (2) information for input into evaluation activities such as team reviews, which have more input.

Together with information from employer followup surveys, results of student followup surveys should be used (1) in occupational awareness and orientation programs in elementary and junior high schools and (2) in student recruitment efforts. Brochures, speeches, and other vehicles for describing CVOE programs to various publics should contain information regarding type of work, income, other benefits, and advancement opportunity of graduates. If taken from recent surveys, such information is far more accurate and impressive than is material from the *Dictionary of Occupational Titles* or typical LEA bulletins.

### Employer Followup Surveys

Some particular uses of results of employer followup surveys are (1) adjusting aspects of placement services in accord with hiring and promotion practices of employers, (2) altering supply and demand estimates, which are used in overall program planning, counseling, and enrollment quotas, and (3) apprising various student-contact personnel regarding competency requirements and occupational outlooks.

## ADJUSTING OCCUPATIONAL EMPHASIS

CVOE programs must respond to student needs and manpower demands. These matters were treated at length in Chapters 5 and 6. A number of evaluation activities should be used to arrive at recommendations and scheduling solutions for modifying total and specific CVOE programs. The major inputs to program adjustment are student interest surveys conducted by LEA's, other manpower forecasts, followup surveys, and factual and trustworthy information regarding economic development, e.g., new establishments.

Some of the kinds of changes which data from such sources suggest are:

1. Deletion of specific programs.
2. Narrowing or broadening of the occupational scope of a program(s).
3. Moving the goals of a program on the responsiblity ladder in the world of work, i.e., raise or lower or expand the levels of occupations graduates enter.
4. Increasing or decreasing enrollment quotas in a program(s).
5. Adding a program(s).
6. Combining programs with declining student and/or labor market demands.

7. Modifying the locale of training stations, i.e., traveling greater or lesser distances or moving toward another segment of the labor market, e.g., another hospital or another government agency.

Often, the best solution is a combination of two or more of these changes in occupational emphasis.

### Summary

In addition to natural checks and balances, program change should result from various evaluation activities. The kinds of statements which result from team reviews are a good starting point for change. Results of other evaluation activities should be translated into conclusions, recommendations, and suggested solutions. Necessary sanctions and approvals should be requested and then solutions should be scheduled for implementation by designated persons in specified time frames, according to stated performance standards. Special uses should be made of data from followup surveys and the several evaluation activities which bear upon decisions regarding occupational emphases. In these and other programmatic decisions, CVOE personnel should involve the kinds of internal and external people which were described early in this book.

### Activities

1. Obtain data from an actual followup study of employers or students. Draft conclusions and recommendations which are justified by the data.
2. Interview a CVOE supervisor to determine how shifts in occupational emphasis occur in the program or programs for which he/she is responsible. Discover the degree to which shifts occur because of student interests, checks and balances of the ongoing cooperative program, or knowledge of labor market trends.
3. Interview two or more levels of personnel in an LEA to discover what evaluation activities are conducted and what kinds of planned changes are implemented because of evaluation results.

# Bibliography

1. American Association of School Administrators. *Public Relations for America's Schools 28th Yearbook*. Washington, D. C.: National Education Association, 1950.

2. American Vocational Association. *The Advisory Committee and Vocational Education*. Washington, D.C.: Publications Committee, 1969.

3. Ashman, Richard D. and Klaurens, Mary K. "Essentials in Educating the Teacher Coordinator." *American Vocational Journal* 44 (1969):28-29.

4. Bailey, Larry J. and Stadt, Ronald W. *Career Education: New Approaches to Human Development*. Bloomington, Illinois: McKnight, 1973.

5. Barbeau, J. E. *Cooperative Education in America: Its Historical Development, 1906-1971*. Boston: Northeastern University, Ph.D. dissertation, 1971.

6. Bloom, Benjamin S. *Learning for Mastery Evaluation Comment*. Center for the Study of Evaluation of Instructional Programs. University of California, Los Angeles: 1 (May 1968): No. 2.

7. Brockstrom, Charles H. and Hursh, Gerald D. *Survey Research*. Northwestern University Press, 1963.

8. Bullard, Lee W. "The Student Selection Myth in Cooperative Education." *Business Education Forum* 26 (January 1972): 4.

9. Burt, Samuel M. *Industry and Community Leaders in Education, the State Advisory Council on Vocational Education*. Kalamazoo, Michigan: W. E. Upjon Institute for Employment Research, October 1969.

10. Coakley, C. B. *Providing Learning Experience Through Properly Used Coordination Techniques*. Paper presented at the Cooperative Education Coordinators Workshop, November 22, 1971.

11. _____. *Tennessee Distributive Education Teacher-Coordinators' Handbook*. Knoxville: University of Tennessee, 17 n.d.

12. Cook, J. E. "Cooperative Education for Rural Students." *American Vocational Journal* 50 (1975): 26-28.

13. Cotrell, Calvin J. *Model Curricula for Vocational and Technical Teacher Educators: Report No. III. Performance Requirements for Teacher-Coordinators.* Ohio State University, The Center for Vocational and Technical Education, March 1972.

14. A Directory of Cooperative Education. *Its Philosophy and Operation in Participating Colleges in the United States and Canada.* Cooperative Education Association, 1973.

15. Evans, Rupert N. *Foundations of Vocational Education.* Columbus, Ohio: Charles E. Merrill, 1971.

16. Farahbokhshira, E. "An Analytical Study of Cooperative Education in the United States and Development of a Plan for Iran." *Dissertation Abstracts International* 28 (1968): 2890-A.

17. Fielstra, C. *Work Experience Education Program in Santa Barbara Counties High School District.* Road Associates, 1961.

18. Glaser, Robert. "Individuals and Learning: The New Aptitudes." *Education Researcher* 1 (1972): 6.

19. Gooch, B. G. *The Status of Tennessee's Secondary Distributive, Industrial, Office, and Part G Cooperative Vocational Education Programs—1973.* Ph.D. dissertation, University of Tennessee, 1973.

20. Heermann, B. *Cooperative Education in Community Colleges.* San Francisco: Jossey-Bass, 1973.

21. Hennessy, J. V. *A Comparison of Course Cost Data of Regular Vocational Courses and Cooperative Education Courses Offered in Selected Secondary Schools and Area Vocational Centers in Illinois During the School Year 1970-1971.* Ph.D. dissertation, Southern Illinois University at Carbondale, 1975.

22. Houstman, James. "The Future of Vocational Office and Distributive Education as Perceived by State Supervisors and Teacher Educators." *Dissertation Abstracts International* 33 (1972): 32251-A.

23. Huffman, Harry. "Cooperative Vocational Education: Unique Among Work and Learner Programs." *American Vocational Journal* 44 (May 1969): 16.

24. Hutkin, R. and Stadt R. W. "Understanding Cooperative Education." *The Educational Forum* May 1970: 541-545.

25. Illinois Board of Vocational Education and Rehabilitation, Division of Vocational and Technical Education. *Advisory Council Member.* Springfield: 1972, Bulletin No. 29-672.

26. _____. *Advisory Committee Organization and Use in Vocational-Technical Education.* (Rev. ed.) Springfield: 1970.

27. _____. *An Annotated Bibliography of Instructional Materials.* Springfield: 1974.

28. _____. *An Articulated Guide for Cooperative Career Education.* Springfield: 1971, Bulletin No. 34-571.

29. _____. *Cooperative Health Occupations Education at Secondary Level.* Springfield: 1971, Bulletin No. 17-371.

30. _____. *Team Member Handbook.* Springfield: 1974.

31. _____. *WECEP Guide.* Springfield: n. d.

32. Kerensky, V. M. and Melby, E. L. *Education Two: The Social Imperative.* Midland, Michigan: Pendell, 1971, 168-178.

33. Kimbrel, G. and Vineyard, B. S. *Strategies for Implementing Work Experience Programs.* Bloomington, Illinois: McKnight, 1972, 1.

34. Knowles, A. S. and associates. *Handbook of Cooperative Education.* San Francisco: Jossey-Bass, 1972.

35. Lanham, Frank W. and Weber, Edwin J. "Cooperative Occupational Training Programs Need Quality Control." *Business Education Forum* (May 1970): 11.

36. Law, G. F. *Cooperative Education Handbook for Teacher-Coordinators.* Chicago: American Technical Society, 1970.

37. McCreery, F. and Shotwell, H. D. *The Coordinator's Job in Follow-up and Evaluation.* Kansas State Board for Vocational Education, Kansas State Teachers College of Emporia.

38. McNally, H. J. and Passow, A. H. *Improving the Quality of Public School Programs. Approaches to Curriculum Development.* New York: Teachers College Press, 1960.

39. Mason, R. E. "Effective Cooperative Business Education Programs, Part I." *Business Education Forum* 16 (February 1962): 21.

40. _____. "The Effective Use of Cooperative Work Experience." *Business Education Forum* (May 1970), vol. 10.

41. _____. and Haines, P. G. *Cooperative Occupational Education and Work Experience in the Curriculum.* Danville, Illinois: Interstate, 1972.

42. Melby, E. "Community Education Can Renew Our Faith." *Community Education Journal* 3 (November 1973): 8.

43. Meyer, Warren G., Crawford, Lucy and Klaurens, Mary K. *Coordination in Cooperative Vocational Education.* Columbus, Ohio: Charles E. Merrill, 1975.

44. Minnesota Division of Vocational and Technical Education College of Education. *A Guide for Cooperative Vocational Education.* Minneapolis: September 1969.

45. Minzey, J. D. "Community Education—Another Perspective." *Community Education Journal* 4 (May-June 1974): 7.

46. _____ and LeTarte, D. "Community Education from Program to Process." *Community Education Journal 3* (August 1971): 7.

47. Mississippi State Department of Education, Division of Vocational and Technical Education. *Handbook for Vocational Teacher-Coordinators of Business and Office Education.* Jackson: 1972.

48. Munisteria, Anthony. "A Study of the Holding Power of Cooperative Education Programs for Male Potential Dropouts, in an East Harlem, New York City, Vocational School." *Dissertation Abstracts International* 32 (1971): 2360A.

49. National Conference on Vocational Education. *Implications of the 1968 Amendments, Notes and Working Papers.* Minneapolis, Minnesota: February 1969, pp. 26-28; 79-80.

50. New Mexico State Department of Vocational Education, Division of Trade and Industrial Education. *A Guide for the Effective Use of Advisory Committees.* Albuquerque: 1966.

51. Ohio State University, The Center for Vocational Education, Product Utilization Section. *A Partial Listing of Cooperative Adult Education Programs.* Columbus, Ohio: 1975.

52. _____. *Abstracts of Selected Cooperative Adult Education Programs.* Columbus, Ohio: 1975.

53. _____. *Discussion of Industry-Education Cooperation for Adult Learning.* Columbus, Ohio: 1975.

54. _____. *Guidelines for the Development and Study of Cooperative Adult Education Programs. Columbus, Ohio: 1975.*

55. Oklahoma Department of Vocational and Technical Education. *This Is a Handbook for Oklahoma's Cooperative Programs in Vocational Education.* Stillwater: 1972.

56. Olsen, Ronald G. "A Study of the Occupational Experience of Distributive Education Teacher-Coordinators and Its Relationship to Businessmen's Ratings of Programs Competencies, and Ratings from the Results of Follow-up Studies on Graduates." *Dissertation Abstracts International* 32, (1972): 3173A.

57. Pender, Albert R. "Selection and Placement of Students in Cooperative Programs." *Business Education Forum* 24 (April 1970): 7.

58. Pennsylvania Department of Education, Bureau of Vocational, Technical and Continuing Education. *Cooperative Vocational Education Evaluation Criteria.* Harrisburg: 1972.

59. _____. *Cooperative Vocational Education General Related Theory Class Outline.* Harrisburg: 1972.

60. _____. *Handbook Distributive Education Teacher-Coordinators.* Harrisburg: 1970.

61. Poe, Janet M. "The Effectiveness of Advisory Committees Serving Distributive Educational Programs in the State of Tennessee." Master's thesis, University of Tennessee, 1971.

62. Public Law 90-576, *Provisions for Dealing with State Advisory Councils.* Title I, Part A, Section 104, U. S. Congress, Washington, D. C.: 1968.

63. Purpel, David E. and Belanger, Maurice. *Curriculum and The Cultural Revolution.* Berkeley, California: McCutchan, 1972.

64. Report: National Conference on Cooperative Education. *Department of HEW, USOE, Bureau of Occupation and Adult Education.* Education Business Labor. Washington D. C.: January 1974.

65. Report of the Panel on Youth of the President's Science Advisory Committees. *Youth: Transition to Adulthood.* Washington, D.C.: Government Printing Office, June 1973.

66. Riendeau, Albert J. *The Role of the Advisory Committee in Occupational Education in the Junior College.* American Association of Junior Colleges, Washington, D.C.: 1967, p. 27.

67. Rummel, Francis J. *An Introduction to Research Procedures in Education.* (2nd ed.) New York: Harper and Row, 1964.

68. Silberman, C.E. *Crisis in the Classroom.* New York: Random House, 1970.

69. Silberman, H. F. "Involving the Young." *Phi Delta Kappan 56* (May 1975): 596-600.

70. Smith, F. S. *A Study of the Importance of and Agreement of National Guidelines for Industrial Cooperative Training by North Carolina Coordinators.* Ph.D. dissertation, North Carolina State University at Raleigh, 1969. (University Microfilms, Inc., Ann Arbor, Michigan.)

71. Stadt, Ronald W. and Jensen, Thomas R. "Functional Advisory Committees for Vocational-Technical Education Programs." *Journal of Industrial Teacher Education* 4 (December 1966).

72. _____. et al. *Managing Career Education Programs.* Englewood Cliffs: Prentice-Hall, 1973.

73. Tennessee State Board for Vocational Education. *Tennessee Cooperative Coordinators Handbook.* Nashville: n.d.

74. Texas Tech University, Home Economics Instructional Materials Center. *Handbook for Home Economics Cooperative Education Teacher-Coordinators.* Lubbock: 1973.

75. Ullery, Jessie W. "A Comparative Analysis of Selected Student Characteristics and Vocational Cooperative Programs." *Dissertation Abstracts International* 32 (1972): 4502A.

76. United States Department of Health, Education, and Welfare, Vocational Education Amendments of 1968, Reports Without Amendments. *Committee on Education and Labor*, 90th Congress, 2nd Session, House Report number 1647. Washington D. C.: Government Printing Office, 8.

77. United States Department of Labor. *A Guide to Child Labor Provisions of the Fair Labor Standards Act*. Child Labor Bulletin, Wage and Hour Division, Bulletin No. 101, Washington D. C.: 1973.

78. United States Office of Science and Technology, Report of the Panel on Youth of the President's Science Advisory Committee. *Youth: Transition to Adulthood*. Washington D.C.: Government Printing Office, June 1973.

79. Vermont Department of Education, Learning Services Division, Vocational-Technical Education. *Guidelines Cooperative Vocational Education in Vermont*. Montpelier: 1972.

80. Virginia Department of Education, Division of Vocational Education. *Teaching Guide for Cooperative Office Education*. Richmond: April 1970.

81. Wallace, H. R. *Review and Analysis of Instructional Materials for Cooperative Vocational Education*. Columbus, Ohio: ERIC Clearinghouse on Vocational and Technical Education, May 1972.

82. Weisman, Lawrence. *School, Community, and Youth, a Statewide Evaluation of Part G Programs in Cooperative Vocational Education*. State of Illinois, Board of Vocational Education and Rehabilitation. Project number SPG-A2-942, 1972.

83. Wentling, Tim L. and Lawson, Tom E. *Evaluating Occupational Educational and Training Programs.*Boston: Allyn and Bacon, 1975.

84. West Virginia Department of Education, Division of Vocational Education. *Cooperative Vocational Education Programs*. Morgantown: n.d.

# Appendix

## Sources of Instructional Materials

American Association for Vocational Instructional Material
Engineering Center
Athens, Georgia 30601

American Technical Society
848 East 58th Street
Chicago, Illinois 60637

California State Polytechnical College
San Luis Obispo, California 93401

Illinois Retail Merchants Association
36 S. Wabash
Chicago, Illinois 60603

Interstate Printers and Publishers, Inc.
19-27 N. Jackson Street
Danville, Illinois 61832

Iowa State University Press
South State Street
Ames, Iowa 50010

J.C. Penney Company, Inc.
Education and Consumer Relations Department
New York, New York 10019

New York Institute of Technology
888 Seventh Avenue
New York, New York 10019

Ohio State University
Agriculture Education
Curriculum Materials Service
Columbus, Ohio 43210

Oklahoma State Board of Vocational and Technical Education
1515 West Sixth Street
Stillwater, Oklahoma 74074

Pennsylvania State University
Department of Agricultural Education
University Park, Pennsylvania 16802

Purdue University
Vocational Trade and Industry Department
Lafayette, Indiana 47901

Teacher's College Press
1234 Amsterdam Avenue
New York, New York 10027

Tennessee State Board of Vocational Education Program
200 Cordell Hull Building
Nashville, Tennesse 37129

Texas A & M University
Department of Vocational Education
College Station, Texas 77840

Texas Technical University
Home Economics Instructional Materials Center
P.O. Box 4067
Lubbock, Texas 79409

United States Department of Health, Education, and Welfare
Washington, D.C. 20202

United States Department of Labor
Bureau of Labor Statistics
Office of Information
Washington, D.C. 20210

United States Government Printing Office
Superintendent of Documents
Washington, D.C. 20402

University of Alabama
Department of Trade and Industry
University, Alabama 35486

University of Illinois
College of Education
Department of Vocational and Technical Education
Division of Home Economics Education
Urbana, Illinois 61801

University of Kentucky
Department of Vocational Education
Lexington, Kentucky 40506

University of Texas
Instructional Materials Service
Division of Extension
Austin, Texas 78710

# Index